ENGENDERING
BUSINESS

GENDER RELATIONS IN
THE AMERICAN EXPERIENCE

Joan E. Cashin

Ronald G. Walters

SERIES EDITORS

ENGENDERING
BUSINESS

Men and Women in
the Corporate Office,
1870–1930

Angel Kwolek-Folland

THE JOHNS HOPKINS UNIVERSITY PRESS

Baltimore and London

© 1994 Angel Kwolek-Folland
All rights reserved
Printed in the United States of America on acid-free paper

The Johns Hopkins University Press
2715 North Charles Street
Baltimore, Maryland 21218-4319
The Johns Hopkins Press Ltd., London

ISBN 0-8018-4860-1

Library of Congress Cataloging-in-Publication Data
will be found at the end of this book.
A catalog record for this book is available from the British Library.

For my parents,
Helen Fritchie Kwolek
and Edmond John Kwolek

CONTENTS

ILLUSTRATIONS

PREFACE AND
ACKNOWLEDGMENTS

This book uses gender as a category of historical analysis and as a central mediator among the workers, managers, and institutional structures of office work in financial industries, as they confronted change between 1870 and 1930. We have failed so far to account fully for the complex relationship between gender—perhaps our most intimate mode of experience—and social structures and imperatives such as business or workplace organization. To explicate these connections, *Engendering Business* argues that ideas about manhood and womanhood shaped both institutions and individual experience in the office workplace and contributed to discussions about the meanings of class and race in white-collar work. Furthermore, it suggests that turn-of-the-century gender roles in financial industries built on the nineteenth-century notion of separate spheres, even as workers, managers, and executives re-shaped that middle-class ideal.

The chapters analyze the gender of business as a series of topical issues rather than a chronology. Chapter 1 provides historical background on financial industries from the early nineteenth century to 1930 and introduces the issues explored in later chapters. Chapter 2 discusses the connections that developed between ideas about womanhood and about the ideal office worker. Chapter 3 outlines the two streams of ideas that structured business manhood—scientific rationalism and subjective sensibility—and explores the contributions of salesmanship to ideas about manliness and management. Chapter 4 sketches the physical environment of urban offices as workplaces and as public expressions of gender ideology. Chapter 5 explores the corporate connections among work, family, and leisure that reinforced older patterns of gender ideology. Chapter 6 charts some of the ways workers tried to restructure business gender roles for their own purposes.

Historical discussions about maleness and femaleness, definitions of gender deviance, elaborate gender metaphors, and gendered spatial divisions all can reveal information about social and economic structures or relationships, in addition to gender itself. Strictly speaking, this book is neither labor nor social history, architectural nor business history, women's nor men's history. It is a conversation with all of these branches, and with others.

When I first began this research in 1983, as a preliminary investigation for a dissertation topic, there was available a grand total of one historical monograph, one statistical study, and a scattering of dissertations on office workers. There was nothing on the history of gender and only the rudimentary beginnings of research into the history of manhood. Business history ignored gender and emphasized a rational, progressive interpretation of economic and bureaucratic growth. Since that time there has been almost an explosion of research in many of these areas, and I am indebted to all those scholars without whose work I still would be on page one. In particular, my understanding of the history of clerical workers is substantially enriched by the work of M. Christine Anderson, Cindy Aron, Margery Davies, Ileen DeVault, Lisa Fine, Margaret Hedstrom, Elyce Rotella, and Carole Srole. Scholars in several fields have expanded our knowledge of architecture and technology, the history of manhood, and the histories of business and the office environment. I am particularly indebted to the work of Daniel Bluestone, Elsa Barkley Brown, Peter Filene, Kenneth T. Gibbs, and Anthony Rotundo. Their work, and that of others too numerous to mention here, has enabled me to suggest a new historical synthesis of the gendered office experience.

Any listing of my scholarly debts would be incomplete without acknowledging Sara Evans, who was arguably the most important figure in this project. As my dissertation advisor, ongoing consultant, and friend, Sara gave me the space and support I needed. In the larger sense, without her ground-breaking scholarship in the history of women's experience my work would not be possible.

Several private document collections provided primary sources for this study. The Equitable Life Assurance Society of the United States Archives, the Metropolitan Life Insurance Company, The New England Archives, the North Carolina Mutual Life Insurance Company, and the Wells Fargo Corporation all gave me access to their corporate records. I am one of the beneficiaries of their commitment to the importance of history. The generous and careful assistance of several archivists made my work much easier. Arline Schneider and Jonathan Coss of the Equitable, James Mann and Daniel B. May of Metropolitan Life, Phyllis Steele of The New England, and Robert J. Chandler of Wells Fargo all located sources, answered questions, carefully read several versions of portions of the manuscript, and—in many ways, most important— took an enthusiastic and knowledgeable interest in the work. My thanks also go to Barbara Peele and Howard Clement III of North Carolina Mutual Life. Howard Clement shared his knowledge of the company's history and his wisdom and vision of the larger purposes of life insurance in the African American experience. I am indebted to the knowledge, friendship, and support of all of these professionals.

Public collections and libraries held a variety of useful documents. Papers at the Baker and Widener Libraries at Harvard University provided information on early life insurance and on insurance buildings. The records of the Bureau of Vocational Information at the Schlesinger Library in Cambridge, Massachusetts, revealed important information about office workers' attitudes. Several collections of personal papers at the William R. Perkins Library at Duke University gave me insights into life insurance sales and the experience of African Americans in insurance and banking. The rich and varied collections of the Hagley Museum and Library in Wilmington, Delaware, gave me access to trade papers, photographs, insurance and banking records, and trade catalogues. In addition, the work on this book would have been virtually impossible without the assistance of the interlibrary loan departments and staff at the University of Minnesota and Kansas State University. Their professional expertise and cheerful competence saved me miles of travel and probably my sanity.

Fellowships from the American Association of University Women and the New Faculty Research Fund of the University of Kansas Graduate School funded portions of this research. In addition a grant-in-aid from the Hagley Museum and Library facilitated access to that institution's wonderful collections and incomparable working environment.

Any book is the product of many minds, and this one is infinitely better for the help of those who read all or portions of it in its various stages or offered comments and suggestions. I am grateful for the insights of Kenneth Ames, Beth Bailey, Ava Baron, Susan Porter Benson, Gail Bossenga, Ileen DeVault, Liz Faue, Alice Kessler-Harris, Maggie Levenstein, Sonya Rose, Ann Schofield, Carl Strikwerda, Mary Yeager, and series editors Joan E. Cashin and Ronald G. Waters. My thanks to Robert J. Brugger and his assistant Gregg Wilhelm at Johns Hopkins University Press, who were always there to answer questions, make helpful suggestions, and shepherd me through the publication process. Judy Sacks's superb copyediting smoothed out the rough places.

The hardest part of writing a book is coming to terms with one's own inadequacies. As a historian of culture, I sometimes found myself struggling through the thickets of obscure economic terms, holding in check my tendency to expand words such as *investment* or *mutual* into philosophical concepts. Sometimes it was hard to catch a glimpse of the human motivations, beliefs, experiences, and tragedies whose material and spiritual expressions created such abstract and, to me, cold institutional landscapes. That in the last ten years I have managed to make those connections between research and life is due to the understanding, enthusiasm, and occasional overt reminders of my friends and family. In this kind of large project, small gestures stand out with great importance. Patrick and Bobby Nolan treated me to stimulating professional discussions and, simply and graciously, took me into their home after a week buried in books. I was enriched by meeting new friends, such as Tom Mertes, whose shared interests in and frustrations with our interdisciplinary topics gave me the sense of having found company on an uninhabited island. The faculty of the Women's Studies Program at the University of Kansas have been enormously supportive. Perhaps my largest intellectual and spiritual debt is to Ann Schofield, who provides a model of friendship and high scholarly standards. My deepest thanks go to Nathan for being there: best friend and most excellent spouse, my tutor in physics and drywall construction. This book took exactly as long as our remodeling project, and there must be a meaning in that.

Portions of this manuscript have appeared as "The Gendered Environment of the Corporate Workplace, 1880–1930," in *The Material Culture of Gender/The Gender of Material Culture,* eds. Kenneth L. Ames and Katharine Martinez (New York: W. W. Norton, forthcoming) and "Gender, Self, and Work in the Life Insurance Industry," in *Work Engendered: Toward a New History of American Labor,* ed. Ava Baron (Ithaca: Cornell University Press, 1991), 168–90.

Introduction

The Business of Gender

I was a 'business girl,' that's what I was. With those brief words, seventy-year-old Alice Peterson summarized her life in 1984.[1] She had worked for forty-five years as a clerk and bookkeeper in a small bank in rural northwestern Minnesota. Confined to a nursing home, her savings consumed by medical care, living on the sufferance of the state, Alice recalled her work in the bank as representing the "real" Alice: the Alice who had been independent, whose life mattered to those she had worked with and to herself. Her definition of that real life used two words—*business girl*—that for her summarized who she was: a woman and a worker.

Alice Peterson's self-definition eloquently suggests questions about the ways individuals conceive of and experience who they are and about the relation between ideologies and institutions, between our sense of self and our social roles.[2] Why would a seventy-year-old woman refer to herself as a "girl"? Why did she call herself a "business girl" rather than a bookkeeper, a secretary, or simply an office worker? Why would an office worker's gender have mattered? Was Alice unusual or voicing a common attitude? Does her language contain clues not only to Alice's life but also to the history of ideas about gender, the history of labor, or the history of financial institutions? This book is an effort to understand at least some of the questions raised by the complex connections Alice so simply asserted. *Engendering Business* assumes that her choice of images was neither accidental nor idiosyncratic. It analyzes the challenges to earlier gender ideals the presence of women like her in the late-nineteenth- and

[1]

early twentieth-century work force represented and the emergence of new kinds of gendered work relations, by focusing on the connections between institutional and personal definitions of manhood and womanhood in financial industry offices between 1870 and 1930.[3]

Financial industries such as insurance and banking were a powerful presence in the American economy and culture at the turn of the century, and women such as Alice became office workers in banks and insurance offices in record numbers between 1870 and 1930.[4] Women's presence in the office work force challenged the Victorian ideal of separate public and private worlds for men and women, with the result that debates over definitions of manhood and womanhood were woven into corporate life from the beginning of the financial industries' modern development. For several reasons, Alice Peterson's statement opens a window onto these developments. One cluster of issues involves the changing nature of work and institutions in the late nineteenth century— Alice's focus on "business." The other grows out of late-nineteenth-century gender ideology—her use of the word *girl*.

The changing nature of work and business in the United States between 1870 and 1930 is well represented by the financial industries, especially life insurance and banking. Although the organization of work, workers, and business has always been gendered, the introduction of women into the office workplace and the growing importance of middle-class consumers in the late nineteenth century gave gender relations a heightened visibility and structural importance in corporate development. In financial industries, conceptions of womanhood and manhood were central to the work experience: executives, managers, agents, and workers used gender to explain and justify office work. Salesmen, for example, were not just people who pushed a product. In sales rhetoric they were "virile," "manly men" engaged in an important public calling akin to the ministry. In the discourse of executives and agents, corporations were not simply investment organizations, they were "mothers" to the public and to employees. A dualistic, gendered language of maleness and femaleness permeated every aspect of corporate experience in financial industries.

Notions about gender became part of the conscious public relations efforts of these industries. By painting the corporation as a benign mother, watched over by wise, "fatherly" executives, financial industry leaders addressed the Gilded Age and Progressive Era's public concerns about corporate greed, unfair business practices, and extremes of wealth. Ideally, if the corporation was a family, it could not also be an alien, pitiless, or evil force in American society. Further, industry executives and agents recognized the increasingly gendered nature of their markets and aimed their products differently at male and female customers.

The insurance and banking industries were important business trendsetters. Their efforts to deal with a multitude of organizational and personal issues helped shape modern corporate life. They were the first clerical sector industries to evolve to a national scale and to incorporate the new technologies and systems of the modern office. At the same time, they continued to have economic and social ties at the local level in sales agencies and branch banks. Beginning with the introduction, around 1870, of office machines (such as the typewriter), new office building types (such as the skyscraper), new forms of internal communication (such as the circular memo), and new kinds of office workers (such as typists and stenographers), financial industries instituted an array of changes in office work and business organization. The banking and insurance industries experienced such changes in organization and work relations as the "feminization" of clerical work, the creation of management and managers, the use of welfare capitalism to deal with labor/management relations, physical job segregation to denote status and gender relations, and the dual hierarchy of promotion and job advancement for men and women. These and other aspects of corporate culture have become central to modern bureaucracies, whether in automobile plants or the federal government.[5]

The financial industries, as service industries, expressed a gendered ideology that was shared to some extent with retail sales but differed from that of manufacturing.[6] It was not that the former were gendered and the latter was not, but that they were gendered in different ways. In both retail sales and the financial industries, as in the helping professions, such as social work, the ideology of service borrowed from widely held middle-class cultural notions of women's particular fitness in caring for others. For example, female insurance agents successfully argued for a place in sales even though insurance sales evolved as a masculinized position. Their efforts were made easier by the increasing number of female customers and by the small-shop atmosphere of the agency system, which allowed for more entrepreneurial flexibility. Manufacturing, in contrast, adopted a masculinized persona based on the connection between artisanal skills and manhood and the ideal of male breadwinners.[7] Female manufacturing workers tended to cluster in those jobs that used so-called feminine skills, such as manual dexterity and the ability to stand repetition, whereas male workers connected their work to notions of men's stronger physique and problem-solving abilities. Thus, while the financial industries participated in many of the broad changes affecting the economy and business in general, they also reveal patterns that suggest the importance of gender to economic development.

All office work underwent changes in the gendered nature of the work force, but those changes were most pronounced in the financial industries. The fastest growing segment of women's labor in the late nineteenth century was clerical work, and the most rapidly growing clerical industries were banking, trust, real estate, and insurance.[8] Women's entry into office work between 1870 and 1930 is a particularly forceful instance of change in the ratio of male and female

TABLE I

Males and Females in All Clerical Occupations, 1870–1930
(in thousands)

	1870	1880	1890	1900	1910	1920	1930
Males	72.4	143.8	307.4	494.0	950.8	1,441.7	1,774.4
Females	1.8	6.6	73.4	214.2	573.1	1,396.0	1,964.4
TOTALS	74.2	150.4	380.8	708.2	1,523.9	2,837.7	3,738.8
Females as percentage of total	2.46	4.40	19.27	30.24	37.60	49.19	52.54

Sources: Adapted from Elyce Rotella, *From Home to Office: U.S. Women at Work, 1870–1930* (Ann Arbor: UMI Research Press, 1981), table 4.1; and Alba M. Edwards, *Population: Comparative Occupation Statistics for the United States, 1870–1940, 16th Census of the United States, 1940* (Washington: Government Printing Office, 1943), tables 9 and 10. "All clerical occupations" includes bookkeepers, cashiers, accountants, clerks (except clerks in stores), stenographers, and typists.

workers in a particular workplace, change that has remained remarkably permanent. The all-male office of the early nineteenth-century United States became, by the twentieth century, a predominantly female place. Between about 1880 and 1930, young, middle- and working-class women entered the labor force as clerks, cashiers, accountants, typists, bookkeepers, secretaries, and stenographers. In 1870, women comprised only 2.5 percent of the clerical labor force; by 1930, 52.5 percent of all clerical workers were female (see table 1). Although African American men and women who worked in offices were for the most part segregated from white men and women in separate "race businesses," they participated in this crucial transition (see table 2).

Men's work in these industries underwent a concurrent revolution: Office skills were devalued and specialized, and the connections between masculinity and white-collar work broke down and were reconstituted. As men moved out of clerical work and into management, they took with them many of the nineteenth-century meanings attached to white-collar work. The salesman, in particular, contributed new ideas about management first to financial industries and ultimately to corporate culture generally. By 1930, on the eve of the Depression, financial industries had come to terms with these changes. The feminized office, housed in a skyscraper and organized in complex, interlocking hierarchies, represented perfectly the modern gendered and racialized corporate workplace.

Connections between economic growth and gender ideals occurred in all industrializing societies in the nineteenth century.[9] British, German, and French culture shared such nineteenth-century notions about middle-class gen-

TABLE 2
Men and Women in Selected Banking and Insurance Occupations, By Race

	All Men	All Women	Total	Black Men	Black Women	Total	All Women as Percentage of Total	All Black Women as Percentage of Black Total
				1910				
Banking								
Bankers & bank officials	22,353	325	22,678	55	4	59	1.4	7.2
Bookkeepers & cashiers	106,130	6,280	112,410	115	36	151	5.6	24.0
Stockbrokers	13,522	207	13,729	32	4	36	1.5	11.0
Accountants & auditors	1,967	115	2,082	1	0	1	5.5	0
Clerks	45,977	3,748	49,725	143	27	170	7.5	16.0
Stenographers & typists	2,001	11,287	13,288	9	26	35	85.0	74.0
Insurance								
Managers & officials	9,376	125	9,501	101	4	105	1.3	3.8
Accountants & auditors	1,215	123	1,338	3	0	3	9.0	0
Agents	82,743	2,521	85,264	1,387	309	1,696	3.0	18.0
Bookkeepers & cashiers	6,385	4,222	10,607	27	113	140	40.0	81.0
Clerks	15,678	6,219	21,897	69	132	201	28.0	66.0
Stenographers & typists	1,334	14,418	15,752	4	58	62	91.0	94.0
				1930				
Banking								
Bankers & bank officials	87,429	5,927	93,356	68	12	80	6.3	15.0

TABLE 2 *(cont.)*

	All Men	All Women	Total	Black Men	Black Women	Total	All Women as Percentage of Total	All Black Women as Percentage of Black Total
				1930				
Banking								
Bookkeepers & cashiers	35,753	36,184	71,937	38	51	89	51.0	57.0
Stockbrokers	69,157	1,793	70,950	90	5	95	2.5	5.3
Accountants & auditors	13,338	1,109	14,447	13	0	13	7.7	0
Clerks	136,386	57,435	193,821	401	78	479	30.0	16.2
Stenographers & typists	1,682	56,287	57,969	6	67	97	97.0	91.0
Insurance								
Managers & officials	27,556	1,752	29,308	409	12	421	6.0	3.0
Accountants & auditors	5,950	1,018	6,968	36	4	40	15.0	10.0
Agents	243,974	12,953	256,927	5,200	1,086	6,286	5.0	17.2
Bookkeepers & cashiers	7,931	18,634	26,565	61	253	314	70.0	80.0
Clerks	34,442	55,986	90,428	259	534	793	62.0	67.3
Stenographers & typists	1,249	75,202	76,451	16	636	652	98.3	97.5

Sources: Compiled from *Thirteenth Census of the U.S. Taken in the Year 1910, Vol. IV, Population, 1910: Occupation Statistics* (Washington: Government Printing Office, 1914), table VI; *Fifteenth Census of the U.S.: 1930, Population, Vol. V, General Report on Occupations* (Washington: Government Printing Office, 1933), table 2; *Negro Population, 1790–1915* (Washington: Government Printing Office,1918), table 22; and *Negroes in the United States, 1920–1932* (Washington: Government Printing Office, 1935), table 27.

der roles as the centrality of the family, men's public and women's private roles, and the connections between white-collar work and middle-class status. However, the pace and type of demographic changes in office work in the United States and in western Europe suggests important differences. Many of the changes in American business and workplace organization and experience occurred as well in much of western Europe, although at a slightly different pace and with different implications. Certain segments of the economies of Great Britain and France, for example, had included female white-collar workers by the mid-nineteenth century. As in the United States, the earliest female office workers were in civil service positions.[10] In western Europe these inroads did not, however, translate into women's expansion into private-sector white-collar work until relatively late, around World War I. England duplicated the increase in female clerical workers which took place in the United States, although at a slower pace. In England, women went from 2 to 20 percent of all clerical workers between 1851 and 1911; they constituted 46 percent in 1931.[11] In France, Judith Wishnia has argued, the government rather than the private sector played the more important role in bringing women into clerical work, instituting an active feminization of the civil service in the 1890s.[12] Industrialization, in other words, did not automatically create specific gender relations or roles; rather, economic and ideological change operated in culturally and historically specific ways. Deep-seated attitudes about gender and class outlined the limitations and avenues of economic change, even as new economic conditions stirred, challenged, and helped create new gender beliefs and class strata.

The gendering of the financial industries contradicts the standard image of late-nineteenth-century business development. Rather than a sharp break with the past suggested by the notion of a "managerial revolution,"[13] the experience of gender in financial industries suggests that the modern corporation remained infused with precorporate work relationships and attitudes. Most business histories, relying on concepts drawn from modernization theory, emphasize the radical break between older forms of employment relations and the modern corporation with its bureaucratic, depersonalized relationships and neutral, rational markets. Most historians of business, focusing on manufacturing, emphasize male experience, especially the activities of male executives as power brokers or of male managers as rationalized bureaucrats. Absent from these interpretations are the continuing ties of corporate life to forms of organization not obvious on charts (such as family partnerships or leisure expressions), the experience of workers and consumers as gendered people, and the implicit assumptions that connected rationalism with masculinity and masculinity with business.[14] Certainly, the transition to rationalism is important to the nature of office work and business practices; systematic management played a major role in creating the modern corporation. However, much of what went on in the financial industries was anything but rational or objective, in the value-neutral sense. How are we to understand, for example, male corporate executives dressed as women playing soccer at a company picnic as indications of bureaucratic rationalism? Or the notion that female secretaries as "office wives" represents modernization? Or the connections among scientific management, efficiency, and new notions of business manhood? These activities may have had a rational explanation or a modern meaning, but those explanations and meanings align as closely with ritual, subjectivity, and privilege as with organizational charts or economic efficiency.

Gendered language often obscured as much as it revealed, mystifying the economic and social relations of the corporation by focusing attention away from the cash nexus of capitalist relations and onto the apparently universal, and morally neutral, biological fact of sex. The financial industries may constitute a unique case because of the demographics of the work force and the nature of their product. However, until we look at the full range of nineteenth-century business and manufacturing development through the lens of gender, we cannot be sure. Given what we do know of welfare capitalism in late-nineteenth-century manufacturing concerns, such as the emphasis on family and leisure, the gendered dimensions of financial industries may be only one, albeit an especially strong, example of the importance of gender in corporate relations.[15]

Finally, the prominence of African American financial industries allows us to explore the connections among race, gender, and economic change. Insurance and banking played a critical role in the labor and financial markets of African American communities and in the growth of a new black middle class, especially after 1900. By the 1920s, African American upper and middle classes had emerged, especially in urban areas, which owned, managed, or worked for black banks and insurance or real estate companies. The gender and class patterns of so-called race businesses differed from those of white-owned companies.[16] Black men and women in insurance clerical work, for example, tended to come from the best-educated among the African American population. Black women more often had jobs, such as bookkeeping in banks and insurance companies, that in white businesses were dominated by men. Race, like gender, shaped opportunities in the financial industries in complex and sometimes contradictory ways.

The changing nature of work and organization in financial industries addresses many of the questions raised by Alice Peterson's description of herself as a "business girl." Specifically, those changes suggest the importance of the gendering of corporate relations and office work. To complete the puzzle of public and private life encompassed in Alice's self-description, we also need to explore some of the issues surrounding nineteenth-century gender ideology. Simply put, *gender* means the cultural expression of biological sex differences.

Manhood and womanhood can seem like timeless categories, as unchanging as the biological markers on which they ultimately are based.[17] While sufficient as a definition, that is not an explanation of why gender is important to historical reconstruction. If gender were simply about how we define our sexuality it would not have much to tell us about anything beyond biology. As a cultural invention, however, gender reveals a great deal. Gender constructions are rooted in the creation of difference, and the ways the ambiguities and tensions of difference open up situations to multiple meanings.[18] Because gender is a model for difference—some have argued that it is the primary model[19]— gender relations traditionally have stood as models for other power relations. Our language is infused with metaphors of dissimilarity and opposition taken from gender and applied to class relations, politics, and nearly every aspect of our lives.[20] Metaphors of gender difference, in fact, are so much a part of the way we think that we take them for granted. Gender, then, is an important aspect of individual behavior, social expectations, experience, and self-definition. Because it bridges the public and the personal, gender can join individuals to society, and vice versa, in visceral and compelling ways. Furthermore, ideas about manhood and womanhood, and about cultural and individual gender roles form within a changing historical context; they are not static, dichotomous categories.

Office work in the late nineteenth century developed in a specific gender climate, one that contemporaries called "separate spheres," which distinguished between a public, male world and a private, female one. Separate spheres emphasized different, inherently biological categories for human experience; it did not distinguish between the facts of biology and the social creation of gender. However, if we define *male* and *female* by their difference from each other rather than by a predetermined set of biological or historical essences, then the gender dichotomy of separate spheres offers merely one way of delineating the duality of male/female; as such, its expressions were specific to its time.[21]

The idea of separate spheres emphasized that manhood/womanhood was a division based on biology but not limited to the biological. In both western Europe and the United States, middle-class culture used gender terms and relationships drawn from biology to describe other, nonbiological phenomena: politics, social relations, morality, education, economics, physical space, and work. Gender analogies explained biological imperatives, describing gender divisions as natural because they grew out of a scientific explanation of biological sexuality (itself a particular manifestation of nineteenth-century thought).[22] The premise of this circular reasoning was that the self was derived "from essences that stand outside of social process," from static categories rather than from a sense of dynamic interaction.[23] Such analogies reinforced connections among the human body, words, and acts, creating a shorthand of the gendered body based on unequally valued dualities: good/bad, matter/spirit, male/female.[24]

The intensive discussion of gender and its ascription to other social systems resulted in a description of social experience infused with maleness and femaleness. By the early twentieth century, gender had become both intensely individualized and broadly social, a legacy of the application of gendered metaphors and language to social and economic structures. Given the centrality of gender to social and self-definition and the interactive process of gender role formation, women's and men's experience at the turn of the century was simultaneously more generalized and more intimate than the static model of separate spheres allowed. In particular, the vocabulary of gender metaphors appeared in unexpected places. For example, just as the apparent rationalism of nineteenth-century science employed the subjective cultural expressions of separate spheres,[25] so the language of work and business expressed complex degrees of status as though those differences were inherently male and female, and inherent in men and women.

Alice Peterson's use of the phrase "business girl" suggests connections between her individual self-conception and widely held ideas about gender in the workplaces of the financial industries. Clearly, for Alice, her work was important in shaping her sense of self. Just as clearly, that sense informed her definition of a worker. Indeed, different labor systems require different sorts of behavior, forms of organization, and sets of personal commitment, expectations, and social beliefs.[26] Just as those connections were critical for Alice as an individual, the interdependence of economic and organizational forms (such as corporations), social constructs (such as gender), and personal experience are central to understanding the history of changes in office work. Written, visual, and spatial expressions reveal the underlying assumptions, the sometimes unspoken beliefs and often covert power relations of office culture. For example, the office environment was open to diverse meanings. The structure and content of buildings and rooms in turn-of-the-century offices suggest struggles and compromises over meaning and use. As space became an arena of disagreement about office work, it revealed both underlying assumptions about status and gender and the modification of those assumptions in new historical situations. Spatial arrangements in offices gave physical form to the abstract social relations of gender and thereby helped create power or status differences among office workers.[27] Participants such as Alice Peterson shaped modern corporate gender relations as they spoke about gender, made gendered spaces, and used symbols, images, and metaphors to connect the world "out there" to the one "in here."

The blurring of gender boundaries called into question the ideal of distinct public and private physical, ideological, and experiential worlds for men and women. The business community and office workers themselves discussed, with varying degrees of insight, this mingling of men and women in office work. The result was a redefinition of socially accepted male and female gender roles within financial offices. These newly defined roles in the workplace built on the conceptual dichotomy of separate spheres but differed critically in their emphases and rationales. *Separate spheres,* in fact, was a complex metaphor in the world of offices. It reinforced women's essential domesticity while encompassing domestic havens in all-male executive suites, and it dictated physical and organizational distance between men and women but incorporated the notion that corporate workers were "family."

The uses of gendered language to describe office work, work relations, status, and corporate organization stemmed from at least two interrelated sources. First, workers, managers, and executives expressed their culture's obsession with categories of maleness and femaleness as signifiers of difference. Second, demographic changes challenged the male-defined nineteenth-century workplace as women entered male space and demanded accommodation, both physical and ideological. Often, women's presence seemed the most salient fact separating the new corporate workplace from the traditional male office. The consuming public, as well, registered larger numbers of women potentially interested in financial products, either directly as workers or indirectly as wives and widows. These factors, taken together, made gender seem a powerful way of understanding and expressing the changing social and economic experience of office work and corporate relations.

Finally, the notion of separate spheres as a gender ideal was part of an as yet imperfectly understood class structure. From the inception of modern office work in the early nineteenth century, most social commentators and scholars have labeled clerical workers as middle class.[28] By this they mean a group that idealizes hard work and delayed gratification, strives for moral and social respectability through the creation of a nuclear family, uses education to effect upward mobility or maintain class standing, performs mental labor indoors at desks (white-collar work) rather than physical labor at machines or outdoors (blue-collar work), and is economically better off than some but not as wealthy as others.

This notion of the middle class, however, has its limits as a tool for understanding social, institutional and economic change in the financial industries. It mingles economic and social status with the role of families and individuals while ignoring gender and race. It emphasizes labor while glossing over life stage, age, family relation, and differences in economic sectors. Most economic analyses argue that families achieve middle-class status when a man has sufficient education or training in white-collar work to support a wife and children without their additional paid labor. Class status thereby assumes a gendered material base derived from the value of a man's wage. If economic class flows from male labor, however, it is not clear what role gender plays in the creation of a "classed" female wage earner, nor what separates the classes from one another. This becomes especially problematic when dealing with female white-collar workers or with shifts in the social meanings of male white-collar work. Further, people can experience middle-class status as individual workers, as family members, or as members of a specific racial or ethnic group.

One useful way to conceptualize the middle class to allow for gender and race is to separate, for purposes of analysis, its economic and social roots and functions. This is not to privilege social over material causes but to recognize that the two interact in complex ways.[29] We label white-collar labor as middle class because of the relatively high wages, the indoor nature of the work, and the level of education required. But the economic and social class meanings of that work can vary depending on gender, race, life stage, or the opportunity such work provides for widening social contacts. Thus, a young woman clerical worker in 1900 whose salary elevated her above factory laborers could have aspired to middle-class social status either as a career secretary or as the wife of a middle-class man, even if her father was a day laborer. If she chose to be a career secretary, however, eventually her work experience would have outstripped her earning power, and as she got older she would have become working class, in economic terms, while retaining the middle-class respectability embedded in the social status of her work. Conversely, a young man who became a typist in 1900 would have faced the steady deterioration of both wages and the social meaning of his work as some office jobs were feminized. For him, clerical work would have remained technically white-collar work but would have held none of the status of managerial labor precisely because it had become a woman's job. His choices would have been to work his way up, and thus maintain both economic and social middle-class status by becoming a manager, or remain in an increasingly devalued position, both economically and socially. Thus, to speak of male and female office workers simply as middle class is problematic, given gender differences and the changing social meaning of office jobs.

The issue of race clouds still further our understanding of class and gender in office work. Most studies of class relations build on an unspoken assumption that to be middle class is to be white, thereby failing to account for race. Further, until the 1920s a black economic middle class was not distinguishable within the African American population, and certainly no large black middle class existed. Rather, due to the relatively limited economic resources available to the African American population and the racism of white society, after 1860 there was an upper class of comparatively wealthy families; a small, economically distinct middle class; and a large working class. Although research in this area is sketchy, it appears that upper- and middle-class blacks largely shared social values. Both groups believed in respectability, church membership, family stability, home ownership, hard work, good education, and refinement.

Further, the black middle class apparently held many of the same gender ideals as whites, if for different reasons.[30] Thus, social beliefs about work and gender did not widely separate the black middle and upper classes from each other or from the white middle class, yet the implications of class differed according to race and gender. The nineteenth-century white middle-class ideals of manhood and womanhood, for example, assumed that the perfect woman or man was white and sexually chaste. This racialized image helped shape the white perception that black women and men were more sexual than whites and increased the importance of female chastity among middle-class African Americans.[31] That emphasis, in turn, may have contributed to the symbolic importance of middle-class African American women clerks as elevating the social tone of office work.

In addition, from the 1860s until the 1920s, the black upper class was not strictly synonymous with wealth, much as white upper-class status was in part a function of birth as well as, or even in the absence of, wealth. Blacks in the old upper class until the 1920s were domestic servants for wealthy whites or owned various types of service businesses, such as barber shops, with a predominantly white clientele.[32] Members of this class included food caterers, teachers, barbers, lawyers, blacksmiths, and dentists in the South and, in the North, civil servants, college-trained clergy, nurses, and social workers. In white class terms, these were middle-class and not elite occupations. In addition, to the extent that one could identify an elite of upper and middle classes, much of their social status and class position derived not directly from economic status but from physical characteristics such as straight hair and light skin, which "afforded economic advantages that were not available to darker-complexioned blacks."[33]

Without divorcing class from a material base or claiming that it is primarily ideological, I will emphasize that a shared ethos marked the middle-class experience—a set of values that elevated female domesticity and male breadwinning, the nuclear family, respectability, education, and clean or physically undemanding work. Of course, identifying a set of distinctive middle-class values does not resolve what those values meant in the gendered or racialized context of office work. In fact, it was the permutations of this shared body of ideas about gender, class, and race that corporate executives, managers, and workers explored in their discussions of office work. In the financial industries, female domesticity and male breadwinning translated into low wages for women (who were not, by definition, breadwinners) and imagery such as "office housekeepers" and "manly salesmen." Issues such as the modernization of business relations, the class status of office workers, the racial components of class in office work, and the connections between class, race, and the ideal of separate spheres all contributed to the gendering of financial industries.

Such issues suggest several important questions that generalize those raised earlier about Alice Peterson's experience. Was the shift from nineteenth-century notions of gender in business complete? What were early-twentieth-century gender work roles? What purposes did those roles serve, and who articulated them? Why and how were corporations gendered? How did the physical spaces of the workplace reinforce or undermine gendered behavior and expectations? How did these ideological and behavioral changes in women's and men's roles, and workplace relations, grow out of and inform one another? As answers to these queries, the stories in this book touch on areas as divergent as family relations and corporate organizational structure, class formation and the nature of bureaucracy, office buildings and company playgrounds, the specifics of individual lives and the movements of economic markets. These aspects of business are connected by gender, and specifically by the ways the various participants in corporate office work used gender both to elide the distinctions between the private and public worlds of family, self, and work and to create status and power differences. An analysis of gender as a body of ideas, experiences, and expressions gives us a window onto complex relationships that Alice Peterson expressed with the phrase "business girl." This book is not the final word on the changing constructions of gender and work in the early twentieth century, nor is it the definitive analysis of the intersection of gender ideologies and business institutions. It is, however, an argument for the pervasiveness of gender in our world and for the insights into our history that the study of gender can provide. I hope that it will generate as many questions as it answers.

CHAPTER ONE

From Six to Forty Thousand

The Growth of Financial Industries, 1840–1930

At its birth in 1867, the Metropolitan Life Insurance Company consisted of six men working in two small rented rooms at 243 Broadway in New York City. In the field, twenty-one agents sold life insurance, collected premiums, and represented the company to the persons it insured. In 1900, Metropolitan Life's home office claimed "more typewriters than any other office building in the world." The company employees—by then both men and women—involved themselves in athletic events, choral societies, newsletter publishing, and a cooperative store, in addition to their compensated duties.[1] By 1929, Metropolitan Life's home office at Madison Square boasted a tower that made it the "tallest habitable structure on earth—fifty floors, reaching 700 feet above the sidewalk."[2] The total work force numbered over forty thousand— "A Family of 40,000," the company's advertising brochures called it—which included men and women, painters, carpenters, doctors, lawyers, clerical workers, masons, elevator operators, chauffeurs, field agents, and engineers. In addition to its landmark tower, the building contained a gymnasium, an auditorium, a radio station, and seven lunchrooms.

This story of one life insurance company tells more than a simple economic tale of business growth and progress, although it is tempting to read it that way. That certainly was the message company executives promoted. Yet what the leaders of early-twentieth-century financial industries presented as linear and essentially inevitable economic progress obscured important, qualitative changes. There were vast cultural distances between 243 Broadway and Madison Square—differences in the nature of the office work force and workplace, the explanations that justified the aims and actions of the business community, and the relations between businesses and their clientele. Metropolitan Life's move uptown from Broadway to Madison Square also encapsulated the growth of an urban, white-collar middle class and the gender and racial separations of that class. In particular, it symbolized the deep-seated connections between office work and the use of ideas and assumptions about gender to create, promote, or dissolve the interests of the white-collar workplace.

The economic history of American financial industries in the nineteenth century is largely a story of the gradual movement of entrepreneurial and investment capital out of the coffers of merchants, families, and mutual aid societies and into the hands of legal entities—corporations—formed specifically for the purpose of accumulating, protecting, and using that capital. The social history of financial institutions likewise charts the gradual replacement of traditional forms of social security and family-oriented business relations with more impersonal, bureaucratic organizations. These have been slow transitions and, as anyone with a family knows, ones that remain incomplete. Families still provide direct funding for the education of children, for example, by paying college tuition. Families often distribute money or in-kind contributions such as room and board in the case of death or divorce of a family member. However, except for the very wealthy, family financial support rarely funds major expenses such as retirement income or capital to begin or maintain a business. Most of these functions have been taken over by financial entities such as commercial banks or insurance companies. This move away from reliance on local or kin-based support networks to impersonal market transactions, which first came to dominate the economy in the 1870s, is what Alan Trachtenberg has termed "the incorporation of America" and Alfred Chandler "the managerial revolution." It is part of a global economic and social process that affected much of western Europe as well.[3]

One of the best examples of these transitions comes in the social and economic changes in life insurance in the nineteenth century as it evolved into a cultural concept, an economic institution, and a marketable product. Insurance is a contract to provide security or protection for something of value. Insurance is an ancient concept, first recorded among the Babylonians, Greeks, and Romans, who insured their merchant ships against losses at sea. Marine insurance recognized the cost of material loss through the vagaries of nature, and this notion that security or protection could be commodified formed part of the basis of modern insurance. Life insurance in the ancient world, however, was shaped by a focus similar to that found in marine insurance. It might, in fact, more appropriately be called "death insurance." It did not recognize the abstract loss of economic value in a breadwinner but did acknowledge the material cost of death itself. The early Greeks, Romans, and Babylonians could acquire burial insurance from private entrepreneurs to cover the costs of seeing a loved one into the hereafter in style.[4] Although this form of insurance did not indemnify the economic value of an individual's life, the idea that the insurance contract itself was a commodity provided the exchange basis for modern insurance.

The second important concept for modern life insurance was the notion of placing a monetary value on an individual's future life—a "potential value." This aspect of life insurance first appeared in the mutual aid societies of the Middle Ages, founded on craft or guild lines or through the auspices of a church or other religious organization. Mutual aid recognized the loss of future earnings represented by a breadwinner's death. In the Middle Ages, mutual aid societies provided funds for burial expenses, including prayers for the dead, but also gave benefits to widows and children in the event of a member's death. Benefits were paid out of a common fund or collected for the event from an organization's members. The mutual aid society denied the commodity or exchange basis of family protection and emphasized instead a gift or reciprocal relationship between members of a self-selected and limited group.[5] As was true of early banking operations, mutual aid existed in addition to rather than instead of direct aid through other family or kin connections; members (and breadwinners) were assumed to be male.

The notions of commodification and potential value were adapted to various forms of life insurance in response to the insecurities of the developing market economy of the sixteenth through the eighteenth centuries. Between 1500 and 1700 in Great Britain and its colonies, for example, "tontines" were a popular form of group life insurance. Tontines were little more than gambling. Individuals in a group each paid an agreed amount into a pool, and the last surviving member, the "winner," garnered the entire sum. Tontines could exist without relation to either mutual aid societies or family protection. Other early life insurance plans, offered by individual entrepreneurs or private companies, allowed an individual to take out a policy on the life of someone else. But these forms of insurance had "grave " problems: In both cases, the temptation to murder sometimes was too strong to overcome. In addition, tontines provided no benefits to the families of any but the last survivor. The abuses of both types of insurance led the British government to prohibit their use in 1773.[6]

Life insurance based on the age of the client at the time the policy was purchased and the period for which the policy was granted dates from 1762, when the Society for Equitable Assurances on Lives and Survivorships was started in England.[7] This type of life insurance incorporated both the notion of commodification and a recognition of potential value. However, the policies of early life insurance companies were available primarily to wealthy individuals or specific professional groups and thus had limited appeal and funding. The

Society for Equitable Assurances, for example, simply stopped taking new members in 1816. The first Anglo-American life insurance company was started by the Presbyterian synod in 1759. The Presbyterian Ministers Fund made life policies available only to affiliated clergymen. There is no evidence among these early plans of any efforts either to insure women or to appeal directly to them as potential beneficiaries. Life insurance companies in this period were dominated by male principals and clients.

Until the late nineteenth century, the poor or working classes and socially segregated groups such as free African Americans continued to rely predominantly on older forms of mutual aid. In 1787 two African American ministers in Philadelphia formed the Free African Society. This group, despite its founders, was based in Philadelphia's free black community rather than a particular religious organization. It was created, as its charter stated, "in order to support one another in sickness and for the benefit of widows and fatherless children." One such society that would become an important economic force for early-twentieth-century African Americans was the Independent Order of Saint Luke, a women's mutual benefit association founded in 1867 by Mary Prout.[8] Mutual aid societies generally were linked to church or work organizations and continued the tradition of providing funds for prayers, burial expenses, and payments to widows and children. Eighteenth- and nineteenth-century fraternal organizations, such as the Masons, Oddfellows, and the Colored Knights of Pythias, provided similar benefits to black and white artisans, shopkeepers, small-scale entrepreneurs, and professional men.[9]

The modern life insurance product combines the notions of commodification and potential value with increased availability, new marketing techniques, and larger organization. The industry relies on policy sales through a system of widespread local agencies that advertise for customers in an open market. The rudiments of the agency system and advertising appeared in Great Britain in the 1790s, and openly available life insurance first came to the United States in 1807 through offerings by the Pelican Life Insurance Company of London. Initially in this and similar companies, however, the principals made little effort to sell insurance, waiting instead for customers to seek them out or offering shares to friends or family. In addition, since distribution tended to be local and personalized, few companies took out advertising in newspapers, journals, or magazines. There were no financial trade papers or national organizations devoted to the industry. The New York Life Insurance and Trust Company was the first, in the early 1830s, to make use of active sales agents. By the 1840s, as the industry began to grow rapidly, more companies adopted aggressive sales techniques and sought out a broader clientele. Trade papers focusing on insurance and banking first appeared in the early 1850s.[10]

Life insurance companies in the early nineteenth century were patterned after mutual aid societies and were financed and organized as "mutuals."

Mutual companies needed little initial investment or operating capital, generating capital largely from the sale of premiums. As in mutual aid societies, the pool of funds provided the money to pay off claims. Mutuals were the quickest and least expensive way to form a company. They held enormous appeal for entrepreneurs with little capital and few connections and enabled young men to get started in their own businesses.[11] Henry Baldwin Hyde for example, founded the Equitable Life Assurance Society in 1859. Hyde had started in life insurance at the age of seventeen, selling policies for Mutual Life; he began the Equitable when he was twenty-five. The Equitable initially sold mutual shares to friends, family, acquaintances of the principals, well-to-do businessmen and self-employed middle-class men. This sort of informality was typical of financial businesses of the period. Banks also could be organized easily; one might begin when someone asked a storekeeper to hold funds for safekeeping.[12] While most companies remained the province of men, Mary Prout's Order of Saint Luke suggests that the more informal economy of the early and mid-nineteenth century allowed avenues for female entrepreneurs. The mutual form of organization may have allowed more room for marginalized groups such as women and racial minorities to become entrepreneurs.[13]

By the mid-nineteenth century, some companies had adopted other methods of organization, sometimes combined with the mutual form. Straight stock companies sold private issues of stock and paid dividends only to investors. Mixed companies sold stock but paid dividends to both stockholders and clients. Like mutuals, stock companies also faced the problem of an unregulated economy, but they provided start-up capital that could tide a new organization over hard times or unwise client selection. By the late nineteenth century, most insurance companies still were mutuals.[14] However, beginning in the 1860s, most stock and mutual companies adopted corporate organization: specialization, stock sales, legally shielded principals, and bureaucratic continuity.[15] An example of these trends is the Pacific Mutual Life Insurance Company, founded in 1868 by two life insurance agents. Operating initially within the local Sacramento community, Pacific Mutual had expanded around the country by the mid-1870s, despite the widespread problems in the nation's economy that had bankrupted its major rival. After the Panic of 1873, the company centralized its agency system and adopted widespread advertising.[16]

In the early years, aggressive sales techniques were not an important factor in the growth of demand for life insurance, and the principals did not see sales or sales personnel as particularly important or critical elements in a company's fortunes.[17] Early agents or brokers, in fact, were poorly paid and operated more like underwriters than salesmen.[18] Most agents were male, and they worked without contracts or training. Many represented more than one company. Competition was stiff and demand high enough by the 1840s to encourage more aggressive sales techniques and higher commissions for agents. Sales agents began to visit prospective clients at home and at work to solicit premiums. Even so, the process remained decentralized until the 1860s. Most agents were men in small towns or urban neighborhoods who sold life insurance as a sideline or to make up for seasonal losses in income. During the 1890s, the agency system became widespread, centralized, and more closely connected to a parent company. Large companies such as Metropolitan Life initiated more formalized agent/company relations through the use of contracts and informative newsletters. The agency system included general agencies and general agents who supervised large numbers of salesmen.[19]

At the base of the simple but innovative approach of corporate life insurance and banking lay two economic concepts: minimizing the risks to the insurer or bank in order to maximize earnings and spreading the costs in order to make the product as cheap as possible for the insured or client. As early as the 1840s, entrepreneurs began to take advantage of the general economic climate to realize the potential of banks and life insurance for generating income through the sale of financial security to the public.[20] Later the development and refinement of new techniques—calculated life-expectancy tables (actuarial science), mass marketing, and specialized types of insurance and banking products—broadened the market for financial services and rationalized financial products.

The growth of life insurance and banking rested on the same dynamics that reshaped manufacturing in the nineteenth-century United States and western Europe. New forms of communication and transportation that facilitated the development of national markets for consumer goods after the Civil War aided financial industries in reaching a wider audience, particularly through advertising and easier communication between the home office and branch offices, banks, or agencies in cities and small towns around the country. A wealth of specialized job functions had emerged in offices by the 1890s, owing largely to the great increase in markets combined with new populations of workers (women, displaced farm workers, and immigrants) and new technologies that speeded record-keeping and communication, such as the typewriter, introduced in the late 1870s. The availability of an increasingly literate, large wage labor force enabled industry leaders to keep wages relatively low and may have contributed to the gendering of the office labor force. At the same time, the specialization or rationalization of production taking place in manufacturing found its way into the financial industries as well. The modern financial industry product—economic security based on complex and precise computations, accurate and thorough record-keeping, and creative financial investments—lent itself to highly specialized labor divisions. Distinctions between managers and other workers, corporate bureaucracy, and division of labor had appeared in financial industries by the 1880s. The insurance and banking industries' increasing use of a corporate organizational structure replicated on a larger and more generalized scale the social security provided by trusts and national workers' unions.[21]

Some organizational patterns could, in fact, transfer quite directly. Metropolitan Life, for example, first used members of a workers' *bund,* the Hildise Bund in New York City, to make its premium collections in the 1870s. Often, one type of organization gave birth to others. This was especially true for the transition from mutual aid to insurance to banking. For example, many of the health, accident, and life insurance companies owned and operated by African Americans began as church relief societies, mutual aid, or benevolent associations before and just after the Civil War. The first savings bank in the country owned and operated by blacks was begun in 1888 as an adjunct of a Virginia mutual aid society, the True Reformers.[22] The first female bank president in the United States was an African American, Maggie Lena Walker. Her creation of the Saint Luke Penny Savings Bank in 1903 built directly from her association with Mary Prout's Independent Order of Saint Luke.[23]

Finally, as had happened in other economic sectors, a few companies in the financial industries became extremely large, even as expanding markets allowed for the continuous creation of smaller companies.[24] Severe and often brutalizing competition and the growth of national markets enormously increased the financial reserves and work force of a few giant life insurance companies and banks. In the 1860s, after nearly two decades of phenomenal growth that witnessed the founding and failure of numerous concerns, there were forty-seven life insurance companies in the United States employing about two thousand people. By 1920, 126 companies did business. In 1924, the Equitable Life Assurance Society alone, one of the largest companies, had over $3 billion of insurance in force and $700 million in assets.[25] The number of incorporated commercial banks grew as well, from twenty-nine in 1800 to about two thousand in 1866 to over twenty-three thousand by 1900.[26] Unlike insurance, however, the average size of banks remained small—about one-half million dollars in assets—which was about the same in 1870.[27] Both banks and life insurance companies went through a process of consolidation and merger from the 1870s to the early 1930s that vastly increased the size and financial reserves of a few companies. For example, National City Bank, the largest commercial bank in the United States, in 1912 had deposits of $252 million and gold reserves approaching those of the U.S. Treasury, and it was affiliated with more than two hundred other banks. It achieved that status by swallowing up other banks.[28]

By 1930, life insurance leaders, with few exceptions, were the same as they are today. Of these, the Metropolitan Life Insurance Company and the Equitable Life Assurance Society were involved from the 1860s in a fierce competitive battle for clients; at the turn of the century, they were among the top five life insurance companies in the country. Corporate growth was both cause and consequence of product specialization. In the 1890s, the Equitable focused on middle-class shopkeepers, small-scale industrialists, and the ranks of upper middle-class professionals, while Metropolitan Life provided primarily "industrial" insurance—that is, life insurance policies for the industrial or working class. The Germania Life Insurance Company, from its inception in 1860, targeted middle-class German-Americans as its clientele. African American companies aimed at both rural and urban clientele but marketed exclusively to blacks.[29] Many small, white-owned companies such as New England Mutual Life Insurance Company, and all African American companies never reached the size of Metropolitan Life or the Equitable, partly because they never focused on growth *per se* or were prohibited by white racism from expanding their markets. Yet smaller companies, whatever their area of product specialization, followed the larger companies in their development of corporate structure, product and job specialization, a large office staff, and social justifications.

From the beginning, the financial industries reflected the racial segregation of American society. In many instances, African Americans started their own life insurance societies after being shut out of participation in white companies. While white companies sometimes took on black agents to canvas African American markets and even invested occasionally in black financial organizations, by the early twentieth century most prominent white companies refused to hire or insure blacks.[30] As reasons, they cited the higher death rates and precarious economic conditions prevalent in most black communities. Those white companies that did insure blacks sometimes offered fraudulent policies or perpetrated outright scams.

Segregation had profound consequences for black financial industries and African Americans generally. Racial exclusion, combined with the fact that white companies left the field open to black entrepreneurs, generated a plethora of mutual benefit societies organized by and for black Americans. There were 106 African American mutual benefit societies in Philadelphia alone in 1849, and families often belonged to more than one. Baltimore had twenty-five such societies before the Civil War, and Charleston at least two. By the early twentieth century, black life insurance companies and banks, many of them direct outgrowths of mutual or fraternal societies, existed in all the southern states and in some northern cities. These companies were important financial and social elements in black communities, providing not just death benefits but investment capital, social welfare activities, and health and educational services. Further, black life insurance companies often were directly responsible for the existence of other financial services. The pattern followed by the True Reformers in 1888 was repeated in virtually every black community with a life insurance company: life insurance premiums provided capital, which the company then invested in real estate and black businesses by creating real estate development companies and banks. In 1930, fifteen African American insurance companies had $235 million of insurance—certainly not a rival for white-owned giants such as the Equitable, but a vitally important capital resource for the African American population.[31] African American companies reflected the same sort of community awareness as white companies, with the difference that racial issues clearly took precedence over or were bound up in issues of legitimacy or public acceptance.

Whatever the size, racial or ethnic orientation, or class composition of the financial industries' clientele, the nature of the product encouraged these companies to become leaders in what would later be called public relations. Since banks, trust companies, and life insurance companies sold an intangible product that was not strictly a necessity, customer relations played a crucial role in the attitudes and business strategies of the financial industries, setting them somewhat apart from the manufacturing and retail sectors. Life insurance entrepreneurs in the early nineteenth century, for example, confronted a reluctant market. Many people resisted the product because they found distasteful the idea of placing monetary value on human life or believed superstitiously that taking out a life insurance policy would hasten death. In addition, forms of life insurance like tontines had given the concept overtones of risk and gambling at odds with both religious beliefs in divine order and traditional mercantilist attitudes.[32] Although these uses of insurance were outlawed, company executives constantly invented new forms which, while not strictly against the law, certainly stacked the profit deck at the client's expense. Metropolitan Life and the Equitable introduced modified tontine schemes in the 1860s based on a "deferred dividend" policy. In this plan, full dividends were paid on a small percentage of premiums; in most cases, lapses of payment or death brought only a portion of paid-in premiums back to the policyholder or his or her family. In effect, those who were able to keep their premiums paid up benefited from the surplus funds generated by those who did not. Manipulations like these continued to haunt the insurance business, culminating in the public housecleaning of the New York state Armstrong investigation in 1905 and the subsequent tightening of laws in New York and other states.[33]

The acceptance of life insurance as a product also was related to structural changes taking place in the larger society. In fact, perceived need for the product must account for a sizeable amount of the industry's spectacular growth in the 1840s and 1850s. First, the industry filled a need formed by the breakdown of older patterns of financial security and support. Organized life insurance enlarged and generalized the benefits provided by guilds, workers' mutual aid societies, fraternal organizations, and labor unions. Rather than tying contributions and distributions to a specific section of the population—a particular trade, group, or voluntary organization—the life insurance industry extended the concept of mutual aid as a general commodity available to almost any individual.[34]

Second, an increasingly secular and urban society found both emotional and economic comfort in insuring the lives of fathers and breadwinners, particularly the growing middle class of small entrepreneurs, white-collar workers, and professionals. These groups traditionally had not formed mutual aid societies but had relied instead on family connections and investments in land or personal property for security. Furthermore, life insurance had a general appeal to an increasingly fragmented population. Urbanites, cut off from the traditional economic support of agricultural lands, found economic security in life insurance and savings banks.[35] For the working class, life insurance provided an alternative or supplement to union supports. In addition, as new groups participated directly in the economy, the life insurance product met new financial needs. Black Americans saw life insurance as both a cushion for the effects of racism and a major entrepreneurial field, particularly after the end of slavery. Women, and especially the increasing numbers of working or self-supporting women, purchased life insurance, acknowledging their economic value. Although many companies continued to be leery of female clients, insurance was available to some women from the earliest years of the modern industry. The Manhattan Life Insurance Company of New York insured its first woman in 1850: Caroline Ingraham of Madison, New Jersey, who listed her occupation as "Woman." The second policy sold by the Pacific Mutual Life Insurance Company of California went to Mrs. Louise Lorette Jackson of Sacramento in 1868. Retirement funds, trusts, or annuities also appealed to a wide clientele and often were aimed at specific markets. Provident Mutual Life and Trust Company of Philadelphia, for example, offered a "Retirement Life Income," which guaranteed monthly payments no matter how long the client lived. In the 1920s, separate advertising campaigns aimed this package at men and women.[36]

Third, life insurance provided a sort of "economic immortality," a way of influencing the living, and of living on through one's legacy, that suited both an inherently unstable economic climate and an increasingly mobile, cash-oriented urban population. Land ownership waned in importance as a source of family wealth, middle-class sons and daughters made their own choices from a variety of possible careers, and the poor and working classes faced increasingly pinched financial conditions. The cash legacy of life insurance allowed a more fluid inheritance than land or a family business, and for many families or individuals it represented a form of savings or investment not otherwise available to them.

Finally, the professionalization of death taking place in the early nineteenth century affected the climate for life insurance. As Viviana Zelizer points out, like professional funeral undertaking and the establishment of trust companies, life insurance "was part of a general movement to rationalize and formalize the management of death."[37] The confluence of these economic, attitudinal and marketing changes made the life insurance industry by 1910 one of the wealthiest and most powerful sectors of corporate North America. Life insurance companies, in fact, were a major source of accumulated funds, rivaling investment banks as sources of entrepreneurial capital. Their investments in a variety of areas, including real estate, municipal and industrial bonds, mortgages, and stocks, represented one of the most important channels of individual capital into the local and national economies of the late nineteenth century.[38]

The expansion of life insurance and banking created important shifts in the composition of the work force, the relations between employers and employees, and the way work was organized. Every business is designed for the same end, to generate profits, but different organizational forms involve workers and employers in particular relationships with one another and with their place of work. In that regard, the precorporate office was a distinctive environment.

Early-nineteenth-century life insurance and banking offices had small staffs who did paperwork by hand.[39] Henry Baldwin Hyde, for example, acted as head of all departments at the early Equitable, spending his mornings in the office and afternoons and evenings out selling insurance.[40] In 1876, the office staff of the Manhattan Life Insurance Company of New York consisted of only 14 people supporting over 450 scattered agents and brokers.

Work space in early offices was cramped and undifferentiated. An office could be housed in two or three rooms divided only by waist-high railings or partitions. Such small-scale enterprises meant that work relations in the nineteenth-century office were more personalized.[41] Given that even by the 1860s many businesses were not far removed from family concerns, one's boss was still likely to be a relative.

In the small, all-male office, each individual theoretically had an equal chance to move from an entry position as an office boy or clerk to the presidency or a secretaryship, and each worker had ample opportunity to come face to face with his employer. Office clerks were closer to their employer in dress, status, and prospects than they were to factory workers.[42] This democracy of opportunity was couched in terms of personal relations rather than standardized tests or promotional tracks, or even equality of skill or training. Office workers constructed an image of office hierarchies softened by the notice of benevolent employers. Asa S. Wing is a good example. As president of Provident Mutual Life Insurance Company in 1915, Wing recalled the close personal ties between himself and his first employer. Wing left his rural Rhode Island home for Philadelphia in 1867 at the age of seventeen to work for the company. For the first few weeks, while looking for a suitable boarding house, he lived at

Members of the home office staff of New England Mutual, ca. 1889, casually posed in the undifferentiated spaces of the early office. *Courtesy of* TNE.

the home of Provident Mutual's president, Samuel R. Shipley, and took his meals with the family.[43]

In office advancement narratives, promotions usually came because an executive paid personal attention to an employee. Typical of this experience was the second employee hired by the Equitable, Thomas D. Jordan, who began as an errand boy because the "actuary liked his looks." Jordan worked for the company for forty-five years and eventually became the comptroller.[44] One Equitable employee recalled that although he began as a clerk, when the president of the company personally noticed his talent for neat, legible handwriting, he was promoted: "Mr. Hyde would sometimes inspect [my] handwriting as he passed through. Finally one day he said 'That's fine young man. I wish I could write as well as that.' Shortly thereafter I was transferred to the Policy Writing Department."[45] Of course, although these stories of advancement stressed democracy of opportunity, unlike Thomas Jordan not everyone made it to the top. Nonetheless, most young men who worked as clerks saw their position as training and probably believed in the possibility of advancement.[46]

The trope of personalized promotion was built, in part, on the foundations of work itself. Because of the lack of specialized work functions, relations between employer and employee in the precorporate structure could be relatively intimate, placing a higher value on general and interpersonal skills than on training in specific areas. B. G. Orchard put it this way in 1871: "Energy, promptitude, tact, delicacy of perception. These, not knowledge of ancient history . . . not skill in essay writing . . . are the results of business education."[47] The apprenticeship system meant that employees' allegiance went to their superiors or the head of the company: those who controlled access to training and rewards. Rather than inviting specific job identification, precorporate paternalism and the apprenticeship and rewards system encouraged personal loyalties. Henry T. Powell constructed a highly individualized relationship between himself and his Equitable employer: "After signing my contract [vice president] Gage E. Tarbell patted me on the back and said 'Now my boy, it is up to you.' He had fulfilled his part—he had given me the contract—it was up to me to make good in good times and in bad. Mr. Tarbell's action indelibly impressed upon me that he was putting the job squarely up to me. This gave me confidence. I had to win—not only for myself but for him."[48] Training schools were available by the 1840s to prepare young men for positions in business, but learning by doing, wherein an informal apprenticeship fitted an employee for a particular company or position, remained the normal avenue for anyone employed in business before the Civil War.[49] The personalized structure of office work and the notion of democratic promotion were strengthened by the fact that offices housed only men.

The links between personalism and apprenticeship were important aspects of the organizational hierarchy of age, gender, and position that shaped the office experience. For example, the widespread use of the term *office boy* to describe the lowest position on the staff had both a functional and a relational meaning. On the one hand, beginning clerks, or office boys, literally could be boys as young as ten to fourteen years old. Morgan S. Bulkeley, the president of Aetna Life Insurance from the 1870s to the 1920s, began as an apprentice at age fourteen with financier and banker H. P. Morgan. George Schaefer started work at the Equitable in the mail room at age fourteen in 1917, and Fordyce Pye as an office boy at fourteen the same year. One employee of a stock brokerage business in San Francisco began work in 1878 at the age of twelve.[50] On the other hand, the term reflected the master/apprentice or paternalistic relationship between the "boy" and his "chief." After the entrance of women into office work, the position of office boy continued, with new status and gender connotations. The term was applied to both male and female employees, since its status at the bottom of the job ranks did not change. For instance, a newspaper advertisement from the early 1920s read, "Wanted—a boy, either sex." However, differences in promotional paths for young men and women meant that the male office boy could "grow up" with the company and assume a man's responsibilities by becoming a clerk, manager, or agency director. A female office boy very seldom could grow up to a high-level managerial or executive position.[51]

The apprenticeship system remained in place after the war, although family ties, money, and personal relations with one's employer played a much smaller, although never nonexistent, role. By 1900 many employers placed a premium on education in business schools, high school, or college as a prerequisite for hiring and promotion. The Equitable, in 1902, started recruiting and training college graduates as agents. The Carnegie School of Practical Life Insurance Salesmanship was started in 1919 to offer professional training in sales. In 1929, the industry codified professional standards for life insurance agents, and its official school, the American College of Life Underwriters, began offering qualifying examinations and certificates.[52] Yet a kind of apprenticeship system has continued in financial industries up to the present,[53] in the forms of entry-level positions for male employees, company-sponsored training programs, formal and informal personal relations among near-peers, and selected mentoring by top executives.

Executives began to rely on training and education as growing numbers of office workers rendered impractical their personal knowledge of everyone in the company. In larger establishments, the subdivision of tasks necessary for complete and systematic record-keeping and communication and the increased scale of production further resulted in the broad stratification of the office labor force into executives, managers, and clerical workers.[54] In the early stages of a life insurance company, executives often were also the owners, managers, and salesmen for their firms—Henry Hyde is one good example of this contiguous experience. In other instances, companies secured the names of socially and financially important or well-known men to legitimize their activities. Until the widespread adoption of corporation organization in the 1860s and 1870s, however, these men were not actual administrators; usually, the day-to-day operations were handled by the man who had promoted the company in the first place.[55] Pacific Mutual Life, for example, made Leland Stanford its first president in 1868, but he probably never set foot in the company's Sacramento offices. Stanford was a prominent lawyer and wholesale grocer, who was also president of the Central Pacific Railroad and a former governor of California. When it appeared in newspaper and trade paper advertisements, his name lent a high profile and an aura of stability to the fledgling company. He also could institute direct contacts between the company officers and other important and influential people.[56] Early "administrators," however, often limited their involvement in companies to this use of their names and contacts.

By the 1880s, executives were working officers who, in concert with boards of directors, increasingly made investment decisions and linked the corporation to the larger financial community.[57] Managerial positions developed to coordinate the work of departments and clerical workers and, at the higher levels, to link executives with the company's day-to-day operations. Clerical workers, also increasingly specialized, were responsible for the hands-on production of records and other paperwork that kept a company in business. The introduction of a stable of office machines between 1870 and 1900 greatly simplified the work process, increased the need for skilled and literate clerical workers, and contributed to the further differentiation of office labor. New recording and communications technologies allowed for the enormous expansion of business in the late nineteenth century, beginning with typewriters and telephones in the 1870s and continuing with the automatic typewriter, dictaphone, addressograph, comptometer, and the pneumatic tube. By 1930 machinery had simplified the letter writing, record-keeping, communicating, and calculating previously done by hand or time-consuming legwork. In life insurance and banking, office machines were critically important for servicing large numbers of clients. For example, the addressograph and the arithmometer (a machine for multiplying and dividing) enabled life insurance companies to process and keep fast, accurate records on an expanding clientele, while bookkeeping machines performed the same service in banks.[58]

Before the Industrial Revolution, clerks were necessary in every type of business to keep books, write letters, and create, store, and retrieve files. The growth of the financial sector in the economy after the Civil War created categories of business, such as banking and insurance, that essentially were "clerical industries."[59] Their primary tangible product was financial capital, and their main production process the generation of paper records. The nature of clerical work—its opportunities, its social meanings, and its gender—changed radically between 1880 and 1930. For white men and women, the position of clerk began a downward revision in both status and duties, even as clerical industries expanded and created job stratification, accompanied by lower wages. Writers in *System* magazine, an important management journal, by the turn of the century depicted clerkships as "detail" work rather than entry-level apprenticeships for young men on the make: "Necessary as clerk-work is . . . and helpful as practical experience in this phase of business may be, the man who sinks into its mechanical routine loses the opportunity for development along the lines that lead to big salaries."[60] Experience in clerical work had been an important nineteenth-century route for men to learn to manage their own businesses. These chances became fewer for white men, however, between 1870 and 1900. As companies in all sectors increasingly consolidated, there were fewer openings for new small businesses.[61] For young white men, clerkships provided fewer avenues for either corporate advancement or training for self-employment.

The growing scale of clerical industries in the post–Civil War period called for more workers, particularly workers who could read, spell, write, and han-

TABLE 3

Stenographers and Typists, 1870–1930

	1870	1880	1890	1900	1910	1920	1930
Males	147	3,000	12,148	26,246	53,378	50,410	36,050
Females	7[1]	2,000	21,270	86,118	263,315	564,744	775,140
TOTALS	154	5,000	33,418	112,364	316,693	615,154	811,190
Females as percentage of total	5	40	64	77	83	92	96

Source: Compiled from Alba M. Edwards, *Population: Comparative Occupation Statistics for the United States, 1870–1940, 16th Census of the United States, 1940* (Washington: Government Printing Office, 1943), tables 9 and 10.

1. These seven are shown as "shorthand writers." Table LXV, *Compendium of the Ninth Census of the United States, 1870* (Washington: Government Printing Office, 1872).

dle interpersonal public relations with diplomacy, tact, and a willingness to serve. Life insurance and banking in particular needed workers who would reinforce an image of responsible public service. One of the largest groups to step in to fill these requirements was that of young, white, educated females. From 1880 to 1890, the number of female clerical workers increased from nearly seven thousand to almost seventy-four thousand. In 1880, only 4.40 percent of clerical workers were women; by 1900, they constituted over 30 percent (see table 1). Further, women took over specific positions within the office hierarchy: Nearly half of all female clerical workers in 1900 were stenographers and typists, so that females constituted 77 percent of the total number of workers in these categories (see table 3). The earliest and most substantial hirers of female clerical workers were the federal government, insurance companies, and somewhat later, banks.[62] One Massachusetts life insurance company hired its first female clerk in 1866. Metropolitan Life hired its first female clerk, Caroline Foster, in 1877; between 1887 and 1889, years of particular growth for the company, the office staff increased by fifty-four, half of whom were women. In 1914, Metropolitan Life's home office employed 2,439 women and 1,376 men.[63]

The precorporate position of clerk carried possibilities for growth and advancement for men. Whether through marriage, patronage, or exceptional skill, clerkship represented a potential stepping-stone to proprietorship. Clerical wages placed such workers within the middle class, and clerks worked under much better conditions, in terms of hours and physical environment, than those of nineteenth-century factory laborers or preindustrial artisans.[64] With the advent of large-scale clerical industries, however, the pay scales and purchasing power of clerical workers decreased relative to other workers between 1870 and 1900, reflecting periodic economic depressions, the entrance of cheaper female labor into the work force, and the separation of clerical functions into higher-paid management and lower-paid machine operations categories.[65]

Entry-level positions in offices continued to be available to middle- and working-class white men, but these opportunities, and promotions, probably constricted after 1900 as formal education became more important than apprenticeship as a job qualification. This pattern was true for Great Britain as well, except it reached a peak after World War I. For white women in the United States, a similar stratification may have occurred, as working-class women, including first- and second-generation immigrants, continued in the less skilled positions while middle-class women dominated in the increasingly feminized secretarial jobs.[66] While conditions in large corporate offices remained much better than in factories, the relative autonomy, independence, and unstructured work day of the precorporate world disappeared.

Conversely, for African American men and women, the appearance of "race businesses" after 1800 meant expanding opportunities in the clerical sector. Particularly for the first two generations of black financial industries, clerical work could provide entry into management. Male and female clerical workers tended to be better-educated than their white counterparts, and because of the high standing and financial importance of many black businesses, all forms of clerical work continued to maintain a high status. Black women, however, experienced much the same lack of promotional opportunities as did white women; in management positions black women usually supervised other women.[67]

It is difficult to characterize simply the class, ethnic, or racial background of office workers in general or of financial industry workers in particular. Cindy Aron has documented the white, middle-class roots of both male and female federal clerks in Washington, D.C., between 1860 and 1900. However, federal employment is a special case, since its patterns initially grew out of political patronage. In addition, other local studies suggest that the class composition of the clerical work force began to change around 1900, the end-point of Aron's study. Anita Rapone's analysis of Albany, New York, shows that middle-class white women continued to dominate clerical work in that city until at least 1925, although the numbers of working-class women increased, especially after 1900. In Pittsburgh after 1890, Ileen DeVault argues, "skilled workers viewed clerical work for their children as consonant with their own sense of social status within the working class." In Boston, Carole Srole has demonstrated, the class composition of the clerical work force was quite varied and depended on factors such as the type of office, industry, and time. Up to 1900 in Boston, the categories of clerk, bookkeeper, and office boy were dominated by white, working-class men. The percentage of white women employed in offices who were from working-class families shrank from 80 percent in 1860 to 73 percent in 1900, while the proportion of white, middle-class women working in offices increased (less dramatically), from 20 percent to 24.9 percent over the same time.[68]

Lee Holcomb has argued that in Great Britain the relatively small middle-class population made it difficult to recruit from this class to fill all office jobs, and most clerical workers continued to come from the working class. Even so, "by 1914 women clerks had become, after shop assistants and teachers, the most numerous and important group of middle-class women in the country." Further, unlike the United States' case, most female clerks in Great Britain worked in commercial offices rather than financial industries. In France before World War I, female civil servants came from a somewhat higher class than men in public service. Jürgen Kocka has stressed that, compared to Germany before World War I, class distinctions in the United States were less pronounced in such areas as dress but clearer in terms of ethnicity. Most United States white-collar workers in 1920 (90 percent) were native-born whites, despite the inroads immigrants had made in white-collar work.[69]

The clerical labor force in the United States, unlike that in western Europe, was further divided by race. Racist attitudes and a lower literacy rate kept African Americans out of most white-controlled office work. Jacqueline Jones has observed that whites who hired black women for office work usually placed them in positions that had no contact with either the general public or white workers. Most white-owned businesses simply excluded black women from office work. Jones also claims that black men usually filled clerical positions in African American companies.[70] However, I would argue that this pattern varied depending on the type of clerical work. With the exception of the general clerk category, patterns of gender segregation in black offices were similar to those in white offices. By 1930, for example, when 96 percent of all stenographers and typists were women, white women made up 95.6 percent of all whites in these jobs and black women made up 92.5 percent of all blacks in these jobs.[71] Yet black women as a whole sometimes fared better than all women in some office jobs. In 1910, black women were 24 percent of all black bookkeepers and cashiers in banking, while all female bookkeepers and cashiers in banking constituted only 5.6 percent of workers in that category (see table 2). This difference may have been because the wives or daughters of African American owners worked in the business and therefore took higher-status and more economically crucial positions. At any rate, by 1930, black women's representation in these jobs nearly equaled that of all women. Further, life insurance may have followed a different pattern, since women were highly visible members of the office and managerial staff almost from the beginning.

The entire home office staff of North Carolina Mutual Life Insurance Company in 1909, for example, consisted of twelve women.[72]

A survey conducted in Chicago and Atlanta in 1931–32 by the U.S. Women's Bureau found that no offices in those cities employed both black and white men or women.[73] Racial segregation in insurance and banking provided economic and job opportunities for black companies and individuals. The same racism that kept blacks from working for white companies encouraged some to create or patronize African American insurance firms or banks. The participation of white insurance agents in lynchings, for example, could increase the business of black insurance companies—in one instance, as much as 800 percent within a month. In Baltimore in 1921, the black community denounced Harry Fledenheimer, a fifty-year-old white insurance agent, for assaulting ten-year-old Esther Short while making his collections.[74] These kinds of activities understandably created bitter feelings toward white companies. Black companies, especially life insurance and banks, also provided important employment opportunities for college-educated black men and women, particularly in the South and in large northern cities, such as Chicago. For both black men and women, unlike the white clerical labor force, clerkship remained a mark of middle-class status and continued to draw on the most literate, best-educated portions of the African American population.[75] However, while black-owned companies were important to the economic and social welfare of African Americans, they were but a small portion of the national business.

An important aspect of the changing job functions and the limited mobility of most clerical workers was the appearance of managers. Managerial positions, dominated by men, took over many of the supervisory and decision-making functions of the traditional clerk.[76] Alfred Chandler's study of the growth of management outlines the causes and effects of this new type of employee for retail and industrial businesses. Even in the 1840s, Chandler notes, "managers" also were the owners or partners of a business firm. The appearance of institutions governed by salaried top and middle managers was a product of the expanding economy and new technologies, which made it more economical to combine many business functions within one company.

The history of financial industries, however, suggests some modifications to Chandler's model. Sidney Pollard has argued that the development of professional management in English industry, beginning in the late eighteenth century, built on both older patterns of nepotism and expectations about new managerial skills. Pollard thus sees the development of industrial management as less revolutionary, less rationalized, and much earlier than does Chandler. Susan Porter Benson's exploration of work relations in late-nineteenth-century retailing presents the management of department stores as a complex process of accommodation among managers, workers, and customers, a process rooted in different class and gender expectations. These descriptions better fit the development of management in financial industries in the United States, which continued to rely on direct family connections and in-house apprenticeships even as they adopted educational requirements and recognized professional management associations. Further, the financial industries fostered complex, gendered relationships among management, workers, and public perceptions of the industry's products, including the use of familial imagery in both internal and public relations.[77] Finally, despite company supervision and centralization, the agency system allowed for a fair amount of freedom in managerial styles and for marginalized groups such as women to have access to managerial positions, to participate in professional organizations, and to redefine the gender relations of office work. Thus, the notion of a managerial revolution driven by neutral firm strategies operating in a rationalized marketplace fails to account for fundamental processes in corporate development.

Chandler's view of managerial hierarchies as a source of continuity, providing a stable *institutional* structure even as individual managers or workers came and went, also is somewhat problematic for the financial industries. As management specialized into various divisions or departments within any given company, the training of managers became more specialized and technical. The development of management, however, both contributed to and undermined the search for business and workplace "efficiency." As management and company ownership separated, managers developed loyalties to their own division, specialty, or gender—often putting themselves in conflict with the goals of boards of directors, executive officers, workers, and other managers.[78]

The intangible product of financial industries took its meaning from the social or economic value placed on it. For clerical industry workers, a specialized production process resulted in a product whose tangible benefits went to owners and whose intangible benefits were a process of cultural definition. Evolving theories of labor control were founded on not only the recognition of this "alienation" from labor but on distinctions among executives, managers, and other workers, revised definitions of skill, and the relationship between these factors and the growing gender differentiation of the work force. In the clerical industries, management primarily occupied itself with the cost-effective use of labor time and office space. While Chandler probably was right to stress that the creation of a class of managers smoothed the mechanics of production, whether of goods or services, the existence of managers and management did not automatically resolve the difficulties of worker control, altered production values, workers' attitudes, and public image that personalism and the ideology of democratic opportunity to some extent had resolved.

Financial industries helped shape two late-nineteenth-century managerial movements to solve these problems: welfare capitalism and systematic management. Welfare capitalism is the name one historian has given to a generalized movement that contemporaries called "welfare work."[79] Welfare work encompassed a wide range of actions designed to bring the attitudes and activities of workers more closely in line with those of owners and managers. Management borrowed many of the elements of welfare work from workers' informal or leisure relations. Efforts ranged from the Pullman experiments of the 1880s, which created an entire company town with parks, schools, and a sailing club, to the development of company sports teams by manufacturing and financial industries beginning in the 1890s, to company-sponsored unions, to the appearance of "house mothers" or personnel officers in the World War I years.[80] Whether viewed as coercion or accommodation, welfare work had an enormous impact on the structure of the workplace and on the gendered experience and meaning of corporate work. Although their methods and gender implications differed, welfare work shared with scientific management an emphasis on what was commonly called "efficiency."

In contrast to welfare work, systematic management is the term for a cluster of approaches that focused on rationalizing the work process and quantifying efficiency.[81] It includes the engineering-driven theories of Frederick W. Taylor, first introduced into factories in the 1890s as "scientific management," as well as the Progressive Era reformist professionalism of personnel theory. Systematic managers all shared an interest in efficiency, although for different reasons and from different perspectives. Indeed, concern with office efficiency predated systematic management. Benjamin F. Stevens, as secretary of New England Mutual, for example, claimed in 1865 that the appointment of general agents for the company would lead to "efficiency" taking the place of "inertness." The officers of the Farmers and Mechanics' Bank of Philadelphia in the 1870s were obsessed with streamlining office procedures, particularly the effect of employee actions on the bank's profit margin.[82] Although it did not have the bestial and noisome ambiance of a steel or textile mill, and its machines were more tied to human than mechanical speeds, the work done in insurance offices, banks, and other clerical industries took on a uniform character merely by virtue of the scale of paperwork required to keep ahead in business. Even before the widespread use of office machines or managerial theory, male clerks stood by their desks in rows while women typists sat at their machines in groups.

Beginning around 1900, two major management journals, *System* and *World's Work,* spoke in favor of applying scientific, rational methods to the work process in offices. Taylor's approach to efficiency, based on the factory assembly line, studied the relationship between time and motion to find the shortest time in which the least motion could produce the most work. Each aspect of a particular office process could be broken down into a series of discrete steps, with each step performed by a different individual. The flow of work—the paper trail of a letter, billing invoice, shipping receipt, or order— dictated the working arrangement of office employees. Scientific management

By 1896, the Industrial Audit and Policy Division of Metropolitan Life had separated female and male workers according to job—female typists on one side of the room, male bookkeepers on the other. *Courtesy of the MetLife Archives.*

theorists maintained that employees should be placed according to where their function fit into the overall flow of the work process.[83]

Taylorism used quota systems tied to a minimum salary and job competition to force clerical workers to care about production. By 1905, advocates of Taylorism were studying the rate of speed and accuracy of a typist, for example, by using a machine that attached to the typewriter. These machine findings were combined with management observation of the tasks the employee performed and how much time she or he spent on each task. In addition, management theorists and educators surveyed employees to outline the discrete tasks of an entire day's work. From these findings they devised a standard (usually taken from the output of the most efficient worker) for the tasks involved in a particular job category, which became the norm for all other individuals in the same category, and set a minimum salary. Those who achieved a higher level of production—measured by number of lines typed in a day, for example—could augment their minimum salary by bonuses awarded for every line produced above the standard.[84]

Quota and bonus systems cut several ways. They could create job anxiety on the part of those who were unable to meet the standard. They could provide a sense of upward mobility, suggesting that workers might get ahead through individual initiative. They could foster competition among workers, so that job approval did not come from one's peers but from the "rewards" bestowed by management, although they also often led to "soldiering." And they tended to separate those in more easily measured clerical jobs (such as typists) from those in less easily measured clerical jobs (such as secretaries). Further, in order to earn bonuses, workers could not afford to spend time chatting or taking long breaks. Those who reported on the success of this system noted that supervisors had less trouble with office workers "wasting" time in personal conversations, absenteeism, or in-fighting.[85] From the perspective of employers, quotas and bonuses were definitely an improvement over more freely structured work schedules. From the viewpoint of employees, however, sometimes including managers, such rigid moves toward efficiency made the day spent in an office much less attractive. The institution of quota systems met spontaneous and subtle resistance in many offices—often from managers who resented attempts to bypass them by centralizing control over the work process.[86]

The unenthusiastic reception of Taylor's theories by both workers and managers did not prevent attempts to introduce his principles into offices. But by the eve of World War I, Taylorism was largely discredited as a managerial solution. A related systematic management movement, personnel theory, took a more humanistic, worker-centered approach that grew out of welfare capitalism, union demands, the professionalization of social work in the late nineteenth century, and feminist demands for a more humane work environment for female workers. Although still interested in the bottom line and the benefits of a scientific approach to workplace interactions, advocates believed workers would become more efficient if employers prevented fatigue, dealt with personal problems that intruded into the workplace, and educated workers to be better decision makers. Rather than seeing workers as cogs in a machine, as did scientific management, personnel theory elevated the human factor as the key to increased efficiency. For example, efficiency expert Lillian M. Gilbreth and sociologist Mary van Kleeck, who were deeply involved in various Progressive Era feminist social reforms, argued for increasing efficiency by instituting shorter hours to combat fatigue.[87] Although systematic management did not enter all businesses at the same time, in the same way, or with the same force, by 1890 efficiency represented the cutting edge of business priorities and outlined the shape of the future.

Managerial theories were attractive because they responded to the increasing differences among office personnel. The escape valve of democratic opportunity disappeared as clerkship separated into routine skills, such as typing, and less easily measured skills, such as planning and decision making. A crucial difference between most clerical workers and managers was that managers had the potential to move up the corporate ladder into executive positions, an ability related to gender. By 1900, male corporate executives in life insurance and national banking concerns had achieved a degree of status undreamed of by early industry entrepreneurs. Executive positions in life insurance included the president, vice presidents, secretary, comptroller, and often the actuary as well. In banking, the divisions were similar with slightly different titles. A large bank's officers usually consisted of a president, vice presidents, cashier and assistant cashiers. Typically, a president oversaw all operations and reported to a board of directors, while vice presidents and, in the case of banking, cashiers, connected the work of individual departments to the president's office. At the most elementary level, the secretary kept track of business conducted by the executives, or, if a lawyer, might oversee the corporation's legal affairs. The comptroller and actuary had more specific functions, the former to manage the financial records of the company (or the financial department) and the latter to devise and implement the statistical tables of life expectancy so critical to decisions on a life insurance company's risk policy. By the 1870s, bank office staffs were specialized into distinct areas such as paying, receiving, and note tellers, or city and out-of-town bookkeepers.[88] In both banking and life insurance, by the late nineteenth century, high-level executive officers were involved in investment decisions, leaving the running of the company to various departmental vice presidents.

The founders and executives of early life insurance companies and banks did not share a common elite or professional experience, and they came from many different backgrounds. They included lawyers, publishers, retailers, and importers, but also former clerks and saw-mill owners. In contrast, corporate executives by the late nineteenth century tended to be upper-class men who moved in the same social circles and who often were related to each other through birth or marriage. Many were the sons or relatives of company officers. Henry Wemple, son of the secretary of Manhattan Life, started work with the company as an apprentice in 1863. He went on to become secretary in turn when his father died in 1882. Frederick and Ewald Fleitmann were cousins, and at different times both were directors of Germania Life. In something of a reversal of the usual order, the ambitious, young Henry Baldwin Hyde brought his father, Henry Hazen Hyde, into the Equitable to lend an air of prudence and sagacity to the business. The senior Hyde was already well known in insurance circles as an aggressive proponent of the agency system. The Equitable's first counsel, Daniel Lord, was the father-in-law of the company attorney, Henry Day, and the father of Daniel D. Lord, a member of the board of directors.[89] Black life insurance and banking followed a similar pattern, although later, at a less grandiose scale, and for somewhat different reasons.

For both white and African American companies, these ties of direct kinship were augmented by bonds of social life and generational proximity. Life insurance executives and bankers attended the same churches, went to the same parties, knew the same people, and ate in the same restaurants and exclusive clubs.[90] Executives frequently moved laterally from one company to another to improve their position. James M. McLean worked for Guardian Fire of New York in 1836 at the age of eighteen, moved to Citizens Insurance Company of New York eleven years later, and became its president in 1859. He was a director of Manhattan Life in 1854 and became president in 1886.[91] Except for the earliest entrepreneurs, executive positions required some experience in insurance and typically were held by men in their early fifties or older. By 1900, the executive financial community was bound together by ties of gender, family, class, age, race, experience, and sometimes ethnicity in a way that made it difficult, but not altogether impossible, for outsiders to attain the highest corporate levels.

The six men in Metropolitan Life's offices in 1867 worked in a different world than did the thousands of men and women employed by the company in 1929. The pre–Civil War office relied on kinship, both literal and metaphorical, between like-minded and sometimes like-blooded men. Early life insurance companies and banks made little effort to supervise workers or agents, allowing gender solidarity and their own hopes of advancement to spur them on. While personalism as a management strategy emphasized the harmony of ideas and goals of all office workers, it also could foster the kind of undercutting and rivalry that later management methods attempted to circumvent. A predominantly white, middle-class, male world, the early insurance or banking office unified the work force through racial, ethnic, and gender exclusion.

By the 1870s, that world was beginning to change. Differences among office personnel—of knowledge, gender, education, race, status—replaced the older unity. The increasing number of female office workers left male clericals in an anomalous position. Male clerks in the 1880s and 1890s often pointed to female office workers as the cause of all their problems—their lower wages, the diminishing status of clerical work, its increasingly mundane and dead-end character.[92] The presence of women shattered the community of males and became the most visible symbol for men of the unwelcome transitions to modern office work. With benefit of hindsight, we know that blaming women for the changed nature of office work was factually inaccurate; the economic transformations of the late nineteenth century were much more complex than that. But hindsight also enables us to understand male white-collar workers' efforts to find a simple, obvious cause for an overwhelming and complex transformation. It was, after all, a transformation that many experienced within their own lifetimes.

Hindsight also can help us understand why men saw the drama of change as a gendered tale. That workers pointed to gender as one of the most salient factors in their work experience was predicated on more than the increasing presence of office women. Because of their ideological roots in fraternal organizations, mutual aid societies, and family mercantile business, the financial industries relied on gendered conceptions of management—of the relation between the family and business—and on an ideal of patrician service that gave these industries a special language to describe the work experience. That language was deeply imbedded in the gender concepts of the nineteenth century, and it shaped the development of twentieth-century corporate culture.

CHAPTER TWO

A "Nation of Silk Knees"

Gender and the
Ideal Office Worker

A writer in *Fortune* magazine in 1935 described the modern business office by calling attention to the presence of women workers. "What kind of nation," he asked, "is this callipygian nation of silk knees, slender necks, narrow fingers, and ironic mouths which has established itself upon our boundaries?"[1] The author identified a critical difference between traditional and modern offices. No one could have described the business office of 1860 as a nation of women, or even as a nation, given the small number of office workers relative to the country's work force. But by 1930, the number of clerical workers in business offices had grown to almost four million, and clerical occupations had been taken over by female workers. Men made up the majority of those who owned and managed businesses, although the numbers of women involved at this level had grown from 6,698 in 1920 to 33,828 by 1930 (see table 4). In all categories, the numbers of women working in offices had grown, but in none so dramatically as "stenographers and typists:" by 1930, that figure had reached 96 percent. The *Fortune* author's metaphor suggests that this "nation of silk knees" besieged and threatened the "boundaries" of masculinized business.

Certainly, women's ideological and physical presence brought the gender of business into the foreground. In that sense, the *Fortune* author's perception of women's central role in creating new office workplaces was justified, but gender relations became an important aspect of office work not because of any inherent qualities of men and women, nor simply because of women's presence. Rather, office work encoded ideas about gender in complex new ways. For

TABLE 4
Proprietors, Managers and Officials, 1910–1930

	1910		1920		1930	
	Male	Female	Male	Female	Male	Female
Proprietors, managers and officials	135,769	4,036	177,767	4,818	227,436	9,775
Real estate & insurance agents & officials	95,302	2,662	129,589	5,389	271,530	24,053
TOTALS	231,071	6,698	306,767	10,207	498,966	33,828

Source: Compiled from Alba M. Edwards, *Population: Comparative Occupation Statistics for the United States, 1870–1940, 16th Census of the United States, 1940* (Washington: Government Printing Office, 1943), tables 9 and 10.

example, the economic forces of job specialization and cost-effectiveness so important to corporate organization would appear to be gender neutral, yet that was not exactly the case. Corporate economic strategies aimed at a work force that expressed the same beliefs, applied the same energies, and made personal sacrifices at the lowest possible wage, whether male or female, for the sake of achieving maximum profits at minimum cost. Economic rationalism thus underlay office relations, and nations of knees and necks were, at base, merely interchangeable parts. But patriarchal attitudes and socioeconomic structures that devalued women and women's role and elevated masculinity and manhood tenaciously persisted in office relations. For example, the office job structure became gender segregated in such a way that women were neither interchangeable with men nor an economic and socially entitled group. As the *Fortune* metaphor suggests, women in business were a separate "nation," perennial outsiders whose weaknesses were many, but especially sexual, and whose strengths were irony and numbers. The bifurcation of the office labor force into managerial or "brain" workers and clerical or "manual" workers had evolved by the early twentieth century, into a division between men and women.[2] The gendered discourse of the late-nineteenth-century business world constructed new ideal work identities for men and women in offices and new connections between manhood, womanhood, and work. Rhetorical images of office workers as gendered first and skilled or positioned second encouraged the notion that workplace arrangements grew out of the same immutable biological laws that governed relations between men and women rather than from social, economic, and cultural interactions. In the process, that discourse obscured the structural aspects of changes in the business world.

Gender segregation meant different promotional tracks, pay scales, and definitions of skill and status, as well as different behaviors for those in management or executive capacities (men) and those in clerical positions (women). Thus, gender differences were built into the new office relations from the beginning, in part the product of men's and women's struggles over meaning and status in office work.[3] As clear-cut and as clearly gendered as this sex segregation seems, it belies female workers' abilities to redefine their position and male workers' sense of being surrounded and overwhelmed.

Patriarchy and labor-market segmentation in the office workplace, and their connections to ideas about gender, therefore, need to be put in the context of contests over meaning and experience. Ideas about the nature of men and women and their relationship to job skills, were as important in forming a male managerial force and a female clerical force as were economic or structural issues. Employers, workers, women, and men used gender to justify, champion, denigrate, and explain the evolving nature of the work force because gender was an authoritative language for expressing and comprehending differences in privilege, status, and experience. By defining particular jobs or positions as more suited to males or females, educators, business theorists, employers, and workers explained as "natural" or "bio-logical" the presence of working women, the displacement of working men, and the systemic job fragmentation of corporate capitalism.

The type of commitment necessary for business work already had been articulated by the time women began to enter offices in the 1860s. Employers stressed apparently contradictory qualities: subordination to business demands and the ambition to "get ahead." One of the primary bases of middle-class formation by the 1830s, in fact, was the ideology of self-control, delayed gratification, and temporary deference that became a form of "capital" for young men in the white-collar workplace. Self-control and self-effacement could ultimately result in rewards: most young clerks fully expected to move into proprietorship and could tolerate subservience, since it was a temporary condition; the gratification of self-employment was not permanently delayed. This, at least, was the hope. And in the fluid economy and open social structure of antebellum America, it was not an unrealistic hope.[4]

Subservience, the ability to adapt to situations, and the denial of self-interest in favor of selflessness were traits the ideal of middle-class manhood shared with the nineteenth-century ideal of domestic womanhood. However, the context in which these traits were embedded was crucial to their meaning. "True womanhood" placed woman's proper role within the family and, especially by the late nineteenth century, in motherhood. The ideal told women to deny the individual self in favor of their work as bearers and rearers of children, as the biological and emotional centers of family life. Women, in other words, were to be subservient to the social and economic institution of the family and to male kin. "True manhood," on the other hand, ideally used subservience in the business world to achieve success through autonomy and individuality. Much like their childhood relationship to their parents, businessmen were subservient to a specific company and specific individual men, with the tacit understanding that such behavior should ultimately be rewarded with proprietorship and independence.

These ideals, of course, interacted with a more nuanced reality. The distinction between public and private supported separate physical worlds for men and women; most middle-class, married women did not work outside the home for wages in the nineteenth century but managed the domestic environment. Most middle-class men worked outside the home, and the workplace took on important symbolic and experiential meanings for manhood. However, for both men and women their relation to work and home, public and private, was complex and fluid. Beginning in the 1830s, middle-class women increasingly acted in the public realm in voluntary associations and political causes such as suffrage, temperance, and abolition; and as professional workers in fields such as teaching, management of educational institutions, literature, and medicine.[5] Men, for their part, created alternative domestic environments in private male spaces such as men's clubs and fraternal organizations. Furthermore, by World War I, a specifically home-centered domestic role for men was well developed. In studying white-collar couples between 1880 and 1920, Joan Seidl has found that although decisions regarding household furnishing usually were made by women, men were part of the decision-making process and sometimes took on the task of designing the furnishings and arrangements of domestic interiors. Men routinely contributed advice on domestic arrangements; Walter Post, for example, a junior clerk for the Northern Pacific Railroad, sketched the plans for furnishing his marital residence in great detail on a piece of his employer's stationery.[6] Middle-class homes, even on the western frontier, sometimes included a "den" or "snuggery," a specifically masculine space within the home.[7] The distinctions between public and private, then, were more complex by the late nineteenth and early twentieth centuries than the rhetorical dichotomy of separate spheres might suggest.

In the late nineteenth century, middle-class masculinity shared with femininity an emphasis on subordination, but it also emphasized ambition and the notion that to be male was to be powerful, active, and involved in a career. Most middle-class advice literature described such activity as "manly." Women's active public involvement, on the other hand, was ideally to support the home, not a personal public career. Whatever balance of public and private experience may have existed between men and women, men still were to be the breadwinners. This connection between earning power and manhood was true for all classes. Elements of the working class had articulated the notion of a "family wage," by which they meant the maintenance of men's wages at a rate sufficient to support a family.[8] To be subordinate was, for a man, to momentarily subsume self into work, emotional relationships, or the hierarchical ladder of military service, fraternal organizations, or family needs, in order to achieve ultimate autonomy through economic independence and patriarchal control. For women, to be subordinate was to fulfill the feminine ideal of economic and status dependence.

Middle-class manhood, then, separated masculine endeavors and privileges from those of womanhood and located the basis of masculinity in men's relationship to their means of earning a living. The number of men involved in mercantile and industrial ownership increased early in the century, and by the 1870s the typical middle-class hero changed from a religious or military figure to the businessman, particularly the "captain of industry." Guidebooks, exhortative literature, and popular stories presented the businessman as the epitome of manliness.[9] Middle-class expectations had so firmly linked manhood and business employment by 1900 that the popular self-help author Madison C. Peters could assert, "the moulding influence of a man's life . . . is employment. A man's business makes him,—it hardens his muscle . . . wakes up his inventive genius, puts his wits to work, arouses ambition, makes him feel that he is a man, and must show himself a man by taking a man's part in life."[10] But what was the believer in manhood's roots in business to make of the insurance agent who cautioned his son against a business clerkship because it had "no future. Could you reach your loftiest aspirations from the top of a high stool? . . . Could you be happy for years in a bank teller's cage?" Or of someone like the fictional character "old Tom Morton nursing his dyspepsia, fighting his neurasthenia, and working, working, working . . . that bald pate, that broken carcass, that shivering whine"?[11]

Such dire predictions could become the fate of a businessman. One particularly poignant example is that of E. Dwight Kendall, a nineteenth-century entrepreneur whose triumphs and frustrations were typical of many young, white-collar men. In talking about his experiences with work, Kendall constructed connections between masculinity and material success or failure. To earn his living, Kendall began, in 1853 (when he was probably in his late teens), to give lectures at rented halls throughout New York, Connecticut, and New Jersey. His early lectures were on electricity and electromagnetism; this type of traveling lecture circuit was common and could include talks on a variety of subjects. There is no evidence that Kendall had any special training in this field, and in fact, his letters to his family suggest that he had no specific training beyond a general education. His father was a dentist in Boston who had connections with several relatives who were in business. Kendall's real desire was to become an agent or representative of a white-collar company. In 1854 he became a salaried agent for a life insurance firm and "puffed," or advertised, the company during the course of his regular lectures. Apparently his "Uncle Yates," who had an insurance agency, put him onto several different job leads. Early in 1854, he wrote his father that he saw four "chances" for himself in New York City. The first two were secretaryships of manufacturing companies, which Uncle Yates could secure for him. The third was lecturing on life insurance, both independently and on a company salary. The fourth was acting as an agent for insurance. In these last two he also was aided by Yates, for whom Kendall occasionally worked, thereby "becoming known to the insurance people." He also flirted with a similar managerial position in a banking house.[12] From 1853 until 1875 (when Kendall disappeared from the historical record) he worked as a lecturer and agent for several different insurance firms, but he never achieved the success for which he had hoped. Throughout the twenty or so years he traveled and wrote letters home to his mother and father, he was repeatedly forced to ask them for loans or funds. The year 1875 found him selling lamps at a fair and still writing on his Uncle Yates's stationery. Apparently he never married. His last extant letter ends the way his first one began: "When these hard times are over I do not doubt that I shall be able to make money."[13]

James Southgate, Sr., was more successful materially but paid for that success with constant worry and impaired health. The founder and owner of his own Durham, North Carolina, insurance agency in the 1870s and 1880s, Southgate spent two months in a hospital in Richmond, Virginia, in late 1883 for a debilitating but undiagnosable series of "nervous system troubles" and a "dormant liver." His health had plagued him for months, alternately allowing him to feast on "oysters and good Beef" and reducing him to agonized sleepless nights of "morphine . . . and . . . vomiting." In July 1883, he lived for several weeks on "chicken broth, beef tea, and mush toast" while traveling on business in New York and North Carolina.[14]

While his father was in the hospital, James Southgate, Jr., ran the business, but not without copious messages and instructions from his father. From his hospital bed Southgate recommended customers, agonized over strategies to keep his rivals from taking advantage of his illness to court his clients, advised his son on sales techniques, and kept up correspondence with several insurance companies he hoped to add to his representation list. He chafed to be out of bed, selling insurance, cultivating customers, and widening his representation: "I am so anxious to be doing something," he repeatedly wrote. At one point during his cure, while out walking, he ran into several "insurance men" and spent time making their acquaintance and comparing notes on the business. Southgate was a loving, generous father and husband whose concerns about money and success were very clearly oriented to making a comfortable family life. He also saw these responsibilities as fully his own, however, and that knowledge weighed on him. He constantly worried over the business, writing to his wife from the hospital that "Jimmie [Southgate, Jr., who was staying in Richmond to be near his father] has been a great comfort to me in my weakness, but . . . I tell him I think I should improve yet faster if I knew he was in the office every day to direct and see after things." He worried constantly about money and even dreamed about it at night.[15]

The rewards of self-employment for Southgate were his ability to pass on his agency to his son and to see his family become important members of the Durham community. Both his daughter and son involved themselves in civic improvement in Durham, Mattie Southgate Jones working for women's suffrage and Jimmie as a trustee of Trinity College. The perils of self-employment, however, were obsessive concern over the competition, the fickleness of clients, and the fragility of his own health. Southgate achieved the business success Dwight Kendall never did; both men's lives, however, suggest the tenuousness of the businessman's position due to the volatile nature of the economy and lack of specific training typical of the late-nineteenth-century insurance business, as well as more timeless difficulties such as ill health. Both suggest constructions of masculinity that hinge on material success; each reveals that success or failure was always potentially present. The thin line between the two gave middle-class masculinity a brittle vulnerability.

The relationship between masculinity and work expressed in Southgate's and Kendall's lives graphically suggests the turn-of-the-century "crisis of manhood" expounded by such national figures as Theodore Roosevelt and identified by later scholars of male gender roles.[16] The changing experience of work for middle-class males was irremediably caught up in notions of manhood, corporate hierarchy, and the increasing specialization of labor; and the evolving nature of managerial capitalism in the late nineteenth century demanded new definitions of manhood. The individual male struggling for upward mobility through "pluck and luck" in the 1870s had been replaced, by the 1920s, by the corporate man—a professional manipulator of people and a team player in the service of organizational duty. The popular definition linking manhood with business attempted to reconcile the sedentary, acquisitive, and consumer-oriented pursuits of business with new physical notions of manhood, and older mercantilist ideas of economic structure and the place of men in society.[17]

A political climate that frowned on economic regulation and restriction allowed free play to the competitive instincts. The unfettered fluctuations of nineteenth-century capitalism involved businessmen in a cutthroat struggle for existence. Herbert Spencer's "social Darwinism," which emphasized the survival of the fittest, provided an important justification not only for business activities but for popular definitions of middle-class manhood.[18] As businessman James Platt put it in 1889, in the seventy-fifth edition of his book *Business*, "life is a sharp conflict of man with man, a remorseless struggle for existence . . . in which the men of greatest skill and perseverance still defeat their fellows."[19] As late as 1906, Orison Swett Marden, the author of advice books for aspiring businessmen and the prominent founder and editor of *Success* magazine, used the popular notion in his recipe for personal attainment: "In this fiercely competitive age, when the law of the survival of the fittest acts with seemingly merciless rigor, no one can afford to be indifferent to the smallest detail of dress, or manner, or appearance, that will add to his chances of success."[20]

Businessmen's rhetoric united violence, conflicts among men, and success. James Southgate wrote to his partner and son that he feared that "Mackey" was out to get him. He told James, Jr., that he was "spiking every gun that Mackey can possibly use against me." Mackey apparently was his rival for insurance customers in Durham.[21] Businessmen also used the language of violence to express paranoia. Dwight Kendall, for example, believed he had enemies who "cut" him out of business in one locale when he was traveling in another.[22] Dealing gracefully but aggressively with competition was an important aspect of business success, one that allowed men to construct a variety of connections between personal and ideal manliness and their work. To contain or limit the destructive aspects of violence or competition in manhood, middle-class commentators stressed that competition and struggle in business could replace war as the arena of masculine contention, thereby obviating men's need to test themselves through bloodletting. Businessmen then could pursue a civilizing mission in their business dealings even as they expressed their higher masculine selves. Further, by believing that both manhood and business were inherently competitive, businessmen could deal with a sense of personal helplessness or individual failures.

In addition to aggressiveness, middle-class definitions of manhood stressed individualism—the need for each man to prove himself on his own, if not on his own terms. What made a man was individual rather than communal actions. The ideology of the "self-made man" built on the notion that character grew out of one's own endeavors, through self-education and not by the assistance of others, formal education, or family ties. In reality, kin connections or other help often made the difference, as Dwight Kendall's Uncle Yates, James Southgate's son, and numerous others make clear.[23]

Individualism and competitiveness in the ideal of the self-made man could have atomized the social structure, resulting in anarchy. Opposing this tendency, the ideals of manhood also emphasized the Protestant tradition of self-control, the stabilizing effect of property ownership, a responsible paternalistic relationship to family and society, altruism, charity, and the religious virtue inherent in fulfilling one's "calling" in life. Religion could create success not only because it was morally proper but because it made a man stronger, both physically and mentally. In turn, evidence of moral propriety was proof of related business skills and hence manliness. As Orison Marden put it in 1899, "If a man's religion is of the right sort, will it not sharpen his faculties, quicken his energies, heighten his self-respect, give solidity to his character, and enhance both his usefulness and his prospects for success? . . . When God calls a man to be upright and pure and generous, he also calls him to be intelligent and skillful, and strong and brave."[24]

In a relatively static economic structure still guided to some extent by the belief in scarcity, it was possible to feel that security and self-esteem could be achieved through frugality and hard work and through saving the fruits of labor and passing them on to the next generation. A man's stature could be measured not by what he could buy but in his legacy of knowledge and property and his stewardship toward his own children and society. During the nineteenth century the religious emphasis on the self-made man gradually altered to favor more pragmatic, work-related qualities such as punctuality, loyalty, and obedience. These were traits more amenable to increased secularization, industrialism, and scientific rationalism, and were of great value to white-collar employers. Nevertheless, the notion of self-improvement retained moral and religious overtones well into the twentieth century even as it took on a decidedly instrumentalist tone. Madison Peters explained in 1908, "with a noble purpose, a high endeavor and a useful end in view you shall make yourself a master in your line."[25] Indeed, professionalism and business success were directly linked. Businessman Albert Shaw argued that there was, in truly great businessmen, a "professional spirit . . . closely related to . . . right intellectual and moral development."[26]

Middle-class notions of manliness also assumed that the businessman who acted with self-control, maintained a sense of social responsibility, and met competition head on would achieve material or occupational success. As Shaw put it, "the greatest pleasure in work is that which comes from the trained and regulated exercise of the faculty of imagination."[27] Success, however, came only to men of "character," to men who were manly. "A man's or a boy's work," Orison Marden noted in 1903, "is material with which to build character and manhood. . . . The exceptional young man is the one who looks upon his vocation as an opportunity to make a man of himself, . . . who is always preparing himself to fill the position above him."[28] The man of character—the man who was rational, honest, generous, dignified, reasonable, gentle but strong, honorable, charismatic, and self-reliant—would automatically succeed.[29] Character could be emulated; it could be learned; but it could never be merely put on like a cloak. As Marden explained it, "One of the best strengtheners of character and developers of stamina . . . is to assume the part you wish to play; to assert stoutly the possession of whatever you lack. . . . By 'acting as though,' and by always being optimistic, by having 'self-confidence,' a man will succeed, will *become* that which he has acted."[30]

A man's character—and, although those who spoke of character sometimes included women in the business world, it was predominantly a male virtue—was his essential self, and success in business constituted proof of manly character. Madison Peters also encouraged readers to make themselves into successful men of character: "They who believe in themselves, who are conscious of their own force of character, of brain and of body, touch the wire of infinite power and can accomplish what would be utterly impossible to those who lack the vital energy which waits on self-concentration and knows not worry."[31] Further, the accumulation of property and enlightened stewardship toward society as a whole and one's family and employees manifested business success. In a clear parallel, "true women" also were made, not born. The emphasis on making oneself, on self-invention, was at the heart of the nineteenth-century middle class. For some, such as Dwight Kendall, the ideology created frustration and a sense of failed hopes. For others, those who were "successful," it could reinforce a sense of wholeness, of ties to family and community, as was true for James Southgate, Sr.[32]

Another persistent aspect of manliness was a concern with leadership or example. Every middle-class man was to strive, ideally, to be a leader of other men and thereby a perfect individual specimen of manliness. To act as a responsible guardian of society was to be a socially useful leader of and mentor to other men. This conception of leadership took the form of discussions of a man's character through most of the nineteenth century and his personality in the early twentieth century. Orison Marden, a major exponent of the success school, proclaimed, "It is natural for all classes to believe in and to follow character, for character is power."[33] Those who described character frequently spoke of it as an almost mystical aristocracy of the spirit, fired by the divine spark of "enthusiasm" and exerting a magnetic, compelling attraction on everyone. The explanation of a man's leadership abilities drew on the same sense of mysterious influence (and sometimes the same language) found in mesmerism and the middle-class preoccupation with spiritualism. Ian Maclaren, speaking of the nineteenth-century Scottish evangelist Henry Drummond, commented, "His influence . . . more than that of any other man I ever met, was mesmeric . . . he seized one directly by his living personality. . . . Men were at once arrested, interested, fascinated by the very sight of the man, and could not take their eyes off him."[34] Madison Peters explained the source of leadership skills as "enthusiasm . . . , the heat of which warms the heart and kindles in the soul noble impulses to worthy actions. . . . In the outburst of enthusiasm the soul reveals its masterful power."[35] Enthusiasm also was the root of physical bravery, "the quality that calls forth the stuff of which heroes are made and makes men rush to the cannon's mouth to court danger and death." Enthusiasm was a divine power which gave men mastery over others, brought material success, and made men of character a potent force in society. Most importantly, enthusiasm was manly—it separated the masculine from the feminine by elevating manliness at the expense of womanly characteristics. Enthusiasm was not effeminate actions nor a "sissy" outlook. The "real boy scout," as one Scout leader put it in 1912, was not a "hothouse plant," nor "hitched to his mother's apronstrings." Rather he was "full of life, energy, enthusiasm . . . self-reliant, sturdy and full of vim."[36]

The need for character and leadership ability, the proof of character in business success, and the emphasis on virility tested in the competitive arena of production all circulated around men's role as participants in the public world of business. No doubt the growth of managerial capitalism in the years after 1865 challenged middle-class manhood and demanded alterations in both notions of manliness and men's relationship to society. Contributing to the intensity of the late-nineteenth-century rhetoric of masculinity was the emergence of new workplace relations. With more men working for wages and declining private ownership of business property, economic independence and ownership could no longer be central to manhood. In addition, life-long wage labor changed the relationship between the individual and white-collar work. In the massive structure of corporate bureaucracy, men seemed like mere cogs in a machine rather than independent actors; they were required to obey rules and regulations over which individual workers seemed to have little control, and they were subjected to spirals of status in which it was possible to exercise power over others but only with the awareness that one was, in turn, dominated by someone else. The older traditions of apprenticeship, of passing on knowledge and occupational learning by working with others, were partially institutionalized and mostly replaced by increased demands for workers with specialized education, first in business schools by 1900 and by the 1920s in liberal arts colleges.

The high-blown language of success manuals reflected the changed structure of the modern corporate workplace, in which masculine gender traits took on new meanings. An advertisement for a life insurance salesman published in 1901, for example, spoke of "a subordinate clerkship as a temporary makeshift." The traditional route to autonomy—clerkship—was no longer an apprenticeship, no longer a stage along the way.[37] Men's subordination at work appeared to many as a permanent condition. As one historian has phrased it, speaking of retail sales, the "pyramid of promotion" replaced the "shaky ladder of success." In particular, the advent of continuous waged labor in offices shared with women challenged the notion that work space was male space.[38] Business commentators addressed these problems by emphasizing an individual's permanent relation to business as an institution or to specific jobs, such as bookkeeper or actuary. It was "the age of the trained man," claimed Madison Peters in 1908. In a variety of fields, professionalism and career were caught up in changing gender definitions.[39]

Employers continued to value aggressiveness and competitiveness for men, but they expected the male wage worker to assert such traits in the service of the company or business community rather than for himself or his family. The ideal corporate worker devoted his attentions and his self-development to working for others. In 1894, Edward W. Bok, the editor and part owner of *Ladies' Home Journal*, described the qualities necessary for the "Young Man in Business." He claimed that employers demanded faithfulness in young men interested in a business career; they also expected them to follow up on the smallest detail, to be alert, to be unafraid of the hardest work, to be able and anxious to please, to possess powers of concentration, and to immerse themselves in the business of their employers: "The successful mastery of business questions calls for a personal interest, a forgetfulness of self that can only come from the closest application and the most absolute concentration."[40]

From the employer's perspective, self-denial and selfless service were key attributes of the ideal corporate worker. Orison Marden, in one of his many career and advice books, asserted in 1889 that "the exceptional boy or young man is the one whose main ambition is to help along the business, to further his employer's interests in every possible way . . . faithfulness, absolute reliability, a single eye to the employer's interest, and close, careful industry are the keys to promotion." The Reverend F. E. Clarke, in his 1884 advice book for young men interested in a business career, observed that the most important thing for success was self-denial: "It is one of the qualities which any good business man would consider in you were he contemplating your probabilities in the direction of promotions and partnerships. It is certainly an important factor in the problem whether a clerk is likely to become a capitalist." Commenting in 1909 on George Phillips, the Equitable's first actuary, an article in the company's management journal praised his extreme commitment to work: "He was never known to take a vacation or holiday, and always arrived at the office long before the opening hour, usually remaining at his standing desk long after the closing hour."[41] For someone who rejoiced in this kind of obsession with work, such behavior was no doubt gratifying. But the ideal defined an individual with no life other than work, no other interests or commitments. It was unrealistic, even as it made clear the all-consuming desires of employers.

In the same vein, the turn-of-the-century ideal for office workers stressed the contiguous nature of public and private life and of work and leisure, as well as the overweening importance of a job as the defining center of the self. F. E. Clarke asserted that certain kinds of amusement, such as "side-shows" or "variety shows," "distracts the minds of the boys from their regular work or study, and makes them less fit for the real business of life." Executives often held their own lives up as examples. In 1917, Samuel Miles Hastings, the president of Computing Scale Company of America, linked his ability to reach quick decisions and hence his business success to his judicious choice of recreations, especially golf, the theater, music, and time spent with a "physical culture instructor."[42] Edward Bok, as head of a publishing concern and a self-appointed career counselor, found clear links between men's work and leisure. He counseled young, aspiring businessmen to devote their entire minds and bodies to their work, eschewing late social hours, hastily eaten or overly sweet meals, dealing with personal matters during business hours, or paying more attention to sports than to their jobs. Employers, he felt, had a legitimate right to extend the commitment to work beyond office hours: "It is not enough that he should take care of himself during the day. To social dissipations at night can be traced the downfall of hundreds upon hundreds of young men. The idea that an employer has no control over a young man's time away from the office is a dangerous fallacy." Bok believed that aspiring young men should structure social contacts to further their business position. Social life could be "a study" wherein one learned how to manipulate people in order to further one's own ends in the workplace: "To know the wants of people, to learn their softer side, you must come into contact with their social natures. . . . It is to his advantage that people should know he exists: what his aims and aspirations are." Bok was a compelling example of his message: he had begun his business career in the United States as a stenographer in 1884.[43]

In summarizing the qualities for success, Bok listed honesty, opportunism, willingness to learn, firmness, decisiveness, abstinence, respect for women and "sacred things," discreet dress habits, and marriage and a home.[44] In a revealing but perhaps not surprising comment, Bok simultaneously asserted the image of white-collar workers as dutiful and ambitious and bemoaned the difficulty of finding such individuals. He claimed that there was no lack of openings for young men starting out in business, but there was a lack of sufficiently self-motivated individuals to fill those positions, particularly workers who possessed that complex mix of ambition, commitment, and subservience: "The average young man in business today is nothing more or less than a plodder—a mere automatic machine."[45] Bok and other business commentators wanted as employees machines that hummed cheerfully as they ran, never wore out or needed repair, and used air for fuel.

Bok and others demanded of young men in business nothing less than the total surrender of self to work, the complete and seamless identification of the self with its institutional position. In a sense, middle- and upper-class employers and educators were asking men to embrace and internalize a total commitment to middle-class imperatives that muffled action, aggression, individuality, and personal autonomy—the marks of perfected bourgeois manhood—in favor of self-sacrifice and ambition in the service of others—aspects of the ideal late-nineteenth-century woman. That there seemed to be fewer young men willing to do so is not surprising, given the changing nature of middle-class work by the 1890s, the challenges to notions of masculinity those changes involved, and the all-encompassing nature of employers' demands.

The qualities these commentators described and the demand for self-sacrifice remained remarkably consistent well into the twentieth century, even as the gender demography of the work force shifted. In her 1934 advice book to young women contemplating business careers, educator Frances Maule repeated the formula. Maule urged prospective female employees to dress carefully, maintain scrupulous honesty, show an interest in their work, and be careful of their personal habits on and off the job. Further, a woman in business should be "a full partner in the business, assuming full responsibility for your part of the work and cooperating to the utmost of your ability to promote its aims, and, through its aims, your own." Maule's list of business virtues included reliability, alertness, politeness, reticence, self-confidence, initiative, adaptability, cooperativeness, discretion, firmness, concentration, and so on, suggesting that workers' first allegiance in all matters should be to their work.[46] The primary quality necessary to make a good corporate office worker—subordination of self to company needs and the channeling of personal desires into institutional forms—changed very little between 1870 and 1930. What did change, however, was the relationship between definitions of manhood and womanhood and their meaning to white-collar work.

The introduction of women into what had been a bastion of masculine self-identity challenged the links between business and manhood by reframing justifications for business activity based on gender distinctions. The growing economic presence of financial industries, such as insurance and banking, and the emphasis on advertising and consumption shifted the overall focus of business ideology away from aggressive competition and toward personal service and the need to please clients—that is, away from masculinized definitions of business and toward feminized ones. Edward Hines, president of a lumber company, argued in 1917 that "service is now as much a part of the transaction as the intrinsic value of the article itself." While a cultural curmudgeon like James Truslow Adams might complain that service was only a new cover for the old American greed for profit, service was becoming an inextricable part of business rationales.[47]

The ideal of the self-made man also came under fire. Admittedly, the reality had never approached the myth. Dwight Kendall and James Southgate, Jr., for example, relied on family and social connections for their business standing. The president of Aetna Life Insurance Company for many years, Morgan G. Bulkeley, promulgated an image of himself as a self-made man in order to further his political career as a "man of the people." However, his father had started Aetna Life, and Morgan Bulkeley's earliest employer, H. P. Morgan, was his uncle.[48] In the antebellum period it may have been more possible to believe such stories, but by the 1890s, corporate capitalism had constricted even the promise of upward mobility. Bureaucratic and managerial capitalism had little room for truly aggressive, self-reliant individuals. The new notions of masculine behavior stimulated by these confrontations emphasized selected older attributes and replaced others entirely. In particular, business rhetoric increasingly conflated perceived gender traits with the duties and behaviors associated with particular jobs, turning an ideology of social gender divisions into a structural gender segregation.

Women themselves may not have been threatening, but what they represented was. Advocates of women's place in business directly addressed the connections between gender and the ideal worker. They acknowledged that wage labor demanded workers who behaved well as subordinates and argued that women's biological and social nature perfectly suited them to the modern business office. Defenders of women's presence in business asserted that women brought unique and necessary qualities to the corporate world simply because they were women—an argument from separate spheres ideology that emphasized women's "higher nature," "sympathetic" understanding, "tender" thought processes, cultivation, and beneficence, all of which would add uplifting character to the selfish, male world of the office.[49] This description of a worker fit perfectly with corporate needs for a malleable and other-directed labor force, at the same time emphasizing women's separateness and uniqueness. Women, some argued, not only made good workers, they made *better* workers than men.

In emphasizing the gendered basis of work behavior, proponents of women's wage labor consciously promulgated the notion of separate spheres as a benefit to the institutional system of the corporation. Discussions of the fit between manliness and business had taken place in a seamless world of apparent inevitability—business was male, and men were in charge of business—but arguments for women's place in that world problematized gender connections, throwing their artificiality into relief. In addition, in asserting female *superiority,* defenders consciously or unconsciously stood the hierarchy of male/female on its head even as they averred that the female self was inherently separate from the institutional relation.

By the 1910s, some commentators were applying the activist perspective of the Progressive "New Woman" to the female business role. In 1915, the director of research at the Intercollegiate Bureau of Occupations, a Miss Snow, painted a utopian picture of an army of female workers in a course held at the New York School of Commerce. She declared that the moral strength and social-minded power of "office women" held "the business of life together" through their influence for good in the masculine economic arena. Women, Snow asserted, could improve the ethical climate of business through the influence of their selfless perspective.[50]

By the 1920s, the argument for women's place in business had veered away from the nebulous benefits of "sympathy" to more concrete practicalities. Edith Johnson, an advice author, commented in 1923:

> Too seldom does the world pause to consider how much kinder and more human business has become since woman invaded the market-place. Her presence there has done more, I believe, than labor's strikes and struggles to shorten the working-day and to improve the conditions under which work is performed. . . . Well-ventilated, well-lighted, and sanitarily kept workrooms, rest-rooms, and other creature comforts provided in factories, stores, and office buildings are largely the results of woman's presence in industry.[51]

Johnson's assertion suggests that such changes did not necessarily occur because female workers actively pursued them. Rather, it was the influence of shared cultural notions about womanhood and about the type of environment women needed that altered the workplace. For some, women's mere presence could relieve labor unrest and make the experience of labor for *all* employees less onerous. The female self, in other words, became a powerful conduit for business morality and ethics, the emotional heart of the public body of the corporation.[52]

The ideal female worker was defined in terms of a particular relation—that of a wife. The nineteenth-century ideology of the ideal wife as self-sacrificing, morally strong, emotionally supportive, cultivated, and gentle had long described the ideal white-collar worker. In 1855, an article in *Hunt's Merchants' Magazine* observed that a mercantile clerk "is to business what the wife is to the order and success of the home—the genius that gives form and fashion to the materials for prosperity which are furnished by another."[53] Female employees had the distinction of making that analogy much more apt. They could literally embody the domestic wisdom, orderly management, and gender subordination of the good wife.

The perfection of this simile led to arguments against middle-class women in the workplace. One reason authors went to such lengths to defend women's office abilities stemmed from the fear that once in the public, male realm, women would either be desexed or lose interest in the institution of marriage. To quell any fears that office women might sacrifice their domestic duties to the public world, supporters noted that business service prepared women to be better wives and mothers by teaching them something of human nature, organizational skills, and self-knowledge.[54] Asserting the links among womanhood, office work, and marriage, advice literature and popular magazine short stories stressed that marriage was the ultimate goal of office women.[55] A woman's persona as a wife thus resonated at both the personal level of male–female relations and the broader institutional level of the corporation. As a worker, she was a "wife" to her male boss or her potential real-life husband and a dutiful servant of the corporation.

From nearly the beginning of women's entrance into office work in the 1870s, apologists for women's wage labor and female commentators and advisors leaned heavily on the more conservative aspects of woman's place. Whether drawn from nineteenth-century notions of private domesticity or the more public orientation of the Progressive Era's "new Woman," the female wage laborer described in popular and business publications was an essentially domestic creature. Justifications for women's entering the office labor force referred to woman's basic orientation to the home, and definitions of womanhood within business lent a personalistic and essentially "private" air to woman's place in the corporate community. That it was relatively easy to subsume women within business without calling womanhood itself into question is a mark of the directions business took at the turn of the century: notions of service emerged, older ideas about masculine individuality collapsed in favor of communal relations, and struggle and competitiveness became minimized in favor of self-denial and efforts to control and overcome the wild fluctuations of an unregulated capitalist economy. Ironically, the factors that allowed the ready absorption of women challenged definitions of manhood. We can see this challenge vividly played out in the evolution of the job of secretary.

One of the thorniest issues in job definition was the position of private secretary, traditionally a man's job that often led to executive status. Increasing numbers of women began to fill this position by World War I, and by 1930 it had become primarily a female job. At some point, the position of secretary lost one of its initial attractions. Edward Jones Kilduff, business educator and well-known author of advice books for office workers, pointed out in 1924 that male secretaries were willing to give up their own personalities in order to be private secretaries because they knew that this was a way to "get ahead" by learning the business and becoming a protégé of the employer.[56] Kilduff held that this applied to both male and female secretaries, yet the evolving reality was quite different. The apprentice/master relationship that made secretaryship a step on the way up was typical of the precorporate office but did not survive in practical terms for women who worked as secretaries. One female respondent to the Bureau of Vocational Information survey of 1925 commented, secretarial positions were "bag ends and few give opportunity for promotion into interesting jobs."[57]

The subservience of secretarial work was, for men, imbued with the hope of promotion.[58] The Bureau's survey, compiled from the results of questionnaires submitted to employers, elaborated on the reasons for men's continuance in this position (albeit in decreased numbers) as well as their different work experience. Male secretaries often were retained if the business required any technical or manufacturing expertise. In addition, some firms created entry-level jobs for male secretaries specifically for their eventual promotion to managerial or executive positions. Some executives had both male and female secretaries, using men when it was necessary to travel, or to do night or weekend work. Other employers felt that men were more respected by other men and thus afforded better protection from importunate callers or provided more status for the executive. Still others believed that men could "stand the guff" better than women or that a woman could not take on as much or as difficult work as a male secretary.[59] These distinctions were based on the employers' sense of appropriate behaviors and expectations for men and for women. It was not fitting for men and women to work together at night or on weekends, away from the protection of other people or the workplace. Men were tougher and more expensive to pay than women, and the power to command them and the ability to pay them thus afforded more prestige. Given all the advantages to the employer of hiring male secretaries, the fact that women came to dominate this job category cannot be explained simply by virtue of availability, cheap labor, or status. Women somehow, fulfilled the gender expectations of the new type of secretary.

As corporate office work became more specialized and the gender composition of the secretarial labor force changed, educators, office workers, and managers wanted more specific definitions of the corporate private secretary. In response to this demand, Kilduff wrote *The Private Secretary: His Duties and Opportunities.* Originally published in 1916, the book went through several editions, remaining essentially unchanged until 1924. As is obvious from the title, the first few editions treated the private secretary as a man's job.[60] In 1924, however, the title changed, and Kilduff spoke of private secretaries as either male or female, reflecting the introduction of women into those positions. In a section entitled "Qualities that Help the Secretary," Kilduff specifically addressed the gender attributes that differentiated men and women and how these attributes affected their job performance: "Male secretaries are more likely not to possess suitable manners than are female secretaries; perhaps because it is man's nature to be more unrestrained and more independent than women, perhaps because men are not so sensitive to the effects of manners as women are and hence do not appreciate their value."[61]

Kilduff had consistently complained about male private secretaries' manners since the 1916 edition. An 1891 article by Clara Lanza about a different job category voiced the same theme. "Women Clerks in New York" claimed that women made better clerks than men:

> Men are troublesome. They complain about trifles that a woman wouldn't notice. The office boys don't suit, or the temperature of the building is too hot or

too cold, or the light is not properly adjusted. Then, if they have a slight head-ache, they stay at home. Most of them are married, and their wives fall ill or their mother-in-law comes on a visit, and all these things are made an excuse for absence.[62]

Kilduff contradicted himself, however, and inadvertently contrasted reality with the ideal: "Woman secretaries, although they know as only women can know the value of manners, often have the faults nevertheless of being careless in observing the amenities of the position and indifferent to the necessity of putting themselves out to accommodate callers at the office."[63] Clearly, neither men nor women held exclusive patent on good business manners.

These gender attributions had been completely reversed by 1930, and the same behavior for men and women was explained in different terms. In a 1929 article in *North American Review,* R. LeClerc Phillips excoriated female office workers for their inability to keep "temperament" out of their job, and their tendency to take everything in the most personal way. Their temperament, Phillips claimed, was responsible for the fact that female office workers earned less than men: "Tears, temper, 'touchiness,' and the strange inability to view office . . . life in a more or less objective light, scarcely make for promotion."[64] A man, Phillips claimed, could be "relied upon to look at his work and his environment in a purely impersonal light. . . . The man is aggressive. The woman is . . . weak."[65] Phillips transformed men's rudeness into indepen-dence and aggressiveness and construed women's lack of manners as oversen-sitivity and emotional weakness. In other words, the behavior of office workers had not changed because it flowed from the nature of clerical work; the relation between gender and behavior, however, shifted to accommodate the new de-mographics of office workers.

Educators and managers spent a fair amount of time attempting to define exactly how a private secretary was different from other clerical workers; they settled on emphasizing personalized functions and self-motivation for secre-taries and measurable skills, speed, and accuracy for clerks, stenographers, and typists.[66] Secretaries and former stenographers themselves echoed these defini-tions in a survey done in 1925 of over twenty-five hundred secretaries (only eleven of whom were men) by the Bureau of Vocational Information. A secre-tary to the Board of Education in Owatonna, Minnesota announced, "I think a stenographic position is more or less mechanical while in a secretarial position one has to use initiative, be able to meet people well, and be prepared to handle many different lines of work."[67] Another young woman encapsulated the differences more succinctly and more cynically: "the ability to write letters as the 'boss' thought he dictated denotes a secretary—She remains a stenogra-pher, however, if she lets him know she's correcting him."[68] This woman used irony to reveal the relationship between the type of work that was part of a particular job and the interpersonal relationships and entitlements it entailed. She outlined what was, in one sense, a straightforward bureaucratic hierarchy: boss, secretary, stenographer. And she implied that to be a secretary—the higher clerical position—one had to practice deference, had to understand the hierarchy of corporate social skills.

The private secretary, unlike other clerical positions, placed enormous importance on the character of the relationship with an immediate supervisor. Specifically, the private secretary had to give up his or her own identity and become one with the employer. Although self-denial was a necessary quality for all workers, in the case of secretaries it was magnified since secretaries had to practice a form of self-destruction in order to keep their jobs. Popular and trade literature consistently portrayed the private secretary as the boss's "alter ego." Henry Horwood, in "The Big Man's Other Self" (1909), described the secretary's function in this way:

> As nearly as he can be described, he is a man who has lost his own personality and found his chief's in its stead. His brain is a plastic fac-simile of his chief's; indeed, like a piece of wax that has been molded to another form, it is so shaped as to think exactly as the chief thinks, . . . he is, in other words, a sort of mental phonograph that never plays its own tune, that never originates but copies perfectly, that furnishes the chief with another extra brain.

To illustrate the total absorption of the secretary in the boss's attitudes and personality, Horwood reproduced a joke about a private secretary who had dinner one night at a friend's house. When dessert was reached, he was offered some rich pastry. "No, thank you," he said, "the chief has dyspepsia pretty badly and never eats pastry."[69]

Edward Kilduff's claim that the main difference between the private secretary and the stenographer or typist was that the secretary had to be able to exercise initiative and submerge his or her personality into that of the chief's reveals an important contradiction.[70] Secretaries simultaneously were supposed to shape their own work (as did managers) yet practice deferential behavior, like lower-level clerical workers. Female secretaries in the Bureau of Vocational Information survey emphasized this contradiction position as the bane and the opportunity of secretarial work. Among the disadvantages of a secretarial position, respondents listed "Close contact with employer if he is not of the right sort," "A girl loses her identity—whenever her work is mentioned, her employer's name must be given," or, most clearly, "you feel almost as though you prostitute (that may be too strong a word) yourself to making money—for you must sacrifice yourself and approach everything thru the point of view of your employer."[71]

Immersion in the status and beliefs of another could have its advantages. One woman noted that she didn't like to make decisions, since it was "quite a mental burden." Another liked the "possibility of association with interesting men (don't quote!!)"; still another disliked "responsibility." Others noted the "prestige" or potential for "mental growth from constant contact with really great minds."[72] In addition, the prescription that secretaries exercise initiative was not always a hollow promise. One respondent claimed that she enjoyed the "full confidence of an upright business man," another that her "chief . . . considered me almost as a partner in his enterprises."[73] Nevertheless, most of the respondents in this survey identified self-sacrifice in favor of someone else's habits, ethics, and moods as the most onerous aspect of secretarial work. One woman emphasized the wrenching possibilities of a loss of self: "Although the secretary is only valuable insofar as she can act independently and spare her employer, she never gets credit for independence, but is known to her associates only as an agent. Her personality must be submerged always, and often in loyalty to her employer's stand she must seem to stand back of principles with which she is not in agreement."[74] The underlying issue for secretaries seems to have been the degree to which all aspects of the job were dependent on the personality, skills, and attitudes of the superior, for good or ill.

Like the management mentorism that is a part of the modern corporate structure, but without its ultimate rewards in advancement, the secretary's relation to his or her superior rested on personality and politics. The private secretary existed in a shadowy area between management's impressionistic skills and the typewriters and dictaphones of the business factory. Kilduff and other business writers pointed out that the secretary had no performance guidelines in the form of measurable product—number of letters typed, or amounts of envelopes sealed. The measures of how well he or she did the job were nebulous and largely involved learning how to get along with the boss. A great portion of the secretary's job entailed "learning how to act"—how to behave toward all the individuals with which he or she came in contact—a skill particularly crucial for the secretary, because the job was composed largely of personal service.[75] Furthermore, there were no set methods or rule books to go by in learning this function, since each individual boss demanded different services and had different working habits. "The desires of the chief can be discovered by *observation* and by *tactful inquiries*," Kilduff explained, and of the two he recommended the former.[76] Interpersonal skills were functions of the job category itself and had nothing intrinsic to do with the gender of the secretary.

Elements of spatial organization accentuated the personal qualities of the secretary's position.[77] A stenographer taking dictation from her chief customarily sat near one corner of his desk and placed her writing pad on a pull-out board situated on the same desk corner. With the introduction of the dictaphone, this personalized moment survived only in the job of private secretary, who still seated herself near her employer and used a portion of his desk for her stenographic tasks. By 1900 this image, had become a popular genre piece, an easily understood sign of status and gender relations in the office. In other words, by the early twentieth century the personalized function of hand-taken dictation survived in a job category that retained overtones of intimacy and personalism both in its job description and its physical proximity between employer and employee.[78] The subservience, lack of ambition, and personalistic relations attached to secretaryship spilled over to female office workers partly as a result of the place of secretaries within the corporate hierarchy. The private secretary was the one remaining instance among clerical workers in which the precorporate, personalized relationship between employer and employee was part of the job description and expectation. At the same time, it was the highest-paid job in the clerical hierarchy precisely because, like management positions, its skills were personal and interrelational and not easily learned or measured. Thus, personal traits that best served that type of position —adaptability, subservience, willingness to subsume one's personality into that of another's—had the highest status among clerical jobs. Anyone with those skills could have filled the job. However, because of increasing specialization in office work, because of ideological assumptions about women's nature, and because increasingly more women than men became secretaries, women office workers were associated with those personality traits.

Although women and men had difficulty coping with employers' demands, for women there was less opportunity for advancement. Grace Hazard, in "A Feather Duster" (1929), described her difficulties in dealing with the capricious, often demeaning demands of various male employers:

I started working for a Mr. Lyons, who owned a good-sized letter-shop. He wanted some one who . . . could take charge of the office and the twenty-some girls who were doing the typing. He had spent four hours in interviewing me to make sure I was the right person. The first morning he handed me the checks to make the deposit and suddenly screamed: "Look at them, look at them, look at them!"

"I am looking at them," I said.

"Now, that won't do," he said. "I may be snappy, but it doesn't mean you have done anything. I have a great deal on my mind."

I laughed and said: "Well, if you are snappy without cause, I'll certainly say something back."

"No. That won't do."

It was eleven o'clock when I left. I had worked for two hours. If only Mr. Lyons had told me when he was interviewing me that he would snap at me without cause and that I must not say anything back to him, I would never have taken the position. When I am screamed at, something inside me happens and before I know it words come out. I can't seem to get experience in saying nothing when I am screamed at.[79]

For men, advancement from clerkship to management still was possible in the corporate structure. In most cases, women did not have access to these routes or were confined to managing women because of the association of women with lower-status clerical work, such as typing, the perception that female office workers were not heads of households, the belief that women worked only until they found husbands and married, and developing assumptions about women's personal role in business.[80] While for male secretaries active subservience was a necessary stage in their general advancement, for female clerical workers it became an end in itself. Coping with a Mr. Lyons was part of the job description.

From the beginning, the presence of women in offices introduced an element of sexuality at variance with the rational economic aims of business. The majority of female office workers during this period were young and single, raising the specter of unchaperoned romantic entanglements that might cross the boundaries of sexual propriety. Advice literature urged female office workers to guard against male advances on the job; in this way, the literature translated to the office setting the notion that women were responsible for keeping relations between men and women nonerotic. In offices men and women were thrown together without the social shields of parents, wives, husbands, other kin, or responsible guardians. The sexually charged atmosphere of the gendered office found its way into popular images of office work almost as soon as women began working in offices. A 1909 postcard represented a humorous variation on the genre image of women secretaries seated at their bosses' desk. Captioned "I love my wife, But, OH You Kid!," the photograph made explicit the notion that sexual expression was an aspect of office experience.

The "typewriter" or stenographer who "married the boss" appeared in short stories and advice literature when women began filling these jobs. Indeed, the percentage of magazine stories regarding employed women remained fairly close to the percentage of employed women in the general population.[81] While such stories cannot be seen as descriptions of reality, they do suggest the sorts of fantasies or images which readers were willing to entertain.[82] The female clerical worker who married the boss remained a remarkably persistent genre from the 1880s into the 1920s, despite its slim basis in fact. However, its message altered subtly over that time.

Donald Makosky has noted that in popular fiction, romantic relations between the secretary-typewriter-stenographer and the employer often grew out of the woman's sense of duty toward her employer and the boss's appreciation of her selflessness toward both him and the job.[83] This emphasis on "duty" and responsible care between men and women kept the basis of the relationship between worker and boss within the bounds of propriety, if not completely asexual. In "The Typewriting Clerk," a young, unmarried stenographer had

Captioned "I Love My Wife, But OH! You Kid," this ca. 1909 postcard uses humor to suggest the widely recognized sexual overtones of the boss-secretary relationship. *Library of Congress.*

taken a job because of family misfortunes. She then inherited enough to live well on, but she chose to remain employed rather than return to the pampered life of "sloth and self-indulgence" of her middle-class childhood. Work provided stimulation and "human interest." She secretly loaned her employer money in order to save him from financial ruin. She is portrayed as "always striving to think only of his welfare" and as his moral savior as well as his benefactor. By expecting him to be a better man than he was, she was rewarded with both his moral elevation and their marriage.[84]

A more humorous tale, "The Typewritten Letter," told essentially the same story. A young, single female "typewriter" discovers that her boss—an older man who was "familiar with the counting-room and its language" but to whom "the drawing-room was an unexplored country"—wishes to marry her. The story stressed that she came from a "good family" and was forced to work. "Miss Gale was pretty, of course—all typewriter girls are—and it was generally understood in the office that she belonged to a good family who had come down in the world. . . . She was a sensible girl, who realized that the typewriter paid better than the piano."[85]

The attitudes reflected in popular literature were well within nineteenth-century conventions of romance and offered no threat to accepted canons of male/female relations. The facts that both parties were unmarried, that woman's role was to elevate and "domesticate" men, and that the "girls" were from good families brought down in the world through financial reverses—that is, of the same class as their employer—simply meant that if the setting for their relationships was unusual, nothing that happened between them was. Stories of this type suggested that female office workers maintained class position, economic security, and social status through marriage, which was the reward for maintaining cultural standards of domestic womanhood within the public sphere of the office.[86]

The stories' stress on female common sense confirmed through fictional fantasy the conservative arguments of those who stressed working women's middle-class domesticity. Miss Gale's typewritten response to her boss/finance's rather bumbling marriage proposal acknowledged that he clearly could use the organizational talents and social skills of a well-trained office worker, at the same time denying any base financial motivations on her part: "I have decided to accept the position [of wife], not so much on account of its financial attractions, as because I shall be glad, on a friendly basis, to be associated with [you]. Why did you put me to all that worry writing that idiotic letter, when a few words would have saved ever so much bother? You evidently *need* a partner."[87] In the 1880s and 1890s, "typewriters" and stenographers performed many of the same duties in small offices that secretaries would later perform in large ones. By World War I, the "typewriter" had become the "secretary" in these stories. As more working-class daughters filled stenographic and typing positions and the work became routinized, middle-class managers and workers alike saw such positions as lower in status.

The evolving cultural image of womanhood included the notion of *companionate marriage,* a union of equal individuals at variance with the nineteenth-century vision of domestic female subordination and separate spheres for men and women.[88] Companionate marriage took a single standard—male—as the ideal for both men and women: companionate wives ideally were sexually "liberated" individuals with their own wants and the right to fill them. Business, however, found the idea of men's and women's sameness at odds with the need for a subordinate female wage labor force. Popular discussions of office womanhood denied the "feminine" qualities of the liberated wife in favor of the dutiful ideal of the previous generation, when men and women were equally important and differently constituted. In 1915, one magazine story incorporated a critical view of companionate marriage into the tale of female upward mobility by introducing the boss's wife into the picture. The story presented the secretary who married the boss not as a vamp or home-wrecker but merely as an understanding woman who appreciated the boss more than did his wife. The wife, in contrast, was a selfish spendthrift, more concerned with clothing and social position and her husband's ability as a financial provider than with him as a person. The secretary not only knew the value of money and respected it because she earned her own living but also shared her employer's interest in his work. Thus, the fact that they labored together became an important link in this ideal relationship, at the expense of the companionate wife.[89]

By the 1920s, popular literature and advice books referred to secretaries as office wives or office housekeepers, even as the notion of marrying the boss became less frequent. Advice literature generally frowned on sexual relationships within offices while stressing the "wifely" nature of secretarial work.[90] A theme in several types of popular literature was that secretaries knew more about men, and particularly about husbands, than did wives. As Mildred Harrington reported in "Too Much Dictation," "she has had a husband ten years, and I have never had one, but I know something about men which she has never even guessed. It is this: Every man in the world needs a woman to brag to. It's the little boy in him." Harrington went on to declare that when sexual tensions erupted in an office, they often could be traced to the man's wife. The modern companionate wife, concerned with her own self-satisfaction and individuality, failed to fulfill her feminine role as other-directed helpmate: "If wives would only cultivate the gentle art of listening, this would be a much nicer world for husbands—and stenographers. And a much safer one for wives!"[91]

The construction of female workers as wives was layered and richly nuanced, reaching outside the office to tie together women's domestic and business lives. In "Business Girls as 'Office Housekeepers,'" Justine Mansfield argued that female office workers could make better preparation for domestic duties, and secure their jobs, by learning neatness, cleanliness, and home decoration while employed in offices. The male business executive was "trained by long tradition to look for neatness and cleanliness in everything a woman does; and especially the housekeeping home-making sense."[92] Because of women's better artistic sense and their ties to home, women could domesticate the office by studying and rearranging the furniture and adding "minor appointments," such as flowers. In this way, women in offices could show men that they were good potential wives by being conscientious office housekeepers. "Lacking in this ability themselves," Mansfield claimed, "men are instinctively drawn to neatness in women as an indication of their housekeeping proclivities [*sic*]. Men unconsciously measure women by the standard of their mothers, and their mother's home-making ways have a deep effect on their psychology."[93]

Finally, the "office wife" image reinforced the function of the secretary as a symbol of man's privilege. Secretaries as daytime wives accented their chief's individuality and business success. For these purposes, a young and conventionally lovely woman was not absolutely necessary, but many women complained that such workers often were chosen over their less physically or personally attractive sisters. The office wife, like a real wife, was a man's possession, a bit of property not unlike the office furniture in her ability to reflect a man's taste and power. Grace Robinson caustically explained:

> Hear the greedy beast—he insists that she shall be well dressed, even though her salary is a modest one. He wants his secretary to appear prosperous in order to impress his business friends. Impelled by the same vanity, or business acumen, he hangs a chinchilla coat and diamonds on his wife. His secretary is part of the office scenery, like the Italian-marble fireplace and the oil paintings. She must be decorative as well as useful.[94]

Literature changed over time to reflect a more realistic picture of actual possibilities, but ideas about the *qualities* the office wife possessed altered not at all. She was still associated with a sense of duty, a willingness to subsume self into work, an unflinching devotion to her boss and his business, and an inherent difference from men. The ideal of the office wife did not keep pace with ideals of women's behavior generally. The "office marriage" was not the companionate marriage idealized between 1910 and 1930, based on equality and sharing. It remained closer to the ideal nineteenth-century marriage. For example, in contrast to constructions of masculinity and work, in which men were rewarded by ascending to control over the workplace, women's idealized reward took them out of the workplace entirely via marriage.

By the 1920s business commentators were able to construct an extended analogy around the notion that women's office role was that of the subordinate and other-directed wife. In a 1935 article in *Fortune* magazine, the voice of the business community, one author argued that women made the office more homelike by the mere fact of their presence and by the qualities they carried with them, as women, to the workplace:

> Their conscious or subconscious intention some day to marry, and their conscious or subconscious willingness to be directed by men, render them amenable and obedient and relieve them of the ambition which makes it difficult for men to put their devotion into secretarial work. . . . [This] indicated that women in their quality of women and by virtue of some of their most womanly traits are capable of making the office a more pleasant, peaceful, and homelike place.

The writer went on to state that men hired women to work in offices not because they would work for less (although he acknowledged the truth of that fact), nor even precisely because they brought womanly qualities with them. Rather, men were willing to work with women because of their altered home situation and the alternative type of domesticity that office women provided. In the process, the author made a direct comparison between the ideal of companionate marriage and the office wife: "The male was no longer master in his own dining room and dreadful in his own den nor did a small herd of wives, daughters, and sisters hear his voice and tremble. He was, on the contrary, the more or less equal mate of a more or less unpredictable woman. And he resented it." The solution, as this author explained it, was that men recreated the gender relations of their father's generation within the office. What an office man wanted was not a pretty, clever, expensive, individualistic wife, but someone to take care of the petty details of his life: pay his bills, balance his checkbook, make reservations, and "take his daughter to the dentist"—someone who would "listen to his side of the story, give him a courageous look when things were blackest, and generally know all, understand all—but not quite forgive all because forgiveness would be quite unthinkable."[95]

The analogy to Victorian wives, or "daytime wives," as the author called them, contained several pointed truths. Female secretaries *were* dependent on the whim of their employers, taking whatever they dished out in order to keep their jobs, even "widowhood." One respondent to the Bureau of Vocational Information survey bitterly noted, "After working as [a] secretary for one man for a number of years, and studying his requirements and whims and becoming really useful to him, he may suddenly die, or retire, and there is usually no room in the organization for his secretary. It means that one is practically compelled to start over."[96]

The definition of a woman's office role as a subordinate wife described not only the expectations for women in offices but the reality as well. Business kept alive a role for women that was gradually changing in society at large. In so doing, the modern workplace perpetuated a nineteenth-century ideal of womanhood. The ideology of the office wife persisted powerfully largely because the structure of business made such behaviors necessary in order to remain employed, and gender segregation within job categories accentuated differences in expected behavior for men and women. The perpetuation of a nineteenth-century gender role model for women served, at the least, the general business aim of worker control by providing a model that working women could internalize. The image of a "nation of silk knees" and "ironic mouths" presented female workers as a disturbing, potent force; it also emphasized women's sexuality and "slender-necked" deference. For many men trying to understand the experience of office work in the new clerical-service industries, the presence of women literally and metaphorically embodied the implications of change. The challenge to manliness in the office environment was met, in part, by redefining manhood in the context of men's increasing dominance of managerial work.

CHAPTER THREE

Science and Sensibility

Manhood and Sales

When Theodore Dreiser introduced Charles Drouet to the reading public in *Sister Carrie* in 1900, he gave life to a familiar American type: the traveling salesman. Drouet dressed in a flashy style with heavy rings, tight suit, and "common yellow agate" cuff links. He was a man always on the lookout for the main chance, whether it was a new business connection or the possibility of pursuing "the delicate task of [a woman's] friendship."[1] In contrast to Drouet, George Hurstwood the manager was the epitome of middle-class blandness whose cruel treatment of Carrie Meeber grew out of his own narcissism rather than Drouet's carefully planned and artfully executed seduction. It was no accident that Dreiser chose a salesman and a business manager to represent the urban men of his time. Dreiser's artistic goal may have been to contrast the men as two forms of self-absorbed evil, but his characters also shared more traits as businessmen than divided them as urban types. Although signifying different classes and different notions of the predatory male, Drouet and Hurstwood represented the links between sales, managerial work, and masculinity typical of the early-twentieth-century business world.

Salesmen and managers were united as the central male figures of the new gender relations of the business world. The female secretary and her sister stenographers, typewriters, and file clerks embodied the feminized ideal for office workers. Even though women's presence in offices had not forced a redefinition of the ideal worker, it had radically changed the gender connotations of work. The fact that the ideal office worker was a female required a redefinition of the connections between gender and work. This redefinition was a critical issue for the association of manliness with work and of middle-class manhood with office work in particular.

Corporate work elevated certain skills but not others, connecting gender and business in new ways. Specifically, the distinction between "managerial" or "brain" positions and "clerical" or "manual" positions maintained the status and skills of a new job category, managers, at a level commensurate with that of precorporate clerks, while denigrating the new, machine-oriented clerical work and its attendant mechanical skills. By the mid-1920s, employers, management theorists, and educators had laid out the ideal traits for various types of business workers. Job qualifications broke into two basic categories: manual skills and personal traits. Clerical workers, such as typists and stenographers and clerks who performed menial functions (such as sorting mail or operating office machines), were to be capable of speed and accuracy first and have adaptable personalities second. As systematic management promoter Frederick Nichols explained it in 1934, in the process reflecting the feminization of these positions, this type of worker "comes into contact with relatively few people, practically all of whom are fellow-workers. . . . Her all-round efficiency is measured in terms of production in a narrow field of service."[2] If they were in a position that brought them into contact with the public (very few of these workers were), physical cleanliness and attractiveness also were necessary. Secretaries were to possess the same traits, in reverse order: first of all to be personable, intelligent, accurate, and adaptable; and second, to be speedy. Mechanized clerical functions had become "women's work" by the 1920s, with a concurrent fall in status of any labor that relied on office machines.[3]

For managers and executives, who normally were men, the desired traits were interpersonal rather than mechanical, including rationality, ambition, thoroughness, "enthusiasm," "personality," leadership skills, and executive ability.[4] Popular views of the mechanistic nature of machine labor enhanced this distinction and made it a commonplace. As one author put it in a poem, "Ode to the Boss," a typist merely followed orders, her status as subordinate predicated on the manual nature of her work:

> You think—and then I pound;
> When you are wrong and I am right
> I never make a sound![5]

Frederick A. Savage, a general agent for New England Life, drew on this idea in a speech to Baltimore City College students in 1906: "The employer is, generally speaking, the man who has so conserved his resources that he is enabled to employ other men to work for him. He hires men with brains, and he pays more to the man who knows how to use his brains than he does to the man who is merely a machine."[6]

So commonplace were these perceived differences between men's and women's jobs and skills that office supply companies used them to sell products. Advertising for office machines, furniture, and supplies stressed an essential distinction between tasks that required concentration, thought, or the ability to make decisions—the mark of executives and managers—and simple, repetitive, or physically oriented tasks—the work of lower-level clericals. Advertisements for office machines such as typewriters depicted women using the machines, while men appeared in ads for larger, heavier office machinery such as massive printers. Particularly after World War I and the last major influx of women into office work, advertisements showed women filing forms or taking dictation, while men more often appeared seated at a desk writing, talking to customers, or bending over female workers as if to give them instruction. When an office supply company wanted to show that a machine or piece of equipment was easy to use, women and sometimes even children appeared manipulating the product. One set of advertisements from 1917 for Art Metal filing cabinets depicted a woman opening a cabinet with her thumbnail to illustrate how easy they were to use. A 1927 advertisement for Shaw-Walker filing cabinets showed a child pulling a drawer open with a silk thread under the headline, "Easy Operation." The Addressograph company marketed its mailing line with a photograph of a woman seated at the Addressograph (which looked remarkably like a small sewing machine) captioned "operation almost effortless."[7] Women, in other words, did those repetitive, often mechanical tasks that required little thought; men, in contrast, engaged in complex tasks that were not machine oriented.

The movement to define management or brain workers as separate categories with their own prerogatives and mission within the corporate system stemmed from two streams of evolving ideology: "systematic" and "impressionistic" management. Based in different premises about how to structure an effective workplace, these theories expressed complex assumptions about gender. Both systematic and impressionistic attitudes about management were present in most financial industry offices, often simultaneously; in that sense, they cannot be strictly segregated from one another. At one level, they represented the battery of ideologies and methods on which managers drew in their efforts to participate in corporate life and exert control over workers and managers. Both sets of ideas—technological or scientific and impressionistic or behavioral—played a part in efforts to manage manual workers. But the technological approach was not as useful for directing mental workers, managers themselves. At another level, each attitude represented a distinct response to the need to redefine the meaning of masculinity in the context of business and to harness middle-class male managers to their bureaucratic role; in this regard, the two approaches emphasized different sorts of masculinity.

Efforts to submit workplace operations to scientific "laws" appeared in movements such as Frederick W. Taylor's "scientific management" in the 1890s and in the fields of social psychology and personnel theory somewhat later.[8] The rationalism of Taylorism grew out of the attempt to apply engineering skills to the work process in factories, and in the field of social psychology from the effort to understand the social basis of consumption and sales motivation. Much broader than the specifics of Taylorism, the movement toward efficiency, order, and rationality based on technological imperatives or scientific proofs underlay the ideology of the late-nineteenth-century middle class, the professional-managerial class; it was reflected in the larger society as Progressivism.[9]

Scientific management theory, as distinct from personnel theory, placed a premium on interpreting the work process in a strictly mechanistic or materialistic way. It postulated that workers could be manipulated by placing them under the guidance of managers, who formed policies according to the dictates of technology. The mechanics of production, in other words, governed the work process rather than personal relations, rapacious greed, or some other human motivation. The rational school of management limited workers' involvement in and knowledge of the larger role of their work in the production process and engaged their individual self-interest through the profit motive. Ideally, manual workers would be distracted from focusing on personal or even class relations; instead, they would face a seemingly irrefutable mechanistic explanation for their employers' and managers' demands. The theory of scientific management posed business operations as mechanical, automatic, impersonal, and measurable, implying that managers only followed scientific or natural economic laws when gauging work product. Scientific management thereby emphasized the logical aspects of the work process and systematic management as a reasonable response to purely technical problems.

The emphasis on rationalism profoundly affected notions of manhood. The mechanical or scientifically rational view of the universe in industrializing America questioned the idea of free will. To the extent that the work process could be measured, and to the extent that it was governed by technological developments and increasing job specialization, it was less possible to imagine a place for the self-made man of character, for social mobility through work, for the opportunity to prove one's manhood by grappling with the vicissitudes of business life, or for physical skill and stamina. As Irvin Wyllie has pointed out, the belief that individual will allowed any man to "make himself over in the image of success, if he would only determine to do so" was a major component of the middle-class ideal of masculinity.[10] Rational management closed a crucial door for self-evaluation by locking out a central tenet of middle-class notions of manhood. However, systematic management's mechanistic view of society suggested alternative avenues for the expression of masculinity: acquiring specialized knowledge, developing such ascribed masculine qualities as rationality, and gaining power over others if not over oneself. Masculinity could be expressed through rational application of mechanical business laws of profit and loss, maximized use of time, and separation from more menial, clerical, female labor. As early as the 1880s, the very scale of business operations made it seem impossible to continue operating on personal hunches and trial and error.[11]

Although specific aspects of Taylorism, such as time-and-motion studies or quota systems, never worked very effectively in offices, systematic management did shape two aspects of office reality. First, it formalized and justified status divisions within corporations. Scientific management spelled out a clear distinction between clerical work with machines and manual skills and managing people through application of a rationalized work process dependent on scientific laws, marking a major departure from the precorporate office. To the extent that this division was recapitulated as a gender and racial division of labor, a rationalized approach to work and specialized knowledge of business mechanics became the property of white males. Second, systematic management theory suggested that managers acted in completely rational ways, instituting programs dictated by natural laws of efficiency rather than by some system of mutual responsibilities or struggles over power and status. The implications were significant: Systematic management and gender ideals together obscured the fact that technological adoptions, the division of labor, class relations, and status privileges all were the result of human choices. Systematic management therefore blurred the socially constructed hierarchies of status—class, race, and gender—in the workplace, making such divisions seem the natural order of things.[12]

Further, by suggesting that human will and self-creation could be replaced by mechanical solutions divorced from moral questions regarding worker relations, scientific management undermined the nineteenth-century focus on ethical character as a central component of masculinity and on personalism as the basis for employer–worker relations. Managerial or professional men could ignore the dehumanizing implications of mechanical labor; they were freed from any personal responsibility for their actions and from the need to identify with those they supervised. The distancing of human agency in favor of seemingly natural economic and biological laws underlay the development of professionalism and specialized expertise in modern office relations. Efficiency, as defined by the rational explication of the natural law of profit and loss, and not human choice governed the work process. Systematic management suggested that some managers acted as they did simply because they were men and therefore efficient and rational; a "masculine style" of management merely expressed universal laws of interpersonal relations and efficient economics. Thus, to the extent that middle-class manhood was identified with rationalized principles of management in the workplace, it was released from ethical obligations.[13]

Personnel management was the "female" version of masculinized scientific management. Both types of systematic management were predicated on the importance of rationalizing the workplace; both focused on the workers themselves; and both grew ultimately out of reformist, Progressive-Era thought. They differed in that while scientific management offered mechanistic methods for cutting down on employee inefficiency, such as dexterity tests or technological solutions, personnel management preferred to deal with problems in workers' lives both inside and outside the workplace. From its inception in the years just before World War I, personnel theory was dominated by college-trained women who often participated in broadly based efforts at social reform. For example, Mary Barnett Gilson converted to Taylorism after she heard Taylor speak in Boston. A Wellesley graduate, she became involved in vocational guidance in 1910. She responded to Taylor's emphasis on managerial responsibility for shaping reasonable workplaces. First as "welfare secretary" and later as "service and employment manager" in a clothing factory, Gilson introduced extensive interviews rather than testing to place prospective workers, pushed for higher wages, and furthered the factory's welfare program.[14] Gilson and other women involved in personnel management introduced moral and ethical concerns about worker welfare to scientific management, without losing their fervor for rationalization.[15]

Rationalized approaches such as systematic and personnel management predominantly spoke to dealing with subordinates. They did not have much to say about how managers themselves were to behave, how they should interact with their peers, and how management skills could be harnessed to the profit motive. These questions were resolved in large part by the simultaneous development of an updated version of the Victorian success ethic: the salesman as a manager of men. Theories of salesmanship played a critical role in the development of professional management theory. In the insurance industry, the connections among sales, management, manhood, and professionalism were highly charged, evocative aspects of the industry's language.[16]

An impressionistic and behavioristic set of management theories sprang up around salesmen in service industries such as insurance. This second management movement did not find scientific justification until the advent of the "human relations" idea in the late 1930s.[17] However, its roots can be found in the development of life insurance sales personnel in the 1890s and, earlier, in the evolving notion of managers in financial industries. Management had been an issue in financial industries since at least the mid-nineteenth century.[18] "Impressionistic management" began to appear in insurance trade papers in the years just after the Civil War.[19] In contrast to scientific and personnel management, which were based in concern over workers, impressionistic management was aimed at motivating, controlling, and shaping the behavior of managers. It stressed skill in dealing with people, particularly subordinates. Good managers were "noble men" who were patient, kind, not pompous or officious, and generous.[20] Men who could adopt these behavior patterns could influence others and become leaders and in that way "manage" their work force and other managers. Commentator Henry C. Fish, for example, emphasized the notion of a life insurance sales agent as an "exponent" of "moral dignity" who would rely on his "good reputation" and "straight forward, open, manly" dealings with others.[21] Clearly, the salesman school of management drew on nineteenth-century notions to articulate ideas about men's success in business.

In contrast to rationalized or scientific management, the impressionistic management movement focused on sensibility: Managing people meant dealing fairly within a constantly shifting context for human behavior. The most effective managers, like the most effective salesmen, knew how to "size up" people, how to be sensitive to shifts in a person's interests, economic or social needs, or any personal ties that might motivate that individual to behave in certain ways.[22] Impressionistic management skills drew on didacticism, example, and empathy rather than rationalized methods. As one sales manager put it, the primary "tool" for this type of managerial expression was "knowledge of human nature. . . . The man who takes pains to study his fellows and ascertains what they need, *and then satisfactorily supplies it,* is . . . a successful Business Man."[23] Impressionistic management was a masculinized version of personnel theory, minus the latter's emphasis on efficiency and mechanistic solutions to workplace problems. It stressed interpersonal skills rather than coercion, along with harnessing male agents' perceived need for competition and aggression to the teamwork of agency or company demands.

By World War I, managerial theory created an ideological niche for both male and female managers that incorporated rather than challenged nineteenth-century gender divisions and complicated the gendering of work relations in service industries. Impressionistic management drew on a mixture of assumptions about gender and sales. On the one hand, it borrowed extensively from the vocabulary and attributes of nineteenth-century manhood. To be a good salesman or general agent was to be "progressive, enthusiastic, ambitious, and manly," as management educator and general agent W. F. Winterble stated in 1928.[24] On the other hand, managers in retail areas such as department stores, which employed more saleswomen, found that some assumptions about women's nature—their empathetic qualities, sensitivity to other's needs, and ability to persuade others—fit perfectly with sales work.[25] It was precisely because the impressionistic aspect of managerial theory became so important to business philosophy that women were able to argue for a female role in business management and insurance sales. Despite the "feminine" qualities demanded of sales work in general, behavioristic sales training for men evolved from nineteenth-century definitions of manly character and work as a calling and emphasized the balance of aggression and empathy, competitiveness and teamwork. Ultimately, both streams of managerial theory, the rational and the impressionistic, contributed to a male standard of sales behavior.

Sales was an important arena for management theory in an economy increasingly oriented to consumption. By the 1920s, male workers in the white-collar labor force were one-fourth of the male laboring population. Most white-collar workers were involved in the burgeoning field of sales, either by selling or by helping others to sell.[26] The number of male insurance agents, for example, increased from only 8,076 in 1900 to nearly a quarter of a million by 1930. While some women were involved in selling insurance (nearly thirteen thousand by 1930), except for department store positions, men and masculine definitions of behavior and personal worth dominated the sales field. Female life insurance agents were rare; before the 1890s, they usually had become involved by taking over their husbands' "debits" (territory or premium list) on his death or incapacity. Further, women remained fairly constant as a percentage of the insurance sales field between 1890 and 1930, at between 3 and 5 percent (see table 5).

The growth in size of insurance companies, the early lack of outside regulation, and the desire by company officers to police agents' activities led to several developments in life insurance sales. By the mid-nineteenth century, companies attempted to centralize sales efforts. As early as 1865, New England Mutual had begun to appoint general agents to cover business in particular states or regions, including New York, Massachusetts, Vermont, New Hampshire, Ohio, Indiana, Illinois, Iowa, and Wisconsin. By 1867, New England Mutual had general agents in eighteen states or geographic regions. In the 1870s, the Equitable appointed "General Agents" to act as managers and liaisons between agents and the company.[27] General agents often sold insurance. Sometimes supervisors or superintendents worked directly for the company, taking little or none of their earnings in the form of sales commissions.[28] As early as 1880, general agents were referred to as "managers" in recognition of the fact that their function within the industry involved leading people, making and enforcing rules, and developing and using relational skills. An advertisement for a general agent in 1880, for example, spelled out some of the personal qualities one company felt necessary in its representatives: "Must be a man with a good record, perseverance, energy and tact."[29] Yet the positions of agent and salesman were far from professionalized by the 1890s. An agent in Pug-

TABLE 5
Insurance and Banking Agents and Officials, 1870–1930[1]

	1870	1880	1890	1900	1910	1920	1930
Insurance co. off.							
Male	762	1,774	1,463	5,227	9,376	14,754	27,556
Female	——	——	4	112	125	306	1,752
TOTAL	762	1,774	1,467	5,339	9,501	15,060	29,308
Females as percentage of total	0	0	.3	2.0	1.3	2.0	6.0
Agents & brokers							
Male	——	——	8,076	117,142	85,926	114,835	243,974
Female	——	——	478	2,141	2,537	5,083	12,953
TOTAL	0	0	8,554	119,283	88,463	90,918	256,927
Females as percentage of total	0	0	5.5	1.8	2.9	5.6	5.0
Bank officials							
Male	2,738	4,421	39,683	14,024	54,387	78,149	87,429
Female	——	——	217	271	1,672	4,226	5,927
TOTAL	2,738	4,421	39,900	14,295	56,059	82,375	93,356

wash, Nova Scotia, who worked for the Glasgow and London Fire Insurance Company in 1890, claimed that in addition to insurance, he sold undertakers' supplies and salted herring.[30]

The agency system in life insurance encouraged close contacts between supervisors and salesmen. Individual salesmen had "territories" where they attempted to sell policies, collected premiums, disseminated information, and filed claims. General agents working out of local offices oversaw other agents and collected commissions based on a percentage of their agents' sales. Agencies, in turn, answered to the home office or, by the early twentieth century, to a branch office.

Whatever other business or educational experiences an individual may have

TABLE 5   (*cont.*)

	1870	1880	1890	1900	1910	1920	1930
Females as percentage of total	0	0	0.5	1.9	3.0	5.1	6.3
Bankers & brokers[2]							
Male	10,631	19,240	35,458	72,984	69,945	60,846	92,509
Female	——	133	510	293	1,246	700	2,079
TOTAL	10,631	19,373	35,968	73,277	71,191	61,546	94,588
Females as percentage of total	0	0.7	1.4	0.4	1.8	1.1	2.2

Sources: *Compendium of the Ninth Census of the United States, 1870* (Washington Government Printing Office, 1872), tables LXV and XVIII; *Compendium of the Tenth Census of the United States, 1880,* part II (1883), tables XXXII and CIII; *Compendium of the Eleventh Census: 1890,* part III (1897), table 8 (claims, commissions, real estate, insurance agents and collectors, and other agents not specified); *Special Reports: Occupations at the Twelfth Census* [1900] (1904), table 1 (real estate agents and trust company officers); *Thirteenth Census of the U.S., Taken in 1910, vol. IV, Population: 1910, Occupation Statistics* (1914), tables I, 14 and 15; *Fourteenth Census of the U.S., Taken in 1920, vol. IV, Population: Occupations* (1923), table 4; *Fifteenth Census of the U.S.: 1930 Population, vol. IV, General Report on Occupations* (1933), table 2; Joseph A. Hill, *Women in Gainful Occupations, 1870–1920* (1929), table 115; and Alba M. Edwards, *Population: Comparative Occupation Statistics for the United States, 1870–1940, 16th Census of the United States,* 1940 (1943), p. 51.

1. This information includes all types of insurance; the census did not distinguish. Figures for 1870, 1880, and 1890 include bank officials and cashiers, insurance and trust company officials, and officials of transportation and trade companies.

2. Includes commercial brokers, commission men, loan brokers, loan company officials, and stockbrokers.

had, insurance sales was and remained an apprenticeship system. General agents were responsible for recruiting and training their salesmen. During the insurance "wars" that preceded the advent of state regulation in the first decade of the twentieth century, most companies followed the common practice of luring exceptional producers away from other companies by the promise of higher commissions. Good agents were constantly in demand, and recruiting was a continual and highly competitive process.[31] The turnover rate went down by the 1920s, but agencies and companies still expected to hire more agents than ultimately would continue working. The turnover rate at Metropolitan Life in 1908 was over 75 percent, and in 1928, still over 37 percent. The assistant supervisor of agencies at New England Mutual observed in 1929 that for every agent hired, he had to talk with or try out twenty.[32]

The public image of sales as a profession underwent a major revision between the mid-nineteenth century and the 1920s. The nineteenth-century salesman was a wanderer-cum-tinker with questionable morals and even more questionable selling practices. Nineteenth-century middle-class anxieties about "confidence men" grew out of the fear of seduction to vice in all its forms represented by the difficulty of evaluating strangers in an increasingly urban society.[33] In Dreiser's *Sister Carrie,* the alluring and sophisticated evils of the city are represented by the salesman Drouet, "an experienced traveler, a brisk man of the world," a "masher," a "lady's man" who preyed on Carrie Meeber's small-town innocence.[34] In the popular imagination, the insurance agent was merely one type of confidence man. As late as 1895, the American Federation of Labor refused to admit life insurance agents into the union on the grounds that insurance was a scam perpetrated by salesmen on working people.[35] By the 1920s, in contrast, popular literature portrayed the salesman as the epitome of the businessman, since business was about selling products, a sense of security, or happiness itself. Fictional and inspirational literature portrayed the salesman as either the ineffective but certainly not evil character of Sinclair Lewis's *Babbitt* (1922) or the riveting, charismatic leader found in advertising executive Bruce Barton's *The Man Nobody Knows.* The phenomenal success of Barton's 1925 sales polemic underlines the pervasive acceptance of salesmanship and business values as an important component of American life. Barton's best-selling book purported to prove that Jesus Christ had been the world's first successful businessman. Far from the physical weakling and feminized "killjoy" Jesus portrayed by popular theology, Barton depicted Jesus as a masculine, "magnetic" leader who "built the greatest organization of all."[36] As was reflected in Barton's emphasis on Jesus' abilities as a leader of other men, early-twentieth-century business stressed salesmanship as a way of managing people as well as a method for producing profits.

The public view of salesmen and of sales in financial industries grew out of shifting class concerns and the changing class composition of the sales force. In the years immediately after the Civil War, life insurance salesmen generally came from among the poor or working class and often sold insurance as a means of augmenting income rather than as a profession in itself. Throughout the nineteenth century, the general public as well as company officials and executives attributed a low status to insurance agents. They were part of the marginalized urban poor and working class, and thus evocative of the middle-class fears elicited by characters such as Dreiser's Drouet.

As companies grew and became more economically important, their national scope gave them and their major executives a certain amount of fame. The massive efforts to legitimize their products achieved some success, especially as women and college-educated men became agents. Some life insurance agents shared this improved image even as others continued to maintain a working-class stamp. After 1875, the Prudential Insurance Company of America began offering industrial life insurance, and some other companies followed suit with a variety of types of working-class insurance. The introduction of these new products, previously only offered by penny savings banks, fraternal orders, or unions, divided life insurance into two very different branches. In the process, new class divisions emerged among agents. Industrial life insurance had a smaller face value, usually a maximum of five hundred dollars, as opposed to the minimum face value of one thousand dollars for "ordinary" life insurance. Agents collected industrial premiums in small amounts, on a weekly basis, by going door to door in poor or working-class neighborhoods. Industrial agents needed to know less about the variety of insurance products or the intricacies of trusts, estates, and personal finances than did ordinary agents, and they dealt with a lower class of customer. For these reasons, industrial agents continued to come from working-class or poor backgrounds, while the class background and status of ordinary life agents rose.[37] In the 1880s, a sampling of Metropolitan Life's industrial agents included John Wilson, a twenty-year-old woolen-mill worker; a sailor and baritone in a touring opera company; a thirty-year-old Austro-Hungarian army officer; Charles Weidenfeller, a formerly unemployed carpenter; and a railroad track laborer. Ordinary agents, in contrast, increasingly came from middle-class or professional families or at least strove for this higher status. Many, for example, were teachers or former teachers.[38]

Concerned about the continued low status of the work, especially compared to the relatively high earnings an effective ordinary salesman could make by the 1880s, general agents initiated various steps toward professionalization in the 1890s. The National Association of Life Underwriters (NALU) founded in 1890, represented an effort to regulate sales practices, elevate the status of life insurance sales with companies and the general public, lobby for effective state laws, and encourage agents to join local underwriters' associations. General agents also hoped to distinguish themselves as individual entrepreneurs rather than mere representatives of a company. The NALU also tried to encourage training programs, at first to be sponsored by individual companies but ultimately provided by independent entities. In 1902, the Equitable established a life insurance selling course in its home office, possibly the first in the country. Evidently, this early experiment was designed to recruit college-educated men into sales specifically to give life insurance sales a more polished persona.[39] All of these efforts—self-regulation, the assertion of expert knowledge, the simultaneous adoption of the notion of professional "calling" and specific training —suggest the standard avenues of middle-class professionalization in the late nineteenth century.

Industrial agents tried a different route toward collectivity, based in part on their different class backgrounds, affiliations, and products. Between 1900 and 1929, the "heyday of industrial insurance selling," some industrial agents attempted to form labor unions. In 1912, for example, agents of Metropolitan Life and John Hancock—two of the largest industrial firms—tried to form a union in Boston. In 1916, the Insurance Mutual Protective Association had six thousand members in Boston, Chicago, Philadelphia, Providence, and New York. They struck against the Prudential in 1916.[40] Labor unions never had the success at recruiting members among agents as did the professional organizations, partly because industrial agents, up to the 1920s, tended to be part-time agents. Given the smaller returns in industrial sales, agents were not as likely as ordinary agents to make a living solely on insurance. Further, it was the NALU that succeeded in defining and regulating the industry's standards. Finally, the professionalization model better suited the national scope of widely scattered agencies and self-employed agents that composed the industry by 1920.

By 1900, more intuitive methods for professionalization were augmented by increasing efforts to apply scientific techniques to sales. The use of psychological profiles and tests, rehearsed sales pitches, and scholarly research on consumer relationships attempted to pin down exactly what agents needed to do to accomplish results. A spate of academic and industry writers used a rather crude stimulus–response model to describe ways to elicit an "instinctual" reaction in the buyer.[41] Such scientific models, however simplistic, did orient sales toward customers, reinforcing the idea that life insurance was a public service.

Reflecting the development of managerial status within corporations and the attempt by general agents to distinguish between the properties of their jobs and those of their salesmen, by the 1920s company title changes and national magazines spelled out in more detail precisely what managers in the financial industries were expected to do. The scientific sales movement spawned several organizations to promote the notion that general agents were managers. The Carnegie Bureau of Salesmanship Research, begun in 1916 largely through the efforts of life insurance general agent Edward A. Woods, was affiliated with the Carnegie Institute of Technology and financed in part by several life insurance companies. The Association of Life Agency Officers, also started in 1916, was more specifically a product of industry activity and was peopled by home-office agency officers. The association spoke directly to the issues of management and agency officers as managers. By the early 1920s, the title of *manager* had come into common usage among field officers.[42]

But even these more organized efforts to link scientific or rational business methods to management and sales were augmented by older connections between impressionistic sales techniques and managerial skills. In January 1926, a new national magazine devoted to the "art" and practice of managing salesmen in the insurance industry made its first appearance. *Manager's Magazine* addressed issues common among insurance salesmen and general agents since the late nineteenth century: how to secure and keep salesmen, how to promote competition without undermining teamwork, the social meaning of selling, and the leadership and organizational responsibilities of general agents. Articles came from insurance agents and managers working for a variety of life insurance companies. In keeping with the qualities necessary for sales work, the articles emphasized psychological manipulation and the art of selling rather than scientific or rationalized methods of management, even though the language sometimes relied on scientific terms. Writers, in fact, used the terminology of science to describe a sensibility: an attitude of awareness, perceptiveness, and receptivity to the client.[43]

As educational levels increased among the general population and companies and agents continued to try to upgrade the status of insurance sales, an intense discussion transpired over the wisdom of hiring "college men." Apparently, their performance in sales had been ambiguous. W. F. Winterble, the manager of the Madison, Wisconsin, agency of Bankers Life Company and an important codifier of sales and management techniques, believed that college graduates could make good agents despite their equivocal track record in insurance sales. On the one hand, college graduates had developed connections with others in the business world, and "are able to step into a good class of prospects early in their career." On the other hand, they failed to see life insurance sales as a profession, or the elevated type of job to which they believed themselves entitled. Winterble's arguments about professionalization continued to call up nineteenth-century images of middle-class manhood. In the process, he melded professional expertise and corporate prestige with older notions of masculine independence and self-employment. Getting the most out of college men, he believed, meant representing life insurance sales as the best of all possible male worlds: it was a "profession," it was "corporation" work, and yet it also gave a man a "business of his own."[44]

In addition to sales agents' concerns over their status, general agents and company officers also sought a way to manage salesmen. Because agents worked alone yet represented the company to the public, their behavior was a source of concern among home office executives and managers. Edward A. Woods, a leading spokesman for the NALU, pointed out in 1927 that "most failures leave the business within six months." By that time, they had probably talked with over one hundred prospects, each of whom had assumed that life insurance had been presented in the best, most intelligent light. "It has indeed been presented, but in a bungling, unintelligent fashion," Woods claimed, "with the result that the subject has been considered and probably dismissed," since if the agent had sold insurance he would not have quit the business. This amounted to a waste of valuable training time, the generation of "prejudice" toward life insurance on the part of the public, as well as bad advertising generally, since the failures were likely to blame their disappointments on the company rather than themselves. Woods calculated, considering these effects, "500,000 yearly are prejudiced against life underwriting."[45]

One of the earliest efforts to standardize and control agents' behavior in the field came in the form of company publications that contained information for the general public as well as advice, strictures, and suggestions for the agents themselves. In 1871, Metropolitan Life began circulating a publication of this type called *The Metropolitan,* which contained stories, health information, admonishments regarding the necessity of life insurance, and words of wisdom and advice directed to agents.[46] For example, one 1894 edition of the magazine contained this classic description of an ideal agent:

> He thinks. It takes brains to win a battle. . . . The Agent can scarcely be too particular about his personal appearance—always dressing modestly, of course —no matter what class of people he comes in contact with. The man who gets on at the business goes at his work resolutely. . . . An Agent who feels that he can produce large results is twice, yes, many times as likely to succeed as the man who doubts himself. . . . A man should always be reaching out for larger work, grander results, always aiming to beat his own record.[47]

The need for intelligence, health, attention to dress, perseverance, resolution, the urge to win, the desire to better one's own efforts, and the sense of one's calling as a battle were standard injunctions to insurance salesmen into the 1920s. They expressed both the economic concern of a company for productive agents and the desire that agents create a good company image with the public. The terminology used, however, emphasized maleness by drawing on the gender imperatives of the nineteenth century middle-class success ethic, the idea of sales as a calling, and war or sports metaphors.

A persistent problem in insurance management was rapid and constant turnover of sales personnel. Agents came and went with great frequency, sometimes lured away by the promise of higher commissions with other insurance companies, sometimes discouraged by the exhausting demands of salesmanship, sometimes going on to open their own agencies. Thus the general agent and his home-office supervisor had to deal with two aspects of management policy that were unique to sales: the need to infuse the sales force with a belief in the value of the product, their "labor," and their ability to sell; and the need to waste as little time as possible training unproductive agents. Managers needed to coerce their agents to produce and to quickly size up potentially big earners, since their own income and their product's prestige hinged on the performance of the sales force.

The emphasis on character in the sensibility of sales technique revealed how secularized economic relations had become in the nineteenth and twentieth centuries. The modern, urban middle-class man was of necessity dependent on himself and his relations with other men. Reputation or character had both an economic and a social exchange value for men concerned about success in the marketplace.[48] For insurance sales agents and managers, the economic and social value of one's character and one's personal network of friends and family were inextricably linked well into the twentieth century. Friendships formed at school, in fraternal orders or lodges, and in sporting clubs were resources from which to draw contacts. A good example of these linkages can be found in the activities of Rencher Harris, an officer and agent of Bankers' Fire Insurance Company, an African American company in Durham, North Carolina. Harris's travels on behalf of the company in the 1920s involved, among other duties, recruiting agents and making connections that would expand the business. Some of his connections built on a web of institutions, including black colleges, churches, and fraternal organizations, all of which were part of racial as well as personal connections. Without public trust in an individual's character, no sales could be made, and trust came in the first instance from personal knowledge or personal references. Further, sales agents depended on their family and friends to provide leads or potential clients by reference, word of mouth, and recommendation. Rencher Harris's wife, Plassie, for example, took an interest in his business associates and fraternal ties, helping to maintain them by entertaining while he was traveling.[49]

The importance of connections and personal interactions in sales built on the traditional nineteenth-century mingling of business and social interactions rather than modern, impersonal bureaucratic relations. Since the mid-nineteenth century, companies had justified their product as social security or social welfare. The service-oriented insurance corporation claimed that the protection of "a widow and orphan children against pinching want" caused by disasters such as fire or a breadwinner's death made insurance a "moral" rather than a "commercial" institution. The life insurance agents' "Chart of Ethics," adopted by the NALU in 1918, claimed that agents were not selling a product but soliciting "fit applicants, who need [the industry's] varied, life-long Services."[50]

As a management strategy, the notion of public service was important precisely because it emphasized manly duty and toiling in the vineyards for a high ideal. In this way, the call to service acted much like systematic management to obscure the multiple needs of sales: individual income, corporate survival, and the validation of personal masculinity. In order to convince agents of the social value of their product, life insurance leaders, such as Haley Fiske of Metropolitan Life and Darwin P. Kingsley of New York Life, stressed the social benevolence, public duty, and selfless communal interests of the industry. Never ones to minimize the importance of insurance, and in keeping with this elevated tone, they insisted that life insurance salesmen performed a sacred public duty by uniting the diverse interests of the nation. Through life insurance they could develop, as Kingsley explained it, "a community of interests with all men."[51] Over and over again, managers and executives told life insurance agents that the social value of their product, and the knowledge that they engaged in a noble calling, sanctified their position as salesmen and reinforced their masculinity. Manager C. T. Lewis announced in 1890, "it is always desirable for us to elevate the pursuits of every day by lifting them into connection with the great forces which permeate and constitute the life of our civilization. And if there is any pursuit known among men which is worthy of such treatment as this, . . . it is the pursuit of those whose business and whose duty it is to make known among men the advantage of life insurance."[52]

Justifications to salesmen eventually lost their overtly religious tone to emphasize that selling was both productive labor and a public service, a shift reflecting the increasing influence of systematic management. Willis Hatfield Hazard, the head of New England Mutual's Department of Publications, wrote about life insurance sales as both social and economic production: "As a matter of public welfare, good salesmanship . . . helps to satisfy wants, and yields the largest surplus of satisfactions from exchange transactions. From the economic viewpoint, salesmanship is a *productive* activity, because those engaged in it are bringing about real economic changes, and increasing economic utilities."[53] Hazard stressed both the search for professional legitimacy contained in systematic management's concern with rationalism and the older ideal of service. He emphasized the benevolent aspects of life insurance and connected it to manhood, which explained why "the whole trend among sales managers is toward a higher type of men."[54] A 1922 article in New England Mutual's company newsletter phrased this connection between productive labor and the social and economic benefits of service even more clearly, addressing directly some of the epithets sometimes hurled at salesmen. "You are a benefactor to your community just to the extent that you succeed in your useful work," the author asserted. "A benefactor—not a leech nor a parasite, nor a drone. . . . Your life is devoted to rendering a service whose value to the community is inestimable."[55]

During a lecture to New England Mutual's training school for agents in 1924, the superintendent of agencies, Glover S. Hastings, cited nineteenth-century life insurance investigator and reformer Elizur Wright on the service and masculinized aspects of life insurance. "Life insurance is the standing together, shoulder to shoulder," Wright said, "of hosts of manly men to defend each other's homes from the enemy that shoots on the sly and in the dark. . . . It is charity without cant which enriches the giver and does not humiliate the receiver."[56] Hastings went on to make the connection between the elevated calling of life insurance and the morally uplifting job of selling: "no field that we know of is more inviting to an ambition" that brought out "the noblest qualities of a sterling man" for the "benefit of society at large and individuals in particular."[57] Managers of salesmen and life insurance executives equated their industry's social role and their salesmen's economic work with the saving of humanity at large. In the process, they argued for an ennobled image of the self that relied strongly on the ethical overtones of the nineteenth-century man of service.

Despite their emphasis on community service, life insurance companies were eager to remind their agents that there was money to be made and ambition to be satisfied in the business. Many argued that life insurance salesmen were uniquely situated to get ahead, to become self-made men. Commentators stressed the distinctiveness of life insurance sales, in an increasingly stratified and circumscribed business environment, as a position from which an ambitious man could climb the ladder of success. A 1901 Equitable advertisement for agents pointed out that fewer and fewer men actually experienced the "rags to riches" stories of the nineteenth century, and in business most men had to content themselves with a "subordinate clerkship" or spend enormous amounts of time and money in preparation for a career in law, medicine, or the clergy. In contrast, the advertisement claimed, the opportunities for life insurance salesmen were "almost limitless; a pursuit which has already attained to the dignity of any one of the so-called learned professions . . . finally he will *reach the top* if he have but the requisite ability and energy." As a sort of bonus, the advertisement declared that life insurance sales provided opportunities for men to exercise "every faculty. It is a noble profession—a profession which will bring into play all the powers of the man of the highest attainments."[58]

Primary among the qualities necessary to make a good agent was hard work, with the accompanying admonition that in overcoming obstacles and difficulties, the salesman not only became better at selling, he became a better man as well. An article in *The New England Pilot* succinctly summarized the connections between better sales and self-creation: "self-supervision is the key to self-improvement, which automatically carries with it financial betterment." The author then observed that "efficiency," which he defined as the increased ability to earn money, resulted from self-supervision and came "only from thought, study, hard work and experience."[59] Hard work meant activity and energy, but not philosophizing if a salesman would be "A Man Who Wins":

> The man who wins is the man who does
> The man who makes things hum and buzz,
> The man who works and the man who acts,
> Who builds on a basis of solid facts,
> Who doesn't sit down to mope and dream.
> But humps ahead with the force of steam,
> Who hasn't the time to fuss and fret,
> But gets there every time—you bet![60]

The active and aggressive man won the "battle"—with his clients, with others, and with himself. Hard work and aggressiveness, for life insurance salesmen, required persistence: "The world hates a 'quitter.' If there ever was a special object of disfavor it is the quitter. . . . No one, however brilliant his talent, can secure the complete respect of others if he is faint-hearted; if he seems to flinch in the hour of trial, or abandon his purpose under discouragement. Persistence is the most masculine of all the virtues."[61]

Persistence, however, was not enough without "enthusiasm," probably one of the most frequently used words in the business vocabulary of the early twentieth century. As one author presented it to Equitable agents, "*The amount of happiness* we will get, and the degree of success we will achieve, depends entirely upon the degree of ENTHUSIASM we put into the chief purpose of our lives. *Just as an engine* cannot run without steam, so a man *without enthusiasm* is a failure."[62] Borrowing a definition from the dictionary, Albert H. Curtis, a general agent for New England Life in Boston, claimed that "enthusiasm [was] an honest zeal in a good cause."[63] More than that, enthusiasm was optimism, persistence, initiative, cheerfulness, and company loyalty: a catch-all word for aggression, competition, and the subversion of self in favor of position and company policy. Sometimes the equation of enthusiasm with the idea of a calling assumed a note of self-parody, as in this exhortation to Equitable agents in 1909:

> *There is no surer way* of fulfilling your obligations to contribute your *full* share towards the Society's *hundred and fifty millions* this year than by completing *at least half* of your task before the close of the *first six months.* . . . DO NOT BE LEFT AT THE POST, but realize TODAY that it will be almost a disgrace for you not to contribute your *full* share . . . and register deep down in your heart without a moment's delay A MIGHTY, RESOLUTE, IRRESISTIBLE VOW that you WILL do it, or *die in the attempt.*[64]

Explications of enthusiasm had changed from the concept's late-nineteenth-century definition as personal power, magnetism, and a mystical-religious spiritual wealth. The term took on further significance through its close application to the sales process as productive work. Instead of personal power in the service of a better self, enthusiasm became the engine of production, a catchword for an active, involved personal attachment to work that would bring immediate material rather than spiritual rewards.

Enthusiasm also was a concept that linked two other important cultural expressions: character and personality. Enthusiasm in its early-twentieth-century incarnation fused the sense of inbred engagement and persistence of the man of character with the more flashy, energetic, mesmeric elements of personality. Character and personality were not the same thing; personality was a modern revision of the older concept. In descriptions of enthusiastic salesmen we can find a precursor to the modern notion of personality as magnetism, charisma, popularity, and leadership abilities. While character was an element of individual being, a kind of genetically encoded gentility and refinement that had to be teased to the surface, personality was a cultivated, learned quality that could be traded for money and status in the consumer economy, measured and charted, manipulated and used to achieve success in the public world.[65] Like character and enthusiasm, personality was a requisite job skill for the successful salesman. Without personality or enthusiasm no salesman could succeed, because saleswork was, after all, ultimately about competition.

Noble powers aside, life insurance sales encouraged a sometimes vicious competitiveness. From the clearly fraudulent to the merely questionable, sales techniques into the early twentieth century were largely of the "anything goes" variety. "Rebating" was acceptable in the late-nineteenth-century commercial context (as it is now in some venues, such as automobile sales). Agents would return a portion of their commission to the customer as a means of cementing a sale. This led to enormous problems for agents. Since rebates came out of the agent's own pocket, carried to competitive extremes they could cut deeply into his profits. "Twisting," another common if less acceptable practice, involved selling policies that were not in clients' best interests in order to lure them away from another company. Companies, general agents, and agents frequently distributed circulars, took out advertisements, or merely spread gossip derogating the integrity, solvency, or policies of rival companies.[66] The point of all these practices was to give one company or agent an edge over another. In the process, life insurance sales drew on notions of men's aggressiveness rather than their higher natures.

Competitiveness became a masculine virtue largely because of the economic shift to free markets and consumption.[67] Competition permeated every aspect of the labor experience for salesmen. The salesman competed against his clients, pitting his willpower and assertiveness against that of the people he hoped to insure. The gloss of social duty and responsibility did not mitigate the bare fact that many people had to be convinced that they wanted the product and that one product was better than another. Although seldom alluded to publicly by those in charge of salesmen, the antagonistic relationship inherent in the attempt to sell a vague product like financial security was one of the main reasons why salesmen needed personality or enthusiasm. In a rare acknowledgment of the adversarial nature of sales, a local newsletter produced by the Louisville, Kentucky, general agents of New England Mutual for their agents counseled salesmen not to be afraid to put pressure on the "prospect": "From the minute that your prospect knows that you are planning a campaign to secure his application, . . . he is fortifying himself against your getting it, and when . . . you again call upon him, you find him intrenched behind a splendid array of excellent reasons why he should not make application now."[68] The author advised salesmen not to worry about crowding prospects too hard; although a particular client might be lost, "there are ten thousand that you have yet to see."[69]

The combination of messianic message and cutthroat methods was in some ways unique to the industry. One insurance commentator, speaking in a later period but describing an essential phenomenon of insurance sales, reflected on this combination: "With almost evangelistic fervor he [the agent] preached the saving grace of life insurance, and at the same time sometimes resorted to questionable methods to effect the sale." This contradiction existed because the salesman simultaneously viewed life insurance as a morally important product and "selling as a battle of wits, a wrestling match. . . . He expected the prospect to show him no mercy in the interview, and generally speaking the prospect lived up to the reputation. Interviews usually were of the high tension kind."[70]

In addition to an antagonistic relationship with clients, salesmen clearly also competed against the salesmen of other companies—and, in an especially fragmenting manner, against one another and against themselves and their managers. "Never lose sight of the fact that sales resistance exists just as much in the mind of the agent as it does in the mind of the dear public," agency manager Louis Paret observed.[71] Yet competition took on positive qualities, perhaps to prevent intragroup conflicts and to harness competitive behavior and attitudes to the sales process. One reason managers and executives constantly touted enthusiasm, perseverance, and hard work was to impress on salesmen that competition constituted the essence of production, their personal worth, and their identity as men. Without it, they were no good to the job, the company, or themselves. Company executives used several methods to spur rivalry among their salesmen. One was to cite examples of those who had or clearly would "make it." Clarence N. Anderson of the Des Moines general agency of New England Mutual used as an example a young man who refused to be stopped by the weather, unlike some other agents who went to the movies on a rainy day. "Ten years from now that slender little personification of Self-Control will have a Superintendent's job," Anderson argued. "This boy will get there—or anywhere he chooses to go. That one quality of his, Self-Control, will put him over, while the other debit-men are wondering where he got his 'pull.'"[72] The "young" man, a "slender," weak boy, was more manly because of his aggressiveness than the slothful cadre of other salesmen the manager supervised. Masculinity was aggressive salesmanship rather than mechanical skill, physical prowess, or successful proprietorship.

Another method of generating a competitive environment to encourage and channel aggression consisted of setting up quotas, often centered around some sort of commemorative activity—the company president's birthday, the anniversary of the company's founding—but usually simply on a monthly basis, with the implication that those who failed to meet the quota were failures in general. In addition, executives used company newsletters, highly ritualized annual conventions, company-sponsored awards ceremonies, and other rewards to publicize those who met or exceeded a predetermined average standard of sales.[73]

Because competition fueled the consumer economy, several aspects of fraternalism also were critically important to the ideology of sales management. Fraternalism brought men together as professionals, as men, and as competitors. The emphasis on a brotherhood of salesmen mediated between the notion of sales as a humanistic calling and as a competitive, acquisitive "business." Managers encourage life insurance salesmen to think of themselves as a brotherhood or community, united in the common endeavor of bringing the benefits of insurance to the general public. In Glover S. Hastings's remarks cited earlier, he used the prestige of Elizur Wright to emphasize the importance of working as a community: "It [life insurance] is the realization of fraternity without the destruction of independence and individuality."[74] The advantage of this community was that it reinforced "independence and individuality," important concepts for men involved in corporate work and indicative of the fine line between the supportive nature of community and the potential loss of self communal membership could invite.

The concept of fraternalism was woven throughout the industry and appeared in many forms. Life insurance had its philosophical and economic roots in mutual aid. In addition, throughout the nineteenth century life insurance competed, sometimes successfully and sometimes not, with fraternal organizations that often provided life insurance to their members. Fraternal societies also performed an important material service in providing an artificial or transient community for salesmen as they traveled from town to town. For example, Glover Hastings, general agent for New England Mutual, was an Odd Fellow for fifty-two years. Percival L. Everett, a director of New England Mutual from 1875 to 1890, was a Mason and became a Massachusetts Grand Master in 1874. Black life insurance agents and company officers also often belonged to fraternal orders.[75]

Mary Ann Clawson has traced the connections between middle-class definitions of manhood and membership in fraternal organizations. Fraternalism was a nineteenth-century expression of manhood that built extrafamilial, fictive kinship ties and allowed men to express emotions in a way denied to them in both their competitive business lives and their domestic context. With the gradual decline of membership in fraternal organizations by the 1920s, fraternal ties were reinforced in the emergence of service clubs, such as the Lions. Service clubs were oriented to white, middle-class businessmen and professionals, and they continued many of the same forms of organization and relations as the nineteenth-century societies.[76] African American fraternal organizations provided many of the same functions as white groups, including business contacts and extrafamilial ties. Since the African American middle class also played an important leadership role within black communities, club membership additionally tied African American men in a direct way to other businessmen, both locally and nationally.

 The bonds of communal fraternity could neither totally obscure nor permanently enhance the competitive nature of sales work. The role of the general agent as manager was to encourage competition and individual effort among his agents but to keep it within the bounds of company policy and communal spirit. Managers approached the task of training potential salesmen by a combination of example, actual sales experience, and encouragement to combat designed to keep agents pushing, but always within the spirit of teamwork. As William May noted in 1926, managers "coordinated" and trained their agents largely by inculcating "vision" and "preach[ing]" ideals: "We must direct and supervise. Above all, we must teach not only by precept but by example."[77] Louis F. Paret called this "creating agency spirit, that intangible force. . . . The motives that create this spirit come more from the heart than from the head. It is a matter of feeling, of harmony, of sympathy, of understanding, of appreciation, of trust." Paret was quick to point out that "agency spirit pays big dividends," and agents might view "the General Agent's motives in creating it from the mercenary standpoint." Nevertheless, the general agent's efforts should "be directed first toward the ideal of service, both to agent and policy-holder. Faithful and efficient service must be the outstanding, urgent desire."[78] Needless to say, this was a fine line to walk, and agents who did it well were of enormous value to their company. Managers who knew how to appeal to such behaviors were doubly important. In managing others, the methods of scientific rationalism were limited. Far more important for dealing with brain workers was the older, nineteenth-century sensibility of management as an art, an intangible but potent expression of character or personality that became the essence of early-twentieth-century managerial manhood.

 That there were contradictions in the construction of sales—that teamwork was as important as individual initiative, that life insurance sales operated on the apprenticeship system, that social and family ties were part of the work, that very few salesmen ever achieved large financial success or moved up the corporate ladder—tempered but did not undermine ideological assertions by managers and executives of the uniqueness of life insurance sales. The mechanistic approach of scientific management and psychological selling, and the mystique of sales as a calling, provided two different but mutually supportive definitions of business manhood. They allowed for competition, but within a contained and restrained environment of cooperative effort; they suggested that professionalism and the possession of expert knowledge marked men of higher status off from other men and certainly from women; and they both avoided manhood's potential role as a moral or ethical agent either by addressing issues in the broadest terms or ignoring their existence.

CHAPTER FOUR

The Domestic Office

Space, Status, and
the Gendered Workplace

Reflecting on the previous sixty years, architect Charles Loring remarked in 1930, "The offices of our grandfathers were without steel frames and files, without elevators and radiators, without telephones,—and without skirts."[1] Loring's remark captures the two most important changes shaping the modern office: the introduction of new technology and the influx of women into public space. Women's presence on city streets and in corporate offices challenged the male-defined arena of business and the perception that urban offices were public, male spaces. Women's presence immediately raised the issue of how these sexually and socially different workers would be assimilated into the masculinized environment of business offices. The evolution of sex-typed jobs within the corporation, the rationalization of work, gender-segregated public areas, and new construction and machine technologies created situations that begged for a reevaluation of the significance of gender.

Any workplace is an arena of shifting rules and behaviors that draws on notions of self-worth, gender relations, and class values, as well as on demographic and economic change.[2] Financial offices of late-nineteenth- and early-twentieth-century America similarly were physical places whose cultural expressions were integral to historical change. They provided enclosures or boundaries for office behavior, but they also were contested, open spaces wherein values, beliefs, ideals and behaviors shaped and defined experience.

Spatial categories organize how individuals orient themselves to their environment.[3] Cultural spatial categories are fluid, not fixed, and respond to a

variety of stimuli. However, even though social spatial organization accommo-
dates a range of experience, it sets boundaries to the possible. For example,
corporations often have "complex spatial norms" that define occupational
hierarchies and individual status.[4] Generally, spatial norms are informal and
unarticulated: individuals may be unaware of their existence. More obvious,
and equally important, is the deliberate creation of physical boundaries to
stress particular spatial relationships or mores. Thus, spatial divisions within
workplaces exist at two general levels: the overt physical boundaries of walls,
stairs, doors, and moveable objects; and the spatial articulations of social
division, status, or position. Both types of space can be avenues of self-assertion
or control over experience and behavior as well as symbolic expressions of
values or beliefs. The construction of offices and office space illuminated problems of status, managerial norms, public imagery, and gender relationships
that were central to this period of technological and organizational change.

Urban financial offices of late-nineteenth-century America were social and
physical geographies where workers, managers, executives, and customers
shared space, time, and culture. The managerial outlook connected workplace
space and time with profits and efficiency. Corporate image makers, designers,
architects and their clients, management theorists, and managers themselves
all fit within this framework, even if not all of these groups or individuals
agreed on every environmental issue at all times. By contrast, workers themselves acted on their environment in ways often at odds with managerial definitions of appropriate workplace attitudes and behavior. These differences generated often covert and ongoing battles. Both groups, however, conceived the
contested terrain of the workplace as though space and time could be used to
reinvent and reinforce gender norms through discussions about men's and
women's place, metaphorical uses of maleness and femaleness, and physical
places built or patterned to accommodate and manipulate gender difference.[5]

The skyscraper building form, first introduced in Chicago in the 1880s and
then in other cities, created a middle-class workplace distinct from both the
small offices of precorporate merchants and the large, machine-dominated
manufacturing plants.[6] The skyscraper was a unique, specialized environment
set within the commercial centers of downtown Chicago, New York, Boston,
Kansas City, San Francisco, and other urban areas. Using a new symbolic
language, architects, designers, and corporate executives articulated a complex
set of public messages intended to explain business motives and attract
clients—messages that relied on gendered images and assumptions. At the
most obvious level, as in department stores, theaters, and hotels, new architectural forms attempted to adapt the male-dominated world of commerce to a
consuming and working public composed of both men and women. At the less
direct level, they subverted the nineteenth-century divisions of separate

spheres, breaking them down and reconstituting them in the interests of commercial success. The public persona of buildings thus contributed to the creation of twentieth-century gender relations in the office workplace. In so doing, such establishments enormously complicated the nineteenth-century gender ideal of separate spheres. On the one hand, they reinforced notions of men's and women's place, domesticity, and the public world by maintaining spatial, temporal, and rhetorical divisions between men and women, manhood and womanhood. On the other hand, they incorporated the private spaces of domesticity into the public world of commerce by substituting a class-segregated for a gender-segregated geography.

Prior to the 1880s, most United States cities had low skylines because it was difficult to build beyond four or five floors on stone foundations, elevators were nonexistent, and cheap urban land was abundant. The buildings of New York City in 1865 did not reach beyond five stories, although by 1875 a few stretched to nine or ten.[7] Chicago, which by 1900 had become the quintessential skyscraper city, was at the time of the Civil War still a level plain punctuated only by small buildings. Most business offices at mid-century consisted of small rooms with relatively low ceilings, natural lighting, and fairly undifferentiated job spaces. They were housed in three- to four-story buildings owned by real estate developers, in part of the business owner's dwelling, or in small spaces within large manufacturing plants. Metropolitan Life's original home on Broadway in New York City was a typical urban commercial building. The rented rooms were divided into two main work spaces: the company president occupied a small rear room, while the front room contained "the remainder of the staff—vice president, secretary, cashier, policy clerk and boy. The entire space was not over nine hundred square feet."[8] In 1859, when the Equitable Life Assurance Society moved into its offices at 92 Broadway, New York City, they consisted of four rented rooms on the second floor. William Alexander, a former secretary of the Equitable, recalled that in its first years the company had no clerical force, and "all the work of the office was done by four executive officers, one physician, a copyist and an errand boy," all of whom were male. The first clerk, James B. Loring, was hired in 1860 to keep the books previously done by the actuary.[9]

Small offices resulted from the lack of emphasis precorporate business put on record-keeping.[10] In the early years of modern life insurance, from the 1840s to the early 1870s, loosely supervised and widely scattered field agents kept primary records, obviating the need for large, centralized offices. As individual life insurance companies grew and asserted more control over agents in an effort to standardize their product, centralized record-keeping became essential, and insurance offices expanded to accommodate both files and customer relations.[11] This need for record-keeping was an aspect of changing business practices not confined to life insurance. By the Civil War, many business estab-

Metropolitan Life's first home office at 243 Broadway, New York City (1868–1870), ca. 1880–1900. The building appears at the far left in this scene of a typical New York business street before the adoption of skyscrapers and large corporate offices. *Courtesy of the MetLife Archives.*

lishments had moved away from family partnerships operated from a residential address toward business organization separated physically and financially from close family ties and catering to the demands of a larger clientele. The insurance industry pioneered the development and use of new architectural technologies to house and regulate the increased organizational demands of centralized record-keeping. The first skyscraper built in the United States was designed in 1883 for the Home Insurance Company of Chicago. While bank building underwent a boom period in the 1890s, banks lagged slightly behind insurance companies in the movement toward tall office buildings; nevertheless, banks and other financial buildings shared many stylistic architectural elements.[12]

The late-nineteenth-century city was an increasingly segregated place. The location of residential, commercial and manufacturing establishments divided the city into living, working, and leisure areas for different groups of people. In this process, for example, the business office of a manufactory often moved to the urban center while the factory migrated to the edge, creating two separate workplaces. Chicago's McCormick Reaper Company moved its business offices in 1879 into downtown headquarters completely separate from its manufacturing plant on the city's outskirts. Office work, which in the early nineteenth century had been peripheral to manufacturing, became by the 1890s one of the most important aspects of any business.[13]

Urban work, for the middle class, took on new temporal and spatial divisions. Separating offices from factories was a way of removing white-collar work from the connotations and locations of factory labor. Instead of dirty factories with their hint of labor unrest and class warfare, urban offices were designed to be middle-class zones: clean, light, healthful, and for the most part racially, ethnically, and ideologically homogeneous. Daniel Bluestone's study of commercial architecture in Chicago in the 1880s and 1890s describes the skyscraper as a city within a city, adopted by upper-middle- and upper-class owners as a retreat from urban congestion and manufacturing's grime. The skyscraper was a middle- and upper-class space, similar to inner-city parks or the expanding rings of suburban dwellings.[14]

The construction and style of offices underwent enormous changes. Beginning in the 1870s, the introduction of elevators, telephones, iron, concrete, and steel frame construction made it possible to construct much taller buildings than four or five floors, while rising land costs due to increased demand for central business locations encouraged builders and speculators to achieve maximum height with the minimum use of ground space.[15] Elevators and telephones facilitated this process, permitting easy access to all parts of a building and to the street no matter how tall the structure.[16] Life insurance companies, in particular, were leaders in the "drive for height" that marked the business building boom between the 1870s and 1930.[17] Metropolitan Life and the Equitable moved four times during that period, from small rented spaces to their own large buildings. The smaller New England Life Assurance Company moved only twice, from rented quarters to its own structure, but underwent several phases of expansion (see the Appendix). By 1930, the organization of business and the profile of the largest American cities had altered beyond recognition. Tall office buildings blocked out the light on the streets below, hemming in pedestrians with walls of concrete, glass, steel, and iron. The urban landscape by the 1930s made a national reality of Henry B. Fuller's description of Chicago in 1893 as a city of "cliff dwellers."[18]

The public exteriors and interiors of tall office buildings reflected new dimensions of public meanings that business owners hoped to attach to the structures.[19] In the 1870s, when many insurance companies began to build their own office buildings, they placed images of these buildings in trade paper advertisements, explicitly identifying companies with their buildings.[20] Owners and promoters of turn-of-the-century life insurance companies and banks wanted buildings that communicated to the public economic and emotional security, civic responsibility, and financial integrity, achieved through a combination of reassuringly domestic images and innovative construction technology.[21] To meet these needs, architects and builders borrowed palatial forms from classic European styles (hoping to annex their stylistic sense of tradition and sophistication) as well as newer bourgeois urban housing. The first spate of urban commercial building after the Civil War, in the 1870s and 1880s, copied freely and widely from the northern Baroque. Equitable's home office at 120 Broadway, constructed in 1870 and enlarged in 1887, used a pattern of repeating columns and pilasters, rusticated ground floor detail, and arched windows that evoked Baroque public architecture. Metropolitan Life's Church Street building and New England Life's Milk Street offices, both finished in 1876, resembled the northern Baroque style of public architecture, represented by the Place des Voges in Paris, or of aristocratic domiciles such as the chateaux at Blois and Maisons designed by François Mansart in the mid-seventeenth century.[22] Classical and Italian Renaissance antecedents also were popular, especially for certain building elements. New England Mutual, the Mutual Company of New York, and Metropolitan Life, in the offices they built in 1873, 1874, and 1909, respectively, incorporated tall towers consciously patterned after the campaniles of Renaissance Italy. The New York Stock Exchange Building, finished in 1865, had precedents in sixteenth-century Florentine bankers' palaces.[23]

American builders focused on the connections among modernity, commerce, domesticity, and style. Advertisements stressed the structures' impressive height, up-to-date materials, design roots in the fine arts, and historical precedents. A Metropolitan Life publication declared in 1908, "the Metropolitan Building is designed in the Early Renaissance style of northern Italy—a style combining dignity with refinement, and of a flexibility readily adaptable to the exacting commercial requirements of the day."[24]

Financial industry buildings relied on the traditions of public domestic architecture and subtly gave the city a domesticated face. Stylistically, these new office buildings reflected a transition from one type of domestic architecture to another. From the late eighteenth century, offices often were part of domestic space, the second or third floor of a residence and a direct part of a family business. The townhouse style of three to four floors, narrow and deep, was simultaneously home, office, and often manufacturing plant. Most early insurance offices used this type of office space, although not actually as a part of a family dwelling. Many early-nineteenth-century banks included living areas for the head cashier or other officers, with separate domestic entrances in the bank building.[25]

The insurance industry moved to the skyscraper form in the 1880s and in the process adopted additional residential stylistic devices. Commercial buildings used many of the same architectural forms (for many of the same reasons) as apartment dwellings, a post–Civil War innovation in middle-class domestic

Metropolitan Life's tower, ca. 1910. Finished in 1909, the building stressed the power and security of the company through its mixture of modern skyscraper technology and Italian Renaissance architectural details. *Courtesy of the MetLife Archives.*

living in large cities. The Broadway Central Hotel in New York City, remodeled in 1871, provided a prototype for the many apartment buildings built in the 1880s and 1890s in the city and other urban areas. Its mansard roof, ten-story height, corniced and pillared window treatment, and elegant detail were intended to replicate the sophistication of Parisian architecture. The hotel, which catered to a clientele of travelers, single men, and wealthy families, was the largest in the country in 1871. Its 650 rooms could house 1,500 guests; its public areas included six parlors and six dining rooms, all decorated with lace, fine carpets, and walnut furniture. On the outside, rich brick and marble facia prepared the traveler for the luxury inside. Completed in 1883, the Berkshire Apartments, at Madison and Fifty-Second Streets, combined a mansard roof with pseudo-Gothic tower façades and individual window treatments to suggest individual dwelling spaces.[26] Apartment house designers borrowed from French Baroque public buildings, much as did designers of urban commercial architecture. Their shared effort to devise suitable public spaces for the urban middle class wedded monumental form with intricate detail, European domestic urbanity with American technical innovations, to create an indigenous urban form.[27] Commercial buildings attempted to negotiate the increasingly fragile boundary between domestic and commercial, private and public life by creating public spaces suggestive in their details of both grandeur and intimacy.

The palatial estates of New York's Fifth Avenue and Newport, Rhode Island after the Civil War, apartment dwellings and hotels, all shared the magnificence and detailing of many tall office buildings.[28] The Baroque palatial domestic style carried the early-nineteenth-century combination of business, home, and family into the early twentieth century, added a layer of meaning to the common term "home office," and replicated the eclectic style of late-nineteenth-century upper-class homes.

The inherently ambiguous message of public commercial architecture—civic duty and familial security combined with aristocratic grandeur—perfectly communicated the enlightened paternalism that financial industry executives hoped to practice toward the public and their own employees. Unlike those devotees of high culture who perceived commerce as its antithesis, the owners of business buildings tried to blur the distinction between the two. They navigated between gross commercialism and altruistic public service, a tension typical of the burgeoning consumer economy. The organizers of world's fairs and expositions between 1870 and 1915, for example, "saw themselves less as businessmen than as curates and educators who stood above the rough-and-tumble world of profit seeking."[29] Furthermore, businessmen perceived their new buildings as "museums" serving the public, or as educational experiences for the "pleasure and edification of the observer," who might learn something of fine art and culture from them.[30] Companies invited the public to identify with their public-spirited values, stability, family or home-centered ties, progressive thought, enlightened management, and restrained wealth.

This aristocratic *noblesse oblige* permeated both financial industry buildings and the business philosophy of their managing executives. Life insurance executives touted their buildings as spiritual refreshment as well as curiosities and marvels of technological progress and efficiency.[31] Brochures for the Equitable building at Broadway and Cedar in the early 1870s pointed to its three passenger elevators, noting that no other business building at the time possessed such a modern convenience. The general public could use the roof, which was higher than most other buildings at the time, to obtain spectacular views of the surrounding city. "The building will thus soon become an object of popular notice, and tenants will be accordingly benefitted," one advertising circular claimed. The roof as garden and viewing platform later was adopted by theaters—such as Madison Square Garden—and upper-class apartment houses in the 1880s and 1890s.[32]

Promotions for Metropolitan Life's Madison Avenue building, opened in 1893, advertised to prospective renters the high quality of the materials used in its construction—"pure white Tuckahoe Marble, of magnificent proportions . . . woodwork of quartered oak, cabinet finish"—and its "fast running elevators . . . mail chutes, plumbing, steam heating, ventilation and electric light plants."[33] Metropolitan Life had grown so quickly that the building at Madison Avenue was no longer available for rental to other businesses, and promotion of the building aimed at the general public. An advertisement for the building in 1910 announced the structure as a tourist attraction famous for its height, style, and its marvels of technology: "The Home Office building . . . has 50 elevators traveling 125,000 miles yearly, nearly 4 miles of corridors, 13 miles of plumbing pipe, 150 miles of iron conduits, 190 miles of electric light and power wiring, 2,460 miles of telephone wire. . . . The tower 700 feet tall is the highest piece of masonry in the world."[34] The ad went on to make a direct connection between the physical structure and what it housed: specifically, over fifteen thousand employees and "more than ten millions of policies in force representing outstanding insurance of over two thousand million dollars."[35] Modeled after the bell tower in the Piazza San Marco, Metropolitan Life's tower was twice as tall as the Venetian monument, rising seven hundred feet above street level. It was higher than any other structure in New York City by almost 75 percent and for a time was the tallest building in the world. Visible from every direction, Metropolitan Life's structure literally towered over the city.[36]

Bankers were concerned with many of the same issues and also displayed their wealth and solidity through architectural style and decorative detail. In 1910–11, when the Wells Fargo Nevada National Bank remodeled its home office in San Francisco after the 1906 earthquake, company executives used the evocative powers of space and materials to draw parallels between the bank's management philosophy and its new building. Advertisements for the new building emphasized both classical conservatism and modern, up-to-date technology and style. The first floor, public interior was both "modern Greek" and "Byzantine," "wholly original and highly decorative" yet "strictly classical" without being "academic." The desired effect reached for a combination of "dignity and atmosphere." The building's interior walls hid the latest in heating and ventilating systems, wiring and lighting, while presenting a surface covered with Italian marble and hand-carved mahogany, ebony, and white holly. Sinclair Lewis used these connections between the physical building and the corporation's product to satirize middle-class beliefs in business when his character George Babbitt considered "how clever he was to bank with so marbled an establishment."[37]

With their emphasis on fine craftsmanship, superb materials, modern technology, and boastful grandeur, business buildings such as Metropolitan Life's and others acted as unique monuments to the aggressive, public-spirited and cultivated image business executives hoped to project.[38] The connections between size and stability, technology and progress, reinforced the goals the companies wished to symbolize. The hints of domestic architecture (although to mansions rather than cottages), subsumed the notions of old families and old money, financial security, the stewardship of monarchy, and the image of corporations as merely larger, and therefore more stable, versions of the precorporate mercantile family.

The symbolic significance of buildings did not stop at their façades but encompassed interior spaces designed to accommodate the public. As was true of department stores, hotels, and theaters of the period, insurance offices and banks hoped to attract the consuming public through the first impressions of the building and its fixtures. "Every stranger coming into a bank is a prospective customer. . . . If your bank furnishings appear aged, decrepit, behind the times—look out!" warned one promoter.[39] Insurance and banking officers sought middle-class male and female clients and the casual shoppers who were an increasing presence in city centers. Like their counterparts in department stores and theaters, the public rooms of commercial buildings were both "palaces" and entertainment.[40] And, like department stores, theaters, and private homes, commercial public rooms encouraged both male and female occupants or visitors but ensured segregation by gender and class.

Inside the lobbies and cashier areas of the Equitable and Metropolitan Life, the relative restraint of the exteriors gave way to thousands of exquisitely rendered details marshaled into an overwhelming magnificence. The lobby of the Metropolitan Life building, built in 1876, was patterned after the Grand Staircase of the Paris Opera, and the building's 425-foot long public Arcade was lined with green marble columns quarried in Greece.[41] Its repeating col-

The opulent public payments area in the Equitable's main offices at 120 Broadway, ca. 1884. Receiving clerks sat at each "cage," with their supervisors behind them. *Courtesy of* ELASA.

umns and archways purposefully evoked the galleries of Versailles. The public lobbies and cashier's cages of Equitable's Broadway and Cedar Building, built in 1870, rivaled the splendor of the most opulent European palaces or the homes of North American millionaires.

Many buildings were designed to manage the public experience of the building interior and could segregate the public and employees in various ways. Areas such as lobbies were open to the public, but for security reasons public access was controlled. In the Victor Talking Machine Building, built in Camden, New Jersey, in 1917, the public was strictly segregated from employees and their employers through the use of carefully controlled ingress and egress:

> There is no promiscuous riding up and down in the elevators and no wandering about looking for people. An entrance hall desk attendant is in close touch, not only with the desk attendant on each floor, but also with every office in the building and can state at once to the inquirer, the direction to, or the inclination toward a visit of the person sought.[42]

The lobby of Wells Fargo Nevada National Bank was arranged so that bank officers could have a complete view from their desks of all employee and customer activities in the lobby. In banks and insurance companies, tellers and cashiers who took deposits or payments were enclosed in "cages" that set them apart physically and symbolically from customers. Cages also separated workers from one another, and a worker could "transact every branch of the business pertaining to his work without leaving it," as one trade paper boasted. Bank customers could use the entire lobby and had free access to officers stationed at desks around the room, but they were not free to wander through the building. Informal seating arrangements structured patterns of interaction while male customers waited to speak to officers. "Retiring rooms" for women were designed to make women customers feel at ease and to separate male and female customers in public areas.[43]

The magnificence and detailed articulation of surface design in banks and insurance buildings was confined to public areas and the suites of top corporate executives. In the early nineteenth century, when offices were small and executives, clerks, and the public participated in the same general space, any luxuriance in interior design added luster to the entire office labor force.[44] By the late nineteenth century, possibly because of the expense of extra architectural detailing, decorative grandeur was confined to a few workers, essentially those who met the public face to face and the higher executives whose offices served as advertisements to other businessmen and prospective investors. This movement toward differentiating levels of design at the turn of the century reflected the necessity of appealing to a broadening audience of customers and clientele, even as office work became more routinized and factorylike.

Changes in technology and consumption patterns encouraged new temporal and spatial partitions of work, domestic life, and leisure. In this context, the commercial buildings of service industries—department stores, theaters, hotels, insurance, and banking—reintegrated the domestic and commercial functions of older urban neighborhood patterns in order to appeal to middle-class consumers as gendered people. Such business establishments, usually located in or near the older central city, drew white-collar workers and middle-class customers out of the pastoral suburbs and into the economic hub of urban living. Men's clubs provided homes away from home for urban professional or middle-class men. Saloons and eating establishments catered to working- or middle-class men and generally did not admit even escorted women. For women there were comparable but different spaces: the tea room in a department store, or the ladies' departments in insurance offices and banks. On the theory that women increasingly had input into family financial decisions and that their presence downtown as shoppers could be encouraged and catered to, banks and insurance offices began inviting women in not only to pay their insurance premiums or make deposits but to linger in special women's "rest rooms," where they could write letters, read books, simply sit and chat, or eat lunch. The physical separation of home and office was replicated within public places as men's and women's spaces, reconstructed homes away from home for customers.[45]

The new construction techniques available by the 1870s made the creation of radically different workspaces possible, allowing managers and workers to articulate new workplace relations. Between the 1890s and 1930s, hundreds of new office buildings were built or older ones converted for corporate use. Fifty new life insurance buildings were built in the United States between 1913 and 1923 alone.[46] The new office buildings relied on artificial lighting, had centralized heating and cooling systems, and were built with exterior curtain walls. These construction features permitted the creation of workspaces quite unlike those of the precorporate office. Rooms could be larger, since supporting structures were on the outside and in the center of the building. Rather than self-contained, one-room offices, large numbers of rooms could be connected horizontally by hallways and vertically by elevators or stairs. Gradually, a depersonalized, bureaucratic organization of space replaced the more intimate business space of the early nineteenth century.

The small spaces of the precorporate office had reinforced close relations among workers, since it was nearly impossible to remove any worker completely from other workers or from employers. An office staff of one to five people, divided from their employer only by a door or a waist-high wooden railing, was well supervised without elaborate methods.[47] With the exception of distinctions among the president or company head, bookkeeper, cashier, and the clerks, the work done in such offices was not *visibly* stratified; in fact, the physical separation of workers, a mark of the division of labor, would have undermined harmonious workplace relations in a small office. The lack of divisions reinforced a kind of democracy of clerkship: Workers relied on one another for assistance. As one former clerk at Aetna Life Insurance recalled, work time was fluid and varied rather than sharply delineated, and an informal work culture encouraged interdependence: "If . . . somebody wanted to go to a ballgame, he would hustle and get all his work done as far as he could go and then ask his desk companion if he would take over if anything unexpected came in. . . . Next week it would be another fellow who wanted to go fishing— or something. The work was always kept up, and no complaints were heard."[48] Precorporate space and work relations lingered on in smaller companies and in branch offices of large concerns. Despite its adoption of the corporate form of organization, for example, North Carolina Mutual Life offices, like those of most African American financial industries, remained small. The company's branch office in Columbia, South Carolina, in 1908 consisted of one room, and its new home office in Durham in 1906 of only two.[49] With economic growth,

In 1908 the Columbia, South Carolina, office of North Carolina Mutual Life was typical of those of small insurance offices. The mantel clock on the far left echoes domestic details found in larger offices. *Courtesy of* NCM.

most companies moved into the larger spaces made possible by new construction techniques. New space brought with it the possibility of new tensions between management and workers and between men and women.

Spatial and temporal issues in the office workplace were part of a larger and older managerial concern with efficiency.[50] Beginning in the 1880s, as insurance companies and banks began to renovate old or construct new office buildings, executives, managers, and designers consciously exploited the relationship between physical space and time and labor efficiency. The concern with efficiency and with status paralleled the division of corporate labor into manual and brain work underway by the 1890s. The corporate order, with its assembly-line techniques, job differentiation, and increased organizational size, demanded a different type of office space and a more regulated and regimented flow of time. In particular, officers in the financial industries were conscious that status could be expressed in physical place and time.[51]

Much as scientific management in industry later would insist on dividing work space and time into smaller and smaller units, many of the life insurance and banking offices built from 1880 on employed spatial and temporal divisions in an effort to regulate and control the production process. Companies built and moved into larger quarters in order to centralize production and thereby limit the independence of managers and workers. Complex divisions of labor according to space appeared as larger interiors were built. Metropolitan

Life, as it took over the whole of its Madison Avenue building between 1893 and 1909, separated departmental functions by floors, attaching managers to the areas they supervised. In 1896, the ninth floor contained the Audit Division, where 287 men worked as bookkeepers and 752 women as clerks. Five hundred of the company's eight hundred typewriters (a name applied to both workers and machines) were in this division. The Ordinary Department took up the entire fourth floor, with 650 clerical workers operating a variety of machines. The top executives, as well as boards of directors, who were responsible for the overall running of a firm, were ensconced on the upper floors, now easily accessible by elevators. Such divisions were geared toward cost-effective use of both labor and machinery. "Every labor-saving device or perfection in system that would operate to keep the clerical force [numerically] within bounds has been inaugurated and successfully utilized in the Ordinary Department," one Metropolitan Life brochure boasted. By 1910, the Mechanics-American National Bank of St. Louis and the Continental National Bank of Chicago, used large tables that accommodated six to twelve male clerks and their typewriters.[52] While office employees continued to maintain some control over their relations with management and their work experience, the buildings they worked in began to institutionalize systematic management in physical form in the 1880s. By 1900, when scientific management was on its way to becoming a popular business ideology, financial industry offices had been using many of its practices for at least fifteen years.

The concern with efficiency was merely one expression of a much larger and more culturally diverse interest in the instrumental and expressive connections among the human body, time, and movement. Those connections took many forms at the turn of the century. By 1900, the experimental and theoretical work of Taylor and the Gilbreths tried to connect human movement to production, while around 1910 the Austrian educator and dance theorist Rudolf Laban (1879–1958) initiated a study of principles of scientific movement in dance. Laban emphasized a "language of movement" that would enable individuals to move in a group as though they were one entity. In the visual arts, the multiple and fragmented Cubist imagery of Pablo Picasso, Georges Braque, Marcel Duchamp, and others refigured the perception of space and time by simultaneously showing parts of an image in different temporal moments. Finally, the invention of film projectors and cameras and the birth of commercial motion pictures in the 1890s instituted a modern fascination with the passage of time and its depiction on film.[53]

Whether or not they consciously articulated systematic principles, executives and managers used the environment in different ways to achieve a variety of goals as the loosely structured work day of the precorporate office gave way to the rationalized manipulation of interior space and work time in large corporate offices. Although they may not have used the terminology of scientific management, architects and clients reached for a rationalized work-place that would channel workers' energies in the direction of efficiency—increasingly the catch-all word for cost-effectiveness and control of the work process. In an effort to sell the services of the Library Bureau (an office supply and furniture company), its San Francisco general manager, Charles E. Myers, argued in 1909 that his company had experts available to work with architects in "laying out rooms . . . to produce a result which insures convenient and economical administration."[54] Describing the recently built home office building of the Victor Talking Machine Company in 1917, a writer in *American Architect* noted the relation between the demands of corporate work and the physical space within which the work occurred: "All floors are different, the arrangement and kind of partitions and the scheme of office sequence and clerking space being dictated by the varying types of work in the different departments. . . . In the main, the broad division of head offices in the front and clerking space in the rear of the stair and elevator halls was followed in all floors."[55] As in a factory, spatial arrangements replicated the flow of the production process, in this case the creation of paper orders, invoices, and shipping or billing receipts.

In financial industries, work areas were divided according to the production process by the 1880s. Some of the earliest divisions simply assigned different work to different desks. The sense of desks as spaces where specific tasks occur is in sharp contrast to the notion of desk space as a small "office" that could encompass all elements of production. The roll-top desk, for example, which achieved the height of its popularity in the 1870s, was both a production and storage space that allowed one individual to control all aspects of his work. Its many partitions, high top, and lockable front gave a clerk privacy and a sense of personal domain.[56] By the early 1880s, banks had created a division of labor using desks and cages that reflected the increasing specialization of bank work. Tellers in the Farmers and Mechanics' Bank of Philadelphia, for example, had been divided into first and second paying tellers, first and second receiving tellers, and note tellers. A bank employee manual stated that the individuals performing these jobs were to "confine themselves strictly to their desks, not leaving their enclosures until they have made their settlements in the afternoon."[57] In this example, not only did desk space divide workers and tasks into several specific jobs, but it also became less a clerk's estate and more his prison.

The relationship between spatial organization and the search for efficient work procedures in offices was fully developed by the 1920s. Office fixtures could serve a variety of bureaucratic purposes. The office labor force in general was extremely mobile; employees typically joined and left firms or merely moved from one department to another. Rather than verbal or written instructions on acceptable social interactions, systematic managers could provide a physical basis for behavior by arranging desks, chairs, cabinets, or water coolers to facilitate particular interactions. Fixtures and spatial patterns could quickly initiate new employees into the status and job requirements of their position. Like a physical counterpart to the permanent bureaucratic structures of the corporation, the arrangement of fixtures in the office environment organized the workplace itself.

Conversely, furniture and fixtures had the advantage of being moveable, and they were cheaper and represented less commitment to a particular arrangement than constructing walls or buildings. Managers easily could encourage changes in job behavior by changing the placement of office fixtures. Management theorist R. H. Goodell described an office in which female workers were distracted by visitors and individuals passing in the hallway. He explained that he modified these clerks' behavior by turning the workers' desks away from the door and their supervisor's desk. This switch in the room's arrangements prevented the women from breaking their routine and at the same time allowed the supervisor to watch them unobserved. Moving furniture forced at least superficial attention to work duties and gave the supervisor omniscience over the flow of outside information into the room. Changing a room or the layout of its fixtures was an attempt to shake loose certain alliances or to forge others.[58]

Executives, managers, or others who dealt with the public also could use office space and fixtures to encourage certain kinds of behavior in clients and other public visitors such as sales personnel. A 1922 advertising brochure for an office supply company applied principles of spatial control when it informed executives that they could limit the amount of time they spent with callers by, for example, making the hat tree less accessible. They also could put a salesman's chair where "the light will strike him full in the face. The executive is then in a position to read the facial expressions of the visitor, learning more than is ordinarily conveyed by tone of voice or words." In addition, the corporate executive's desk space retained the precorporate sense of desk as domain. The office supply company's "efficiency desks" were at the "heart of the hive," the space in which the real work of the office transpired—problem-solving and policy- and deal-making.[59]

By the 1930s, the connections between the physical workplace and workers' efficiency had become a management commonplace. Between 1930 and 1933, an alliance of life insurance executives and professional office planners spawned a detailed articulation of the managerial uses of physical work space based on forty years of experience. The Life Office Management Association sponsored a study of life insurance home office buildings built since the turn of the century. The purpose of this study, interpreted in the publication that resulted, was to provide interested executives with guidelines for planning the construction of new offices. It analyzed and compiled architectural specifications on forty-six life insurance home offices. Seven life insurance executives from various companies composed the committee in charge of this study, and these gentlemen made clear their belief in the connections between physical work space and worker activity. In deciding on the shape and content of new buildings, they encouraged builders to nullify the "existence of antiquated procedures caused by reluctance to modify early office systems due to gradual evolution or personal qualifications within the company." In other words, by changing the building, executives could shake loose old habits and relationships at all levels of the corporate ladder. In addition, the "health or efficiency of employees" could be improved. As the connection of these two terms by the word *or* makes clear, industrial design issues such as air quality, climate, and lighting were as intimately bound up with the question of cost-effectiveness as with workers' comfort.[60]

The committee used the language and philosophy of systematic management to divide work space into four categories based on status and function: space for executive officers, department heads, clerical employees, and maintenance or service workers. The spatial allowance for clerical "units" was about sixty square feet, "sufficient for desk and chair and immediate aisle space" if not for "filing equipment."[61] Echoing the terminology of Taylorism, the report noted that there was a "certain amount of lost motion and time in clerical processes because of relatively large spaces between desks." Instead, desks should be placed close together (only three feet apart), facing in the same direction, with easily accessible aisles so that workers could "get in and out without disturbing anyone else." The references to scientific management— "time," "motion," "units"—and the formality of the report were in essence an adoption of prevailing language rather than the introduction of new ideas.

In emphasizing the managerial functions of space, the committee noted that employees should be placed "in front or around the person having authority over them."[62] Like the moveable desks in Goodell's management system, the placement of employees enabled supervisors to keep an eye on their activities. Physical space thus represented an approach to management with a wide variety of solutions, from the drastic course of erecting a new building to the simpler movement of furniture or restriction of traffic patterns and therefore of worker interactions. The purpose of such devices was to give supervisors more control over the behavior of workers and to provide structure for the work process.

Spatial arrangements were one way to maximize the time workers spent at their tasks. Another was to institute a more rigid chronological structure through the use of punch time clocks, gongs, or bells. Bells or gongs signaling the temporal parameters of the workday had been common in industrial concerns since the advent of the factory system in the late eighteenth century. They were, however, an innovation for office workers of the late nineteenth century.

Before the use of time signals in offices, employers controlled the comings and going of workers by using verbal or written strictures. The employee instruction book of the Farmers and Mechanics' Bank of Philadelphia in the 1870s and 1880s, for example, entered presidential pronouncements on employee behavior in handwritten form in a book available to all workers. This early version of the circular memorandum included procedures for balancing accounts at the end of the year, information on vacations, and numerous entries describing the time frame of the workday. Entries told clerks to "confine themselves to their desks as much as possible during business hours" and to be "at their desks not later than 8:45 A.M." But merely writing it down did not ensure compliance. The book's earliest entries were made in 1872, and the president's concern with employees' time began to appear in 1873. The need for the instruction book and the increasing number of names listed in the company employ suggest that as the numbers of workers went up, an executive's ability to monitor their behavior became more difficult.[63]

Various timekeeping systems could facilitate monitoring. By the 1890s, so-called master clock systems were in use in manufacturing concerns and in many offices. One exhibitor at the Chicago World's Fair in 1893 displayed a typical clock system, which controlled "slave" clocks in various parts of the exhibition by one main clock, the "master."[64] From at least 1900, automatic time devices in large life insurance companies divided work into segments, separating working time—time owed the company—from employees' personal time—taking breaks for the restroom or lunch.

A manager's time, in contrast, continued earlier nineteenth-century work patterns. Fluid and unbroken, managerial work time could include time spent at lunch, on the streetcar, at home, or in leisure activities. The types of timepieces used in workplaces reinforced status differences. Punch clocks and clerical clocks usually were devoid of extraneous ornament and "watched" over workers from prominent sites on workroom walls. Executives' clocks often were ornate, such as the massive grandfather clock in Metropolitan Life's home office, which also was notorious for its accuracy. As the reputation of Metropolitan's clock suggests, the managerial demarcation of employee time brooked no outside appeal.[65] Managers and executives ultimately controlled the clocks, deciding which type of system to institute and then regulating the activities of workers according to that system. Rather than buzzers or "slaves" connected to master clocks, executives and managers used their own engagement calendars and appointment books to schedule their workday. These tools, which had become common in trade advertising by about 1910, indicated that managerial time also was susceptible to rationalization. However, executives "penciled in" their encounters with others rather than responding to bells or whistles: they structured their own time.[66]

Despite the emphasis on efficiency and the apparent neutrality of management approaches, the work force was far from a set of interchangeable parts. One of the most visible and thorny differences among workers was their gender, a difference that did not escape management's notice. Systematic managers discussed the gendered nature of work and tried to incorporate their expectations into the office environment. Workers, sometimes openly and sometimes covertly, brought their own sense of gender into the office.

Women's presence sexualized the office, creating several logistical and ideological management problems. Executives and managers assumed that sexual attraction inevitably would result from the physical proximity of men and women in the workplace. Management's role was to minimize this attraction, for several reasons. First, cultural assumptions regarding the special frailty and sexual vulnerability of middle-class women led male managers and executives to prescribe a protective attitude toward female workers. But that protective attitude undermined the ideal of a rationalized use of business time and space. Second, innumerable rules of polite behavior reinforced gender differences. Men were expected to rise when women entered a room, and male language contained at least two vocabularies—one for exchanges between men, and one for men and women.[67] As one employee of the Equitable put it in 1933, "now-a-days one is surrounded by an ocean of permanent waves and one's requests (not orders) are received with a smile while one's vocabulary has been refined to such an extent that 'Oh Well' is about as near as one can come except that the 'Old Timers' occasionally relapse into the old version."[68] Finally, the general public's fears for young women in offices had to be acknowledged. From at least the 1890s, advice literature to young working women emphasized that females needed to guard against male advances in the office, where men and women were thrown together without the social shields of parents, wives, husbands, other kin, or guardians. To mingle these public and private behaviors threatened the impressionable nature of women, upset canons of respectability, strained traditional male methods of interaction, and undermined management's search for efficiency.

Systematic managers tried to solve their gender concerns in several ways. One of the most important was the invention of a kind of bureaucratic kinship, wherein a company as an institution assumed the role of women's protector and guardian. Out of concerns for efficiency, smooth employee relations, and a positive public image, executives and managers presented the corporation as the custodian of employee morals and social interactions. Custodianship was expressed in welfare work and the ideology of corporate domesticity; it also emerged in the adaptation to the work environment of the nineteenth-century segregation of men and women. Separating workers could remove the possibility of encounters, or at least put them under management's control; it also set men and women workers apart in ways that both reflected and lent credence to the distinctions created by salary differentials and gendered work skills.

Time was a critical element separating male and female workers. Time held symbolic meanings in relation to office work, and temporal divisions came to express gender divisions. The division of time into rationalized and nonrationalized segments coincided with the managerial revolution's division of labor into manual and brain work. As their numbers in jobs such as stenographer and typist increased, so did women's assignment to office machinery such as dictaphones, typewriters, and addressographs. By 1910, women dominated the routine clerical positions that utilized machinery, and women were the manual laborers of the office factory. Advertisements from the early twentieth century invariably show women operating most office machinery. Exceptions to this typecasting were lettergraphs—usually shown being run by boys—and heavy printing machinery—shown operated by men; both types of machines typically were located in company mail and print rooms, which remained male spaces in the office building because these tasks had roots in the artisan print shop, a male-defined craft.[69] Unlike managers and executives, who mostly were men, office machine operators, who mostly were women, were paid by the hour. The interest of hourly workers in the passage of clock time naturally would be more personal than management's interest in the relation between work time and company efficiency. Despite the fact that workers' revolt against structured time was genderless, both employee and managerial wisdom implied that female workers were particularly prone to be "clock watchers." Observers described clock watchers as uncommitted labor; committed labor was oblivious to time.[70] As the gender segregation of labor developed in corporate offices throughout the period, the gendered nature of temporal divisions increased. For executives and managers, work was to be an unbroken continuum rather than twenty-four hours divided into work and the rest of their lives, which coincided with the middle-class emphasis on men's work as a defining attribute of male existence. "Manual" employees, however, who increasingly were women, found their lives regulated by punch clocks and "gongs." Women workers were, by definition, uncommitted to their work and thus deserving of less pay and fewer promotions. The structure of work time, and the presence or absence of a particular type of clock, served as a demarcation of pay, gender, status, and a mark of commitment as well as a general feature of worker control.[71]

Another area of gender segregation grew up alongside the development of gender-specific job categories and the application of systematic management principles to building design. The new construction methods introduced in the 1870s, which allowed designers to create enormous office spaces that could hold many workers and which led to the division of rooms or entire floors according to procedure, often meant gender divisions as well. For example, at Metropolitan Life, floor plans from its new building built in 1876 included whole rooms devoted to "clerks."[72] Interior photographs of the home office taken in 1896 showed rooms with female and male clerks all engaged in related activities but stationed on opposite sides of the room. In 1908, company publications and photographs indicated the continuation of these trends toward the physical segregation of workers according to organizational division and job specialization.

The "pooling" or aggregation of workers that resulted often affected male workers. Banks, which did not hire large numbers of female clerical workers until World War I, frequently pooled male clerks and bookkeepers.[73] Nevertheless, the largest concentrations in these work groups were women, simply because female clerical workers increasingly outnumbered men. The Audit Division at Metropolitan Life in 1908 employed 752 women clerks—nearly half the 1,533 women employed by Metropolitan in that year. In describing the Stenographic Bureau, a company brochure of 1908 explained that of the over 200 stenographers, "125 are in the Stenographic Bureau. A clerk desiring to dictate applies to the head of the bureau by telephone or electric annunciator and a stenographer is at once sent, returning to the bureau to transcribe the letters, which are later distributed by messenger for signatures." Clearly, the company management intended to generate a smooth flow of paperwork by pooling:

> Experience has shown that more efficient service is secured at less expense by grouping the stenographers. Where individual stenographers are allotted to a clerk or division it is impossible to so regulate the correspondence that at times there will not be a dearth of work and at others more than can be promptly handled. Again, a stenographer continually taking dictation from one person or in one division cannot compare in general efficiency with one who comes in contact with many persons and with the work of many divisions.[74]

The Mailing Department of E. I. duPont de Nemours main offices in 1921 was separated into three divisions. The first consisted of three female clericals and the male manager. The second was composed of twenty-two men in the Mail Division who worked as messengers, carriers, wrappers, and mail boys (who worked at night). The third was the Addressing and Enclosing facility, which employed thirteen women. The Mail and Addressing divisions were in separate areas.[75] Such pools facilitated the efficient generation of paperwork; they also immensely depersonalized the work experience, isolating workers from the higher levels of management and executive positions and fragmenting the production process. By 1930, grouping workers according to job or division in physical space had become common practice, replicating the gender division of labor. The physical arrangement of the office thus reinforced gender as a work category and displayed that difference for all to see and experience by creating different work spaces for men and women.[76]

Spatial organization also addressed the relationship between work areas and status. The relative size of allotted work space was a good indication of an individual's place in the hierarchy, but often as important were the objects or the degree of decorative articulation of a given place. For example, in the Victor Talking Machine Company, large entrance areas were contrasted spatially with "more intimately considered" areas, such as waiting rooms and the offices of high-level managers. In keeping with their status in the corporate hierarchy, "the president's room and the board room were keyed to a higher pitch of [design] elaboration than any other rooms." Nonpublic clerking areas, in contrast, were functional and spare, with little or no ornamentation.[77]

Corporate designers used objects and spatial arrangements borrowed from nineteenth-century domestic architecture to demarcate the status divisions between managerial and manual workers. The Life Office Management Association spoke openly in its 1933 report of the status distinctions possible in the private office and its appointments. The report asserted that planners should consider who could have private offices, how large they should be, who should have windows, and whether there would be rugs or fireplaces (an increasingly nonfunctional item in buildings with centralized heat).[78] The corporate offices of many executives, from at least the 1890s through the 1920s, created domestic spaces within the public, corporate realm. The boardroom of Metropolitan Life, built in 1893, had gold leaf on the ceiling, leather walls, a fireplace patterned after one in a French chateau, and special chairs. The Equitable's boardroom also was luxurious. In addition, executives often had their own dining rooms as well as offices with overstuffed chairs and massive fireplaces.[79]

Domestic decoration manuals of the late nineteenth century, which aimed at a middle-class audience, treated the fireplace as an image of familial togetherness, "warmth," "comfort," and bourgeois status. It denoted a room set aside for family contemplation. Fireplaces and animal skins also were repeated emblems in "dens," masculinized rooms that served as retreats for the contemplation of domestic masculinity in a culturally feminized realm, the home. In addition, fireplaces, animal rugs, chandeliers, and other costly ornamentation drew on upper-class notions of refinement and luxury. These diverse meanings came together in corporate executive suites, peopled by men of both middle- and upper-class backgrounds, many of whom were *nouveau riche*.[80]

Most new buildings built after 1890 had centralized heating, but fireplaces remained as a symbol of the "domestication" of executive offices, which were smaller and more intimate than the large halls where clericals worked. Metropolitan Life's executive library and dining room used furniture and fixtures found in middle- or upper-class homes, including a bearskin rug. When officials of the First National Bank of Lebanon, Pennsylvania, remodeled their office in 1906, they placed a massive stone fireplace topped by a thick wooden mantel with a central mirror next to the heavy doors of the bank's modern steel vault.[81] Agents' offices for North Carolina Mutual Life had mantel clocks and

The executive library at Metropolitan Life, ca. 1900, replicated a domestic library or parlor in the corporate "home office." *Courtesy of the MetLife Archives.*

carpets, even though other fixtures in the room were spartan. Similarly, the executive offices in New England Mutual's Milk Street building from the 1920s to early 1940s could have been domestic parlors or libraries. Leather couches, fireplaces, paintings, and carpets replicated both the symbolic and literal experience of domestic interiors.

The use of domestic fixtures and furniture in offices was paralleled by the introduction of office-type furniture and fixtures in domestic dwellings. From about the 1870s, many office supply companies handled both office and home furnishings, varying their designs and sales pitch slightly according to whether a piece of furniture was aimed primarily at a business or a middle-class domestic consumer.[82] The "cabinet secretary" office desk, for example, had a duplicate in a home "mixing center." Likewise, a space-saving office "rotary case" applied the same design principles as a contemporary china closet. Cheryl Robertson has observed that the impetus for these adaptations came from the general movement by the late nineteenth century toward reliance on scientific principles.[83] As offices became more "scientific," the job of housekeeping took on a professional persona with the appearance of college training courses in "domestic science." These influences, however, flowed in both directions: The initial prototypes for office fixtures probably came from the "gentlemen's study."[84] Thus, business fixtures reappeared transformed in middle-class kitchens and dining rooms, and the furnishings of men's domestic rooms transferred to the office.

Since there were no antecedents for office furniture, and since early offices had indeed been domestic spaces, it should not be a surprise that the connections between public offices and domestic space lingered in the household fixtures of offices. But the connections were more than just a holdover to earlier times, more than just anachronisms. The movement to domesticate the public workplace was as consciously ideological as the push to rationalize the home. Architects picked up the theme of the domesticated workplace from their clients in a variety of fields. The owners of the Victor Talking Machine Company in 1917 wanted "the interior of the building [to] have a domestic character." Their architect noted that, "this idea is carried out in all public parts of the building, and in the major private offices and their reception rooms." The owners of a commercial collection agency in 1922 wanted an "artistic, home-like appearance" in their new offices. Architects explained this desire for home-like surroundings as a function of personal taste; a businessperson was the same individual whether at home or at work, and most people spent more of their waking time at the office than at home. Articles on office decoration appeared in domestic popular magazines such as *House Beautiful* and *Country Life*. Even the unofficial journal of scientific management, *System* magazine, touted the domestic office in the early 1920s, suggesting that the desire for this type of office space was widespread and long-lasting even among devotees of rationalized office management.[85]

Emphasis on the separateness of the business and domestic realms overlooks the degree to which executives and managers—and sometimes workers as well—tried to link the two. Just as scientific rationalism legitimized the domestic labor of women through home management and domestic science, corporate domesticity authenticated the ultimate purposes of business: for men, self-fulfillment and family security; and for young women, training for their journey toward marriage. In light of these aims, the class and gender connotations of domestic symbols in the office (fireplaces, animal skins) were both complex and revealing.

Domesticated private offices communicated a great deal about business manhood. Recreating a man's domestic, private space within a public place strengthened corporate claims of executive "fatherhood," and it encouraged the identification of personal life with corporate, public existence. As one author put it in 1929, "he brings his whole life to his office now, where before he left part of it at home, for there was no place for it in his commercial existence. His office is now *his* office, where before he seemed merely to be occupying a space apportioned to him."[86] As this quotation suggests, the man in a private office was a man of property. He did not actually own the space, but it was nonetheless his. With their careful, rich detail, private offices removed their occupants both symbolically and literally from the general herd of employees. In the often noisy, crowded environments of large office buildings, a private space was the most sought-after mark of status. Irenée duPont, who in 1911 was in charge of plans for the new duPont office building, wrote in a letter to his father, the president of the company, that the Smokeless Powder department had more office space than was allotted to similar departments. This was because "there are very few clerks and lower grade men and a very large proportion of [higher grade] men that could not properly be 'doubled up.'"[87] Private offices validated the manhood of those who possessed them by emphasizing individuality and personal freedom. Male workers not blessed with such spaces were both lower in status and less manly. Lest anyone miss the point, the female secretaries who visited private executive offices were referred to as "office wives" or "office housekeepers."[88]

Plumbing also distinguished workers' spaces in many office buildings. The offices of mid-level managers often contained sinks and running water; those of top executives had complete toilet facilities as well as sinks. In the late nineteenth century, most executives but few workers probably had these amenities in their dwellings.[89] Blueprints for the Pennsylvania Railroad's Broad Street offices, built in Philadelphia in 1929, demonstrated the careful articulation of status. The eighteenth floor, which housed the financial officers of the company, including accounting and the treasury office, contained two communal men's toilets, at opposite ends of the floor, and one women's toilet. There were seven stalls in each men's room and only five in the one women's room. Clearly, this was a floor dominated by males, willing to let female workers wait. However, not all men were created equal: In addition to the two general men's rooms there was an "officer's toilet" for the mid-level managerial staff and three vice-presidential toilets, one in each executive's office. Only one of the executive offices had a decorative fireplace, and this official's name was the only individual name to appear on the blueprints. The other offices were designated by function. Even the new offices of E. I. duPont de Nemours, which in 1911 showed a remarkable democracy of toilet facilities, delineated the executives from the clerks.[90] Office workers used communal spaces and facilities that reinforced their status as cogs in the corporate machine. Their privacy at work was nominal, whereas executives' separate refuges for bodily functions reinforced the notions that they were too busy to leave their offices even for the most urgent personal reasons and, conversely, that their work encompassed such private needs. Similarly, executives took their meals in separate dining facilities in most large financial concerns, or in one of many upper-class urban men's clubs. Such segregation suggests an almost ritual taboo or ceremonial function, as if the executive's body and its products were too powerful or important to be shared or mingled with those of lower-status office workers.

Men's restrooms can be found on nearly every floor of office buildings from the 1880s to 1930. Despite women's increasing numbers as workers, however, women's restrooms often were spaced on alternate floors, with a greater number of stalls than men's rooms, even in new buildings. Women's and men's restrooms sometimes were separated from one another by a good distance, even though this must have created design problems. Women's rooms usually had anterooms that contained couches or chairs and could be used, literally, as "rest rooms." The "girls' rest room" at New England Mutual was locked, and anyone wishing to use it had to obtain a key from "a designated person" in each department. This room was for resting when female workers felt ill (presumably during menstruation), and "Conversation [was] strictly forbidden in this room."[91]

Compounding the increasing gender segregation in job categories, the physical arrangement of the office also reinforced gender differences.[92] Given the use of large female clerical pools and the absence of women in management positions, most female office workers occupied the less public office spaces. In the Victor Talking Machine building, built in 1916, the "men's toilet" was placed within easy access of the public area (to accommodate the nearly all-male clientele as well as high-ranking employees) and near the elaborate public stairway. The "women's toilet" was located at the end of a crooked corridor, behind the vault and the service stairway. Emphasizing the status difference of these placements, the men's room was convenient to office space that would have housed predominantly men—managers, salesmen, and clients—while stenographers and clerks, mostly women, had to make their way down the entire length of the building to reach the women's and men's rooms.

The use of domestic imagery and the segregation of clerical and managerial time and space, which replicated the gender and status segregation of the work force, did not exhaust managers' efforts to structure the work experience. Managers also attempted to control movements *outside* work areas, as well as the time workers spent inside the building but not actually working. Evidently, efficiency covered personal behavior and included expectations about gender difference. The 1895 edition of Metropolitan Life's employee handbook stated that "separate entrances, hallways and elevators for men and women must be used exclusively as provided." This prohibition continued until at least 1921 and was enforced by the imposition of (unspecified) penalties. Similar regulations were in force at Aetna Life Insurance in 1910 and at other companies. New England Mutual provided lounges for women where employees could read and hold "quiet conversations." In addition, the company provided separate "rest rooms" for women only.[93]

Gender-segregated eating facilities were common. In the early 1890s, female clericals at Metropolitan Life were not allowed to leave the building during the lunch hour without permission; after 1893 lunchrooms were provided in the

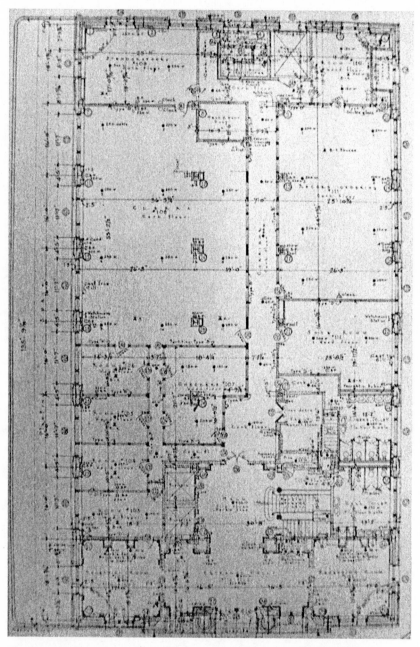

The floor plan of the Victor Talking Machine Company, Camden, New Jersey, 1916–1917, displays the architectural gradations of gender and status in its placement of restrooms and clerical offices. *The American Architect 151 (28 Mar. 1917): 2153.*

One of the lunchrooms reserved for women only at Metropolitan Life, 1898.
Courtesy of the MetLife Archives.

building as alternatives. Lunchrooms also were divided into times for male and female use and, in some concerns, into separate rooms. At Wells Fargo Nevada National Bank in the years after World War I, separate lounges for male and female employees allowed eating, napping, reading, and conversation. The women's lounge and lunchroom included kitchen facilities where women could purchase lunch. By the early twentieth century, both male and female workers were eating in their office buildings. A 1911 publicity brochure for Metropolitan Life's home office observed that the two thousand female employees ate lunch in the same building lunchroom at different times. The thousand male employees had their meal "in a large room in another part of the building." At New England Mutual there were separate lunchrooms for men and women as late as 1942. Although men could purchase their lunches in the women's room, they had to eat in the men's lunchroom.[94]

In part, the creation of corporate lunchrooms was a response to the fact that in the earlier period, few if any public lunchrooms on the outside were available to women. One employee of Metropolitan Life recalled that in the early 1890s, male office workers went "to a nearby cafe for a glass of beer or wherever a free lunch counter was in vogue. . . . As for the women I don't know? I suppose they either brought their own lunch or patronized Childs or Dennetts depending on the weather." By the time such facilities were common, the corporate lunchroom had become a fixture, and discount lunches could stand in place of paying employees more so they could buy their lunch at a place of their choice outside the building.[95]

Several possible reasons explain the gender separation in nonworkspace areas. The rapid growth of business may have crowded existing facilities, making it necessary to have certain portions of the work force arrive, leave, and go to lunch at different times. Norman Cushman recalled that in the early 1890s male employees began work fifteen minutes before women because the 650 total employees taxed the capacity of the building's one passenger elevator.[96] Metropolitan Life's handbook for clerical workers, issued in 1915, stipulated that men go to lunch at 12:00 on the eleventh floor, women at 11:55 and 1:10 on the eleventh and twelfth floors. Crowding, however, does not explain why work forces were divided by *gender* for purposes of allocating lunch hours, elevator usage, and recreational facilities. Separation of this sort seems particularly inefficient, since it meant the added expense of devoting more space solely to recreation or eating and the necessity of moving food and utensils around the building. The fact that men and women sometimes worked in the same rooms suggests that segregated conditions reflected management's desire to control the issue of gender in public space during private times as well as in work areas.

The segregation of men and women everywhere in the work environment indicates that management philosophy shared common assumptions regarding women in public life and the workplace. Priscilla Murolo has suggested that in the case of Aetna Life Insurance, President Morgan G. Bulkeley did not approve of the presence of women in offices and thus tried to make them invisible in public areas.[97] This attitude was fairly common, judging from the amount of ink expended on justifying why women should be allowed in offices. In addition, the segregation of women in offices followed similar patterns developing in other types of urban space: Department stores, hotels, and banks of the time often had separate entrances and facilities for women. The Union National Bank of Delaware, for example, advertised its separate rooms for "ladies and gentlemen" in the safe deposit and vault facilities. Segregation by gender also was based on the idea that women needed protection in public life.[98] This belief certainly helps explain the fact that female clerical workers at Metropolitan Life could not leave the building during lunch time without permission, but men could.[99] Finally, prescriptive literature from the 1880s to the 1920s showed an enormous concern among both managers and workers with the possibilities for unbridled sexuality that women's presence in offices created. Metropolitan Life's employee handbooks, for example, stipulated at least until 1933 that female clerks were "not allowed to take down their hair in the office nor in the lavatories."[100]

Segregation also diffused what systematic managers saw as another major disruption: the formation of alternative cohorts and friendships not based on management's needs. Workers—both male and female—found different meanings and uses for the time they spent in office buildings. Men and women asserted their relationship to employers and other workers through their own uses of corridors, furniture, lunchrooms, and nonoffice space and time. Whether viewed from the perspective of management's continuing frustrations or workers' often bemused contempt, office life abounded with workers who lingered by the water fountain, chatted at one another's desks, combed their hair in restrooms, met on corporate rooftops, wandered from the office for lunch and a beer, or shopped on their lunch hour. For example, in the 1860s and 1870s, male employees at Mutual of New York routinely used the basement vault area for fistfights to settle office disputes.[101] An employee of Metropolitan Life recalled a physical fight in the 1880s involving three men in the Audit Department, which was broken up by the supervisor. No record exists of what the fight was about, in part because the combatants refused to answer the supervisor's questions. Their refusal suggests an awareness of differences between workers and managers and a group solidarity among the male clericals. In 1912, when told there would be a social dinner for all home-office staff, some female workers at Provident Mutual Life cried because they believed their attendance was mandatory. They expressed concern that their jobs might come to hinge on their performance in such "informal" social settings. Throughout the 1870s and 1880s, the employees of the Farmers and Mechanics' Bank in Philadelphia were told repeatedly to be on time, to stay at their desks, to keep working until they had finished all their tasks for the day, and to not sit on the windowsills and desks. The bank clerks not only did not heed this advice, they complained about it among themselves and with people outside the bank. Finally the president, in a burst of peevish impotence, notified the clerks that he felt he had "done all in his power for those employed, and being tired of hearing complaints from them, will be glad to receive the resignations of any who are dissatisfied with existing arrangements." This did not end the clerks' complaints, but the two groups apparently came to some kind of understanding.[102] Clearly, spatial segregation did not resolve all the issues that divided workers and managers.

Goodell's description of moveable desks focused on managerial manipulations of space, but it also can be used to illuminate the underlying differences in how workers used space and time. From the clerks' point of view, the shifting of desks might have had a quite different effect. What managers saw as distractions from the goal of efficiency, workers probably saw as welcome breaks from

In this 1918 cartoon from Metropolitan Life's management publication, *The Home Office,* male and female workers dawdle in the main hallway on their way to work. Although corporate lore suggested that women were more prone to be uncommitted to their jobs, this cartoon suggests that men and women were equally reluctant to be at their desks. *Courtesy of the MetLife Archives.*

One section of eight in the Industrial Audit and Policy Division at Metropolitan Life in 1908, with the supervisor's "throne" set off physically and symbolically by a low railing and his high-backed roll-top desk. *Courtesy of the MetLife Archives.*

the routine of paperwork. Observing visitors and the passing crowd gave clerks a way to vary their routine, pay attention to office events that may have had an impact on themselves, and keep an eye on their supervisor so they could modify their own behavior according to his or her presence or gaze. Sinclair Lewis, in his novel of office life, *The Job,* satirized the importance of the water cooler as a place where workers could retreat from work: "The shifting of the water-cooler from the front office to the packing-room may be an epochal event to a copyist. . . . The moving of the water-cooler may mean that she must now pass the sentinel office manager; that therefore she no longer dares break the incredible monotony by expeditions to get glasses of water. As a consequence she gives up the office and marries unhappily."[103]

Getting a drink of water, like using the couch in the restroom, fulfilled biological needs difficult for management to deny completely. Workers could take advantage of this by using such places as havens from supervision. Sometimes workers clearly were aware of the managerial uses of time and space. An employee of Metropolitan Life, speaking of the Audit Division in the late 1880s, observed, "George Gaston had attained unmistakable control of the Division. This was indicated by his occupancy of a platform (the 'Throne') in the center of the room and by the Clerks called to the platform to explain delinquencies."[104]

Management's efforts to defuse the sexuality which gendered offices encouraged also were to little avail. Workers, in fact, treated the workplace as much like a personal, social resource as a workplace. Sinclair Lewis cleverly explained part of the reality of office relations: "The office is filled with thrills of love and distrust and ambition. Each alley between desks quivers with secret romance as ceaselessly as a battle-trench, or a lane in Normandy."[105] Employee newsletters and official company journals recorded with either avid interest or frustration the personal lives of employees. *The Pacific Coast News*, the 1920s Metropolitan Life's employee newsletter for the San Francisco office, contained a column titled "Social Notes" that documented the parties, illnesses, marriages, vacations, and deaths of employees and their family members. A good deal of speculation centered on the romantic potential of the young woman who had just begun work in one office, or a young man's frequent trips by a young woman's desk. Often, employee newsletters recorded the wedding plans of employees who had met and furthered their romance in the office. In 1918, the Provident Mutual newsletter *Between Ourselves* announced the wedding of Marguerite Knoedler, a company secretary, to John Leo "of the Auditing Department." After a list of engagements, one editor of Metropolitan Life's *Pacific Coast News* observed in 1921, "The Metropolitan is some Matrimonial Bureau."[106]

The newsletters cited such social occasions to emphasize the qualities managers hoped to find in employees. A lengthy announcement in the Wells Fargo *Nevadan* in 1919 gave the complete employment histories of Clarice Koon and Arthur Durbrow, a recently engaged couple. Koon had begun in the Transit Department and at the time of her engagement was assistant to the head of the Department on City Collections. The paper described her as "like her fiancé . . . a thoroughly good worker and . . . one of the most important women on our staff." Artie Durbrow had worked his way up from a bookkeeper to head of the bank's Liberty Loan Department. In addition to his usual work, Durbrow also was known for his social efforts to promote "the esprit de corps" of the bank.[107] However, Clarice and Artie clearly also had more personal "investments" in their work, as their engagement made clear.

Building design between the 1880s and 1930 communicated corporate ideologies to the public through architectural imagery and to consumers and workers by levels of design elaboration in personal work spaces. Interiors could be manipulated to define spaces for the consuming public, the parameters of work behavior, the permutations of hierarchy, and gender distinctions. Notions of maleness and femaleness were reinforced by domestic decorative details and by gender separation in space and time. The sheer presence and permanence of buildings not only provided continuity in structuring consumer relations and a mobile work force but gave visible, environmental impact to consumer interactions in public and worker behavior. Business buildings thereby reproduced the social relations of the work force by supplying a physical envelope for the corporate organizational system. At the same time, architecture reshaped the gender and class dimensions of the public urban environment.

In public arenas or spaces viewed as inherently "male" or "female," those of the other gender who used such spaces may have felt uncomfortable. William Leach, for example, has argued that department stores developed separate entrances, elevators, and departments for male and female shoppers partly to ease the psychological threat to men entering public spaces culturally defined as female.[108] The idea that architectural place delineated and displayed gender attached the cultural sense of private and public, femaleness and maleness, both to space and to the activities that went on in a given space. Physical segregation sorted out and clarified gender role boundaries, at the same time allowing those boundaries to overlap by providing clear-cut situations for behavior. Gendered architecture offered a pragmatic solution to the incorporation of private values and images into public life.

Ultimately, the office was not the efficiently divided work environment managers and employers wanted. Nor was it the personalized space workers attempted to achieve. It was, however, a world that replicated the gender arrangements of white, urban, middle-class private families, a world in which social rituals such as courting frequently went on. Employers who used domestic imagery and furnishings to engage workers' commitment consistently were frustrated by workers' much more intimate and personal approach to their work. In contests over space and time, gender relations were used for many purposes, not the least of which were to replicate private relations within a public environment and to extend the corporation beyond the workplace itself. In the process of defining the meaning of corporate work, all the participants acted through and on the environment, inventing the complex spatial, temporal, and gender divisions of the modern office.

CHAPTER FIVE

The Family Way

Corporate Domesticity, Kinship, and Leisure

In 1906, President John Hegeman of the Metropolitan Life Insurance Company wrote to congratulate John Bayer on his fifth year as a company agent. Hegeman made special mention of Bayer's ten children: "May his boys and girls all grow up to be good and useful members of the community. . . . May the sons all become leaders in the Metropolitan and the daughters all marry Superintendents, and may they never go back on the precepts and especially on the example of their illustrious and industrious parents." In a series of puns on life insurance terms, Hegeman asked the supervisor to "convey to them all the assurances of our unlapsable, nonforfeitable and incontestable consideration." Later, in 1910, Bayer's family—which by then included eleven children—posed for a portrait that appeared on the front page of the company newsletter. At the family's feet, letters spelled out the word "Metropolitans." The company thus claimed John Bayer, his wife Laura, their seven daughters and four sons as members of the figurative Metropolitan family.[1]

Bayer's story reveals that the rationalized, bureaucratic setting of the modern office remained infused with older, familial traditions of the precorporate era.[2] Indeed, the nineteenth-century middle-class family was an important model in financial industries. Domestic imagery contributed as much to the development of financial corporations as the organizational structures of the railroads and the military. The family model moved in two directions: outward to the public and inward to corporate workers.

Insurance agent John P. Bayer and his wife and children in the cover photograph on a Metropolitan Life company agents' newsletter, 1910. Company president John Hegeman congratulated Bayer on both his large family and his large portfolio of clients, claiming all the Bayers as corporate representatives. *Courtesy of the MetLife Archives.*

Because of their emphasis on security and family protection and their concern with creating a positive public image, insurance and banking executives
tended to think of their mandate in social terms. Social legitimacy was particularly important in life insurance, which fought an uphill battle for public
acceptance well into the early twentieth century. Although any business relies
to some extent on reputation, a good image is critical in industries like insurance and banking, which "manufacture" and sell financial security. The intangible nature of the product and the all but invisible process of production make
public good-will of paramount importance. Life insurance executives looking
for ways to make their business appealing found gender imagery both a "natural" and a useful tool.[3] Executives hoped that by presenting the corporation as
a "woman," and focusing on the paternal, fraternal, and domestic vision of
corporate relations, they could serve the dual purpose of winning public acceptance and preventing employee unrest. Corporate domesticity dealt with this
problem in a variety of ways. Among the earliest was the use of female figures in
advertising and promotion. From the 1850s on, symbols of womanhood emphasized the security of the financial industries by implying that a company
was to the public as a mother was to her children. Company logos and advertising stressed the nurturing, protective aspects of insurance and banking with
images of domestic womanhood. The use of female figures to describe an
organization was paralleled by traditional feminine attributes given to ships,
nations, churches, or allegorical figures. The symbols used as company logos
grew out of the convention of allegorical images, which used female figures to
represent abstract concepts, such as liberty or justice.[4] In 1859, for example,
the Pennsylvania Company for Insurance on Lives and Granting Annuities
represented the company with an image of a standing woman clothed in flow-
ing, classical robes. She held a banner that read, "A Prudent Man Foreseeth the
Evil." Her left hand also held a mirror, traditionally the symbol of vanity. This
allegorical image bridged the older notions of *vanitas* and the sixteenth-
century *memento mori* with the sound commercial instincts of the "modern"
man. It reminded him to buy insurance rather than contemplate the state of his
soul if he really cared about his and his family's future.[5]

By the 1870s, female allegorical figures were common in trade advertising.
Increasingly, companies either substituted images of real widows and orphans
for abstract female figures or added realistic figures to the image as representative women and children, borrowing directly from similar imagery that workers' mutual benefit societies used in the mid-nineteenth century.[6] Atlantic Mutual Life showed a mother and two children seated in an upholstered chair
within a shield. The Provident Fund and Life Insurance Company of New York
used a winged female figure who held her arms out protectively over a weeping
woman carrying a weeping child. Included in this tableau were an elderly,
bearded man leaning on a cane—a reference to the use of insurance policies as

retirement funds—and a young woman seated on the ground in front of a funerary urn.[7] This complex tableau, with its reminders of the frailty of life and family responsibility, was less typical than simpler figural groupings. Allegorical images seem to have been relatively interchangeable: The Provident Fund image, for example, also appeared in advertisements for the United States Life Insurance Company in the early 1870s, although the two companies seem not to have been directly connected. The image was produced by the Continental Bank Note Company of New York and may have been a stock trade image.[8]

By the 1890s, financial institutions were more proprietary about their individual company symbols, tailoring them to represent particular corporate entities. Even so, the use of female figures continued to draw on the rich symbolism of traditional allegory. Both Metropolitan Life and the Equitable used a mother to suggest the protection and care offered by their companies. In 1859, the Equitable adopted as its logo a vignette of an allegorical female figure with shield and spear protecting a mother holding a child in her arms.[9] This vignette varied slightly over time, modifying but not abandoning the symbolic link between the company and motherhood. In an advertising theme of 1900, a more realistic portrait of an actual mother cradling a child, titled "The Equitable Mother," referred to the security of families insured by the company. What had been an allegory had become a direct connection between the company and a protective, nurturing, late-nineteenth-century mother. New England Mutual used a picture of a woman at her spinning wheel, Priscilla Alden, to illustrate the company in 1886. Between 1908 and 1954, this image was used as an illustration on life insurance policies and on some promotional items.[10] The symbol was both a localized reference to colonial antecedents and a larger invocation of nineteenth-century associations of domesticity. By the 1920s, Provident Mutual Life had adopted a standing woman, swathed in classical drapery, holding one child in her arms and shielding another with her hand; in the 1930s, the company used a shield with a cross and, in the center, a young woman in Renaissance garb cradling an infant under the banner "The Provident Mother."[11]

These metaphors were not only visual. In 1895 an article in the *Baltimore Underwriter,* an insurance trade paper, commended the "devotion" of Equitable agents to their company by feminizing the corporation and playing on notions of masculinity: "The company is their sister, their mother, their wife, whose honor they are ever ready to defend." R. A. McCurdy, president of Mutual of New York, in 1899 elaborated a complex metaphor describing the "birth" of the Equitable from MONY, likening the relationship between the two companies to that between mother and child. Womanhood was a multifaceted image that could convey a variety of themes. By far the most common usage of feminine imagery was the evocation of motherhood. Office equipment companies advertised their products using the contrast between young female type-

The Equitable logo, as represented in a living tableau at a Merchants' Carnival, ca. 1900. Women as allegorical figures often were used to represent insurance companies in the late nineteenth century. *Courtesy of* ELASA.

writers and elderly, male clerks to suggest the progressive, up-to-date office.[12] The employment of college-educated Susan Gille as a stenographer for North Carolina Mutual Life in 1906 was both a local curiosity and publicity for the company. The presence of a black woman lent a moral tone to the company, and her background in an upper-class black Ohio family and her education brought "culture and class" to the company and the city.[13] In the early twentieth century, Metropolitan Life president Haley Fiske used corporate domesticity to address "labor problems" generally and especially those in his own work force. His formulation was a particularly articulate example of what had, by World War I, become a common industry attitude. In an address of 1920 entitled "Mother Metropolitan," Fiske told a gathering of sales agents that the Metropolitan was a mother to both its clients and employees. In the process of arguing that the company should continue to provide group insurance, Fiske claimed that it was worth the high overhead expense and enormous paperwork because "the working people are the children of Mother," and the company was charged with protecting, guiding, and educating (and insuring) everyone. Referring to his audience as "my dear boys," Fiske stated, "if Mother is this great Company, and if these millions of people [clients] are her children, then you are the elder brothers," whose job it was to become part of the client's "family circle," to become their "confidante and advisor," and to point out to them "opportunities and responsibilities."[14]

Fiske urged managers to create among employees a sense that the company was a family whose head acted as a benevolent guide and father figure to his "children" by providing benefits designed to improve their health and mental well-being. Advocates of this perspective theorized that if management extended such concern, employees would feel they were part of a community dedicated to the furtherance of their own careers and happiness as well as the company's fortunes. In addition, customers would feel that their best interests were a corporate concern. Fiske charged agents to serve their public with "courtesy; kindness; the handshake; the smile; the question about their health; the searching for the need of nurses; the offers to help in times of trouble."[15]

In a memorial service delivered on Fiske's death in 1929, Vice-President Frederick Ecker accented the former president's choice of "Mother" as a metaphor for the company:

> What was his favorite term when he spoke of the Metropolitan? He didn't say "Father"; he didn't say "business enterprise"; he didn't even say "corporation with a soul." He chose the term—"Mother." . . . Is there any word in the English language which means so much of what he meant this organization should be to every man and woman connected with it? Sacrifice, to begin with; brooding thought and care, and painstaking desire to provide for her children. He chose the term "Mother," because it tells the whole story.[16]

Fiske patterned his ideal of motherhood and corporate service on that of the nineteenth-century middle-class woman visualized in hundreds of insurance company logos: a nurturing and benevolent figure. To round out the gendered image, within the corporate family male sales agents were the eldest sons, carrying the ideal of service to the consumer/child. Fiske's audience was, no doubt, entirely conversant with such imagery and its emotional overtones. So common did the notion of corporate motherhood become that an anecdote reprinted in a 1923 edition of Metropolitan Life's employee newsletter used the metaphor to make a humorous point about company loyalty: "A certain agent was asked by a prospect why his company was any better than any other company. 'Why is your mother better than any other fellow's mother?' was the agent's reply, which settled the matter."[17]

Symbols of corporate domesticity tied the product to its production process, articulating an ideal of employee and customer relations. Executives had three interconnected purposes in mind when they used images of family life: to calm the public's fears, to stimulate sales, and to encourage a parental relationship with employees. The language executives used outlined a set of fictive kinship relations that executives hoped would address the alienation of workers and personalize bureaucratic relations, suggesting corporations were the economic and emotional equivalent of a supportive family. The industry's vision of companies as "mothers" to the public, for example, harmonized with descriptions of the paternal relationship between executives and employees. Morgan G. Bulkeley, the president of Aetna Life, attempted to maintain the personal relationships of the precorporate office even as Aetna's staff increased from twenty-two to three hundred by 1904. He ordered the creation of an athletic association for clerks and officers, encouraged activity among employees in Republican party politics, and closely supervised management policies.[18] Allusions to fictive fatherhood also expressed the paternalistic methods of corporate employee relations. Many executives at one time or another referred to their companies as "families."[19] In 1915, the president of Provident Mutual Life, Asa Wing, described his attitude toward his employees as "the feeling of a father for his children." Employees of the North Carolina Mutual Life Insurance Company referred to company president H. H. Spaulding as "Papa."[20]

While this emphasis on families initially came from the roots of the business in the family partnerships of the early nineteenth century, by the 1920s, Metropolitan Life's "family of 40,000" described an ideal of harmonious public and employee relations, not reality. To bridge the gap between ideal and reality, executives and managers in the financial industries developed a theory of management that supplemented nineteenth-century paternalism and twentieth-century systematic management with corporate domesticity.[21]

Among the most important expressions of the new managerial style was a remarkable adaptation of earlier gender ideology, wherein leading life insurance executives articulated a philosophy of worker control that incorporated notions of "social motherhood." Promoters of social motherhood in the late nineteenth century had argued that women's place should expand into the realms of politics and public welfare because the unique qualities of womanhood would bring sympathy, nurturance, and enlightened responsibility to the public arena. In this way, educated women could become the mothers or guardians of the whole society.[22] Financial industries employed large numbers of women compared to manufacturing and based their product's appeal on emotions. Therefore, they used this version of corporate domesticity as a description of labor–management relations and a public persona. A major departure from the vision of business as a public, male arena peopled by men and masculine values, corporate domesticity became part of the general ideology of business service.

The Metropolitan, Equitable, New England Life and others provided various benefits as a means of convincing employees that companies were concerned with their welfare.[23] For example, in 1913, Metropolitan Life opened a sanatorium at Mount McGregor, New York, for tubercular employees. In 1921, the Equitable inaugurated a health camp for "Equitable girls who are convalescent or whose state of health demands a period of rest and quiet." The camp also could be used for "vacation purposes." There was no charge for this service (except for vacationers), and the company deducted no time from earned vacation periods for recuperative stays. It was clear, however, that the company hoped to encourage a more productive work force: The stated purpose of the rest camp was to keep "our people well and *efficient*."[24] Healthy employees had fewer sick days at company expense and created less job turnover and consequent training of new employees. To further ensure health, as early as 1896 Metropolitan Life provided lunchrooms with free tea or coffee, and athletic facilities on the roof. Later, it supplied free lunches, dental care, and a gymnasium for the use of its employees. The company gave free course work for male and female employees who wished to advance within the company or simply "improve" themselves. In addition, companies took over the informal group athletic clubs that had existed in the late nineteenth century, sponsoring intra- and intercompany sporting events and contests. By the 1920s, these ventures included full-scale outings at seaside resorts or in the mountains, where employees of all classes theoretically would mingle under the benevolent eyes of the heads of the family.[25]

Initially, welfare work included the gender-specific belief that female employees required special maternal protection and guidance, since they were far from home and family, prey to a variety of temptations, and potential victims of unscrupulous persons. After the personnel management movement began, Metropolitan Life created a Welfare Department around 1915, headed by Mrs.

Women playing softball in the Metropolitan Life gymnasium, ca. 1900. Many corporations provided athletic facilities for their employees, which were segregated by gender. *Courtesy of the MetLife Archives.*

Gean Cunningham Snyder, to oversee the health and job satisfaction of the company's female employees. Metropolitan hoped to "increase the efficiency and happiness of its employees." Snyder explained the department's purposes:

> We keep careful watch upon the health of our girls, ordering each of them who appears anemic or unrobust to go daily to the dispensary for a milk-drinking! That, with our short hours, rest periods, gymnasium, roof garden and free luncheons . . . is very apt to build up a frail girl into a 100 per cent. efficient employe. And it is the 100 per cent. worker who earns the "living wage" and never loses her job.[26]

Snyder suggested that Metropolitan Life's discovery of corporate motherhood echoed the activities of other companies, not all of them in insurance: "Other great corporations are coming to see it our way. It is now pretty well understood that there is no real economy in the underpaid, underfed, overworked helper. The company which assists its employes to attain high efficiency is not only the benefactor of the nation's women, but the truly successful business organization."[27]

The Welfare Department's mandate clearly grew out of the need to push for efficiency and undermine worker discontent. An industrial relations circular produced by the University of Wisconsin's Extension Service in 1920, for example, observed that "inter-plant contests in girls [sic] indoor baseball, basket ball, and bowling would do a great deal to break down the caste and clique spirit which is too prevalent among female employees."[28] Wells Fargo Nevada National Bank by World War I had a well-developed corporate welfare system, with recreation, sports events, and a newsletter.[29] The National Cash Register Company initiated the earliest employee welfare program in the United States in the mid-1890s that included many of the same features later found in the life insurance industry—chorale or sport societies, dining areas, and "rest rooms" for women.[30] Questionnaires collected from personnel supervisors or directors between 1918 and 1920 by the Bureau of Vocational Information of Boston suggest that corporate welfare had become a widespread phenomenon. Indeed, welfare directors held positions in banking, insurance, manufacturing, mercantile establishments, and telephone companies from Cincinnati to San Francisco.[31] In contrast to financial industries, the NCR plan and those of manufacturing concerns generally did not extend all benefits to male workers and were not used to sell products. In insurance, companies provided various forms of community welfare outreach, from public health nurses to holiday food baskets for the needy.[32]

The welfare idiom often took on specifically gendered tones. Metropolitan Life created a "house mother" in 1921 whose duties were "indicated by her title":

> She is glad to consult with women Clerks as to their relations with their associates and superiors in the office, their domestic affairs, and their personal worries. She will willingly advise them in regard to any difficulties in or out of the office, or their residences and surroundings. Women Clerks who do not live with near relatives may feel free to ask her advice about boarding-places or living accommodations.

The house mother extended corporate domesticity to males as well. The company stressed that while the house mother "is expected, primarily to be of assistance to the women Clerks, . . . yet she is only too glad to advise with any men Clerks to whom she can be of help."[33] Athletic facilities at Metropolitan Life were open to both men and women, as were courses in "self-improvement." For women only, Metropolitan provided sewing rooms and instructors so that female workers could make their own clothing.[34] Higher wages would have enabled women to buy clothing, but wages would not have expressed so directly the company's message of parental benevolence.

Corporate domesticity justified and softened paternalism, emphasizing the nurturing and guiding role of the corporation in the lives of its employees and clients. At another level, images of mothers and fathers, brothers and sisters, domesticated the public persona of these industries, rendering them benign by analogy. Linking corporate aims to the powerfully charged symbol of nineteenth-century motherhood and the protective insulation of the middle-class family attempted to assuage the era's highly vocal fears of corporate monopoly, greed, and irresponsible masculine competitiveness. From these beginnings, it was but a small step to the professionalized personnel departments and human relations theories of the late 1930s, which in part represented a social science formulation of the financial industries' vision of corporate domesticity.

The image of the family was not solely metaphorical. Another type of corporate family existed among those whose ties of blood or marriage connected them as relatives within a corporation. Corporate nepotism was merely a bureaucratized form of the earlier pattern of favoring family members with choice positions, but it also reinforced the metaphors of kinship promulgated by executives.

Blood ties were present at every level of corporate experience, from executives to the clerical staff, and included both men and women. Particularly at the executive level in insurance and banking, directorates and company officers often were bound together by formal blood or kinship ties. Life insurance agencies encouraged the hiring of relatives in sales, management, and clerical positions, perhaps to keep profits and clientele within a family. Race businesses hired more than their share of siblings and relatives, probably because of the pressures of segregation, which limited the opportunities for educated African Americans.[35] In some instances, women and men seem to have been treated as essentially the same in terms of their kinship ties in corporate work; in other cases, gender determined different traditions of inheritance and participation.

Sons took over merchant houses, manufacturing concerns, or small businesses from their fathers and were promoted into their fathers' businesses. This type of kin connection also was evident in large-scale financial industries and encompassed many executive positions. In 1894, Robert McCurdy, the son of the president of Mutual Life Insurance Company, was appointed to run the company's London office and, by extension, all their European business. James Hazen Hyde, the son of the Equitable's founder, Henry Baldwin Hyde, became a company officer in 1899 when his father died.[36] Inheritance remained an avenue to a business career well into the twentieth century. J. Stinson Scott started as an agent in his father's insurance firm in 1926 and was promoted to general agent, probably on the senior Scott's death, in 1931. John R. Hegeman, the son of Metropolitan Life's president John Hegeman, was an officer of the company from 1892 until 1921. Richard T. Dow, the son and grandson of New England Mutual executives, began service in the Actuarial Department in 1954.[37] New England Mutual retained four family lines at the executive level, two of them notable for their extensiveness and longevity. The Homans family supplied three company physicians—father, son and grandson. The Foster family provided four executives, from Dwight Foster, who was counsel for the company between 1868 and 1884, to his son, grandson, and great-grandson, who variously served as counsels, president, chairmen of the board, vice-presidents, and treasurers, finally bringing the dynasty to an end in 1960. North Carolina Mutual Life's tradition has emphasized the importance of generational continuity at all levels.[38] The Alexander family of Boston contributed six officers to the Equitable between 1859 and 1951: three directors, two presidents, and a secretary.[39]

Direct inheritance from father to son and the hiring of sons and grandsons were typical forms of kin-based succession, but young men also could become "sons" by marrying the boss's daughter. In 1890, an insurance trade paper announced the marriage of the daughter of a life insurance agent to a member of her father's firm, probably a partner or a son of a partner.[40] In the early 1940s, Robert C. Jordan married Alison Warren Smith, the daughter of George Willard Smith, president of New England Mutual from 1929 to 1951. Jordan later became chief financial officer of the company in 1968 and also served on the board of directors from 1971 to 1983.[41] Sometimes, kinship ties reinforced or continued blood ties or simply resulted from propinquity. In the early twentieth century, the directors of the Union National Bank of Wilmington, Delaware, for example, became part of a complex genealogy when James Price, the president in 1908, married Margaret Tatnall Starr, the widow of former director Isaac Starr and the sister of director Edward Tatnall. Thus, president Price was related by marriage to two of the bank's directors, and Margaret Tatnall Starr Price's willingness to marry within the business kept its resources and control in family hands.[42] At North Carolina Mutual Life, the three principals were united through marriage: Fannie Jones, stepsister of founder John Merrick, married president C. C. Spaulding, who was the nephew of company officer Dr. A. M. Moore.[43]

Siblings sometimes worked at the same company, occasionally, as in the case of Vivian and Walter Schlump of Provident Mutual Life, in the same department. Black insurance companies often included siblings. Sisters Dora, Bessie, and Pearlie Whitted, for example, all were clericals in the home-office staff of North Carolina Mutual Life in the early twentieth century.[44]

It was uncommon for fathers to include their daughters in businesses, yet in the sales area of the insurance industry, quite a few daughters joined their fathers' agencies. These familial links include some of the earliest references to female insurance agents. In 1880, Fannie Stocking succeeded her father in his insurance agency after his death. When her father died in 1890, "Miss E. L. Buel" continued to run his agency and was appointed agent for all the companies he had represented.[45] This pattern of female inheritance was uncommon

The North Carolina Mutual Life Quartet, ca. 1920. Left to right: Hattie Livas, Lyda Merrick, Susan (Gille) Norfleet, Martha Merrick, Bessie A. J. Whitted. Interconnected family relations were common in the financial industries but were especially important for African American companies. All of these women worked for the company and were the wives, daughters, or sisters of male employees. *Courtesy of* NCM.

in manufacturing industries; insurance agencies, in fact, may have represented a special avenue into management and high-ticket sales for the daughters of white-collar men, partly because these businesses retained vestiges of the older familial organizational form.

One outstanding instance of a father providing a daughter entree into the financial industries is the case of Lucy Jane Wright. Her father, Elizur Wright, was a famous abolitionist who went on to become one of the first actuaries in the nation. Wright was widely connected in the insurance world, acted as actuary for several companies, and was for several years the insurance commissioner of the state of Massachusetts. In 1853 he invented a machine that could calculate reserve valuation tables quickly and accurately. As a teenager, Lucy Jane trained in the practical applications of mathematics, particularly civil and mechanical engineering. For eight years she was Wright's principal assistant while he was insurance commissioner, and in 1866, at the age of twenty-four, she became actuary for the Union Mutual Life Insurance Company of Maine, working out of its home office in Boston. Lucy Wright surely was one of the youngest female actuaries ever and one of the only female actuaries in the nineteenth century. Her position clearly resulted from her father's connections.[46]

A combination of inheritance and marital ties also allowed female executives to act as the heads of large and small companies. Sometimes a woman became an executive or chief of a board of directors by virtue of her relationship with her husband. Margaret Tatnall Starr Price helped cement and maintain a banking directorate simply through her role as a wife. There is no record, however, that she took any active role in running the bank. Tradition in life insurance stresses that women first became agents by taking over a husband's debits when he became ill or died.[47] This practice was in keeping with longstanding methods of business operation in which widows or married women could operate as *femes sole* in their husbands' absence or death. Alice Pratt Berdell Pedder became the secretary-treasurer of the Conservative Water Company of Los Angeles in 1910 because her husband Wilmer had been president. She succeeded her husband as president of the company on his death in 1932 and ran the company until she died in 1947. Sometime in the 1890s, Debbie B. Coleman became a director of the First National Bank of Lebanon, Pennsylvania. Although her relationship to the bank is not entirely clear from the surviving evidence, she was probably the widow of one of the first directors, G. Dawson Coleman. Two other Colemans, possibly their sons (one was named B. Dawson Coleman), continued as directors after 1905. This pattern of executive relations also obtained in race businesses. When the founder and chief officer of Atlanta Life Insurance Company, Alonzo Herndon, died in 1927, his wife Jessie Gillespie Herndon became first vice-president. Women also could use their marital relationships to extend themselves into other business ventures. In 1880, Laura D. Maxwell, who worked as an agent in her husband's insurance firm, was admitted to the bar in Iowa. She probably acted as attorney for the firm but may also have used her position as a springboard for other legal work.[48]

Some female executives actually directed their companies. Alice Pedder, for example, managed not only the water company but extensive real estate holdings as well. Others may not have been active in management. Debbie Coleman probably left the management of the family bank to her sons. Jessie Herndon, although a director of Atlanta Life and its major stockholder, left the actual management of the company to her stepson Norris, Alonzo's son by a previous marriage. However, even female executives who did not participate directly in the affairs of their companies were more than mere figureheads. They played important roles in keeping social networks intact and thereby maintained their companies' social and economic position. Good connections were critical to success. In order to nurture the political relations that might secure favorable legislation, for example, and to ensure a company's financial well-being, elite men and women cultivated relationships with prominent people outside the company. Like the all-male clubs and fraternal organizations or the interlocking directorates of major financial companies, executive women's informal entertaining or formal charitable work could provide an aura of community legitimacy. Jessie Herndon, for example, was one of the most important social figures in black Atlanta, and she kept the company's profile high and respectable. In addition to her executive duties, Alice Pedder was involved in the American Red Cross, the Women's Auxiliary to the National Council of the Episcopal Church, and several philanthropic social clubs.[49]

Metropolitan Life's Bayer family represents the third and most common type of corporate family: those involved in a metaphorical and organizational kinship structure by virtue of employment. These fictive corporate family ties were created, expressed, and integrated into the office bureaucracy largely through leisure. The physical envelope of the office building was only a portion of the corporate space in which work relations were articulated and experienced. The fictive corporate family was constructed in offices but also in people's homes, at outdoor picnics and field days, and in conferences at resorts. The resulting corporate family was not always a happy one; divisions of gender, class, and race expressed the differing goals of executives, managers, and workers, and of men and women. It was, however, a complex mixture of harmony and discord that perhaps mirrored actual family life better than its promulgators supposed.

Even wives who never took executive titles could perform as social functionaries, using their family circle as a business setting for entertaining their husbands' employees. J. R. Ford, superintendent of the New Haven, Connecticut, John Hancock office, was visited one evening at home by "the whole of his office staff and many friends." The agents presented Mrs. Ford with an album with photographs of all sixteen of the office agents. "Refreshments were served and the evening spent with music and song" and Ford's stories about his twenty-one years as an insurance salesman. The wife of superintendent Hill of the Greenpoint, Long Island, district of the Prudential entertained her husband's entire staff "in her spacious parlors. For several hours business troubles were cast aside, and music, recitations and a bountiful repast were enjoyed."[50] At a supper given by a Metropolitan Life agency superintendent for his staff in 1890, his wife and the wives of several staff members "were present and added . . . to the brightness and pleasure of the evening."[51] Some of these gatherings were not limited to workers and included the families of both employers and employees. The superintendent of the Cincinnati Prudential office, early in 1890, gave "an elegant supper" in a local business building—possibly the office itself—during which his wife and the wives of several agents entertained the guests by singing.[52] At these celebrations the distinctions blurred between home and office, public and private, real and corporate families. Women's presence reinforced the festive leisure atmosphere, and women's domestic labor provided food and a pleasant environment. The social work of "corporate wives" cut across class divisions, although their social entertainments differed vastly in content.[53]

By the 1920s, official management wisdom had enshrined the role of wives in the success of life insurance salesmen. Louis F. Paret, an important codifier of management thought in sales work, observed in 1926, "the cooperation of the agents' wives is an essential factor in agency spirit-building." He believed they should be included in social gatherings for their own enjoyment but also as official speakers who could address the importance of family support for building agents' confidence. W. F. Winterble, another influential management thinker, emphasized that it was important to have a man's wife present when trying to recruit insurance salesmen. Her support or lack of it could make the difference.[54] Wives of financial industry professionals often attended conventions with their husbands and became involved in their planning and festivities as chairwomen of committees, as players in golf and tennis tournaments, as musicians, and occasionally as speakers in informal settings. Wives of agents also were encouraged to become familiar with the insurance offerings so they could generate interest in them among members of their women's clubs.[55]

The mingling of work and leisure and of employers and employees that took place at domestic gatherings had long been an aspect of work. Artisans traditionally boarded apprentices, and merchants adopted this pattern for their clerks in the eighteenth century. In the offices of the early nineteenth century, clerks sometimes were apprenticed to merchants with whom they lived.[56] By the late nineteenth century, employees seldom lived with their employers, but the less structured relations of the precorporate era continued in smaller offices. It was not uncommon, for example, for insurance agents or clerks in branch offices to join their supervisor for a supper or party either at his home or in a restaurant or club rented for the occasion. On New Year's Eve, 1889, the superintendent of People's Insurance Company in Pawtucket, Rhode Island, "gave his staff a supper. . . . The boys all had a good time, and spent an evening long to be remembered." In 1917, Wells Fargo agent J. T. Middleton of the company's Sedalia, Missouri, agency gave a turkey supper for the "boys" in the office the day after Thanksgiving.[57]

Some large, company-sponsored events ritualized the more informal gatherings of the small office and connected executives to others within and outside the company. In April 1897, the board of New England Mutual gave an elaborate dinner honoring the fiftieth anniversary of the election of Benjamin F. Stevens as the company secretary. The dinner, held at the posh Exchange Club

Top and bottom: C. C. Spaulding, the president of North Carolina Mutual Life, joins his employees and many members of their families for his birthday party in August 1923. (Spaulding, in glasses, is standing just above the word *Mutual.*) "Papa" Spaulding was an important father figure to both the company and the African American financial community of Durham. *Courtesy of* DUL.

in Boston, included a ten-course meal, which began with oysters on the half shell. Fifty-three men attended to commemorate this anniversary.[58] At a party in 1923 honoring the forty-ninth birthday of North Carolina Mutual's president C. C. Spaulding, ninety-one staff and family members got together at the company's home office for a celebration. The party even included seven young children aged about three to ten and one baby.[59]

In the gray area between work and family relations, the metaphors of corporate domesticity so common in the financial industries often described actual work relations. The fact that social events were reported in trade papers, and later in company newsletters, suggests that their function in cementing office ties and furthering business aims was well recognized. In fact, such informal events often took on a formal, or at least ritual, quality: in many reports, everyone always enjoyed themselves, and gifts often were exchanged. Storytelling and reminiscences encouraged those present to work harder by creating an atmosphere of camaraderie and fellowship. Gatherings reinforced the alleged democratic team spirit of office work, at least for some workers, by bringing together employees and their families with the boss's family.

This type of activity continued in such forms as office birthday or retirement parties. However, managers and executives in large companies or offices also promoted more formalized interactions between unequal members of the corporate hierarchy with large company or organizational outings. For example, in 1904 the manager of the Des Moines Equitable Life agency "gave a combined love feast and battle rally" to his agency staff. About fifty people attended, and after eating they were exhorted to sell more insurance and were presented with prizes based on the amount of business already done.[60] Although some of the specifics of this event were identical to less formal entertainments, the overall tone was quite different. Instead of an intimate evening with co-workers and family, the Iowa "love feast and battle rally" was a large, formal event. The intent of the two types of event was identical: to create a feeling of group solidarity. But in large gatherings, the end was reached by an expanded set of relationships, a more formal setting, and a sense of ritualized events rather than the more informal, at-home suppers of the smaller office.

To some extent, the differences in these two types of office event charted a change over time. Spurred by the growth of many companies by the early twentieth century, large corporate gatherings became much more common and more integrated into management strategies, even as more informal events continued. The shift to large-scale corporate organization replaced personalized, informal leisure activities with bureaucratic, highly structured leisure relations. By the early twentieth century, corporate leisure activities had formalized the familial relations of the early nineteenth century master/apprentice system. Three essential types of corporate leisure had evolved by World War I. First, company-sponsored leisure activities ranged from formal suppers for select staff to large outings or vacations for an entire office. Second, professional organizations used leisure as a way to bring together disparate and geographically separated members of the professional community for mutual education and socializing. Finally, in company-affiliated leisure activities, people played together because they had generated friendships in the workplace. In all three types, systematic management tried to capture the meanings of leisure for bureaucratic purposes. How well it succeeded is uncertain, but it is clear that corporate leisure became an important part of the experience of office work.

Company-sponsored gatherings initially emphasized business relations. They normally included everyone in a firm and were designed to encourage "family spirit." Among the earliest of such events were the organized recreations provided for industrial workers, such as the facilities at George Pullman's company town on Lake Calumet, south of Chicago. By 1882, the skilled employees and other residents of Pullman could attend annual regattas and track-and-field competitions. One grandstand on the company's recreational island accommodated seven thousand spectators.[61] The National Cash Register Company's annual outings began in the early 1890s. Employees traveled on trains paid for by the company to Indiana or Ohio for camping and other outdoor activities. The NCR trips grew to huge dimensions: In 1905, seventeen hundred workers vacationed in Port Huron, Michigan, at company expense.[62] This type of event began to appear just before World War I in financial industries. The Provident Mutual Life company started what became annual "Get Together" meetings in 1912—dinners for all home-office employees, where they listened to inspirational speeches delivered by the company officers. Company president Asa Wing observed at the first gathering that such meetings were necessary because the company had grown so large that it was impossible for everyone to get to know one another during the normal course of business. "We no longer knew each other as well as we should have wished," he told the assembled company. Meetings were not simply social events; they also were about business. President Wing observed in his closing remarks, "I hope that from this time forward we will cultivate what we hope to call the 'Provident spirit,' that each one has a real part in the work, and that each one feels just as much responsibility for the Provident as the president does." In a similar event in 1917, Wells Fargo Nevada National Bank sponsored a dinner at the Palace Hotel in San Francisco to celebrate the renewal of the bank's charter. Ten officers and about two hundred employees attended.[63]

By the 1920s, formal company outings were structured events, with printed programs advertising ball games, track events, music, and dance, including pages for exchanging written comments as mementoes. Outings closely resembled the field days of industrial recreations.[64] Reports in employee newsletters included the winners of sports contests, humorous anecdotes, and photographs.[65] In the early 1920s, for example, New England Mutual's pilgrimage to the seaside resort of Swampscott, Massachusetts, was an important event. At the 1923 meeting, about 200 of the 279 members of the home-office staff were present at Swampscott, including many executives and managers.[66] Some outings encompassed invitations to the entire office; others were for selected groups, such as general agents. Corporate employees, their families, and friends were invited to all these types of outings.[67] By the late 1930s, the Provident Get Together had evolved into a field day, where employees of the home office in Philadelphia joined in food, games, dancing, and other outdoor sports during one weekday in summer.[68] This type of outing involved intergroup mixing, as executives, high-level managers, supervisors, and clericals mingled. In some cases, the company-sponsored outing could become a community event as well. In 1917, Provident Mutual put on an athletic carnival for a large local audience. Patterned on the Olympic games, participants engaged in basketball, potato races, and a "girls' ten-pin race."[69]

An important aspect of company gatherings of professionals and managers was the notion that such meetings reinforced the sense of a company as both a literal and a metaphorical family, at the same time targeting certain groups within the company for special treatment. General agents' meetings were common in insurance companies, usually under the auspices of a local or national professional organization or only loosely unified by company affiliation.[70] One good example of the complex meanings such events expressed is the meeting of New England Mutual's general agents on four weekdays in July 1927, at Mackinac Island, Michigan. Executives (including the president), general agents, their wives, and in at least four cases their daughters vacationed together on the island. Company executives designed the outing so that a minority of the time was spent in meetings. Participants devoted most of the time to sports, games, and "the social side."

Important to making this meeting a success was the participation of the agents' wives, who were treated as both honored guests and members of the company sales team. They were introduced to the company president "alone, . . . no mere man was allowed in the room." President Daniel F. Appel addressed the women specifically as corporate wives, with the message that their interests in the company were vital "because the Company is the bond of unity that draws us all together." An unofficial report of President Appel's talk centered on the observation that while he did not preach to the wives, he nonetheless inspired them to be "more content, more helpful, stronger, and therefore better fitted for the tasks and the fullest enjoyment of home." For their part, the women made a formal presentation to the president's wife, telling her they had "felt at home. The lovely, friendly atmosphere that you and the other wives of the official family created here . . . made it a real homecoming." They were "thrilled" with the spirit of togetherness and grateful for the "big-sisterly interest" Mrs. Appel had taken in them and their families. Mr.

Appel also conferred "artistic miniature silver cups" on four daughters of agents. Both men and women also were awarded prizes for "the [golf] putting and bridge contests."[71] The Mackinac Island meeting, and others like it, clearly made the incorporation of managers' or agents' families a priority of company policy. Whether or not this report's effusions represented the genuine emotions of those present is impossible to gauge. Nevertheless, using metaphors of family relations, along with special treatment and rewards, executives and their wives encouraged the agents and their families to identify the company as "home" and its personnel as kin.

For those involved in race businesses, socializing had additional importance: It could strengthen ties within and among black communities. North Carolina Mutual Life Insurance Company's outings, which began in 1904, were designed to bring together not only the company personnel but the local black population. The first was an agency meeting at the North Carolina Colored State Fair. Trains brought the "Mutual Family" to the fair, where the agents and managers mingled with the general crowds, enjoyed themselves, and incidentally advertised the company. The prosperous-looking Mutual agents suggested the company's affluence and security. In 1908, the company began "superintendents' conferences" at the home office; they were not only important managerial meetings but also vital summer events for black Durham.

Socializing also was one extension of the material support African Americans provided one another in segregated towns and cities where public facilities might not be available. During the North Carolina Mutual Life conferences, agents and managers who came from out of town stayed in churches or with church- or company-affiliated black families, since there were no African American hotels in Durham. While the product of segregation, mingling with the local community reinforced the ties between the company and powerful institutions such as the churches. Furthermore, since the mission of such conferences was partly to educate the public and heighten the company's profile, staying in homes or churches more easily incorporated Mutual agents into the community and the community into the company. In addition to the purposes Mutual's outings shared with financial industries generally—reinforcing fictive kin ties and encouraging class identification—the company's outings also spoke to important racial issues.[72] In segregated markets, socializing strengthened the solidarity of the black business sector and helped with customer relations. Rencher Harris, an officer of the Bankers' Fire Insurance Company of Durham, noted that on a business trip to Memphis, local people treated him to supper and a ride through the city's business section. At home in Durham, his wife entertained visiting fraternity brothers by organizing a recital.[73]

For race businesses, company gatherings could be important sources of information and solidarity. In 1921, North Carolina Mutual Life's president C. C. Spaulding inaugurated Saturday morning "Forums." These meetings began with all participants singing a chorus of the company song to the tune of "Old Time Religion." The Forum was a kind of pep rally based on a ceremony Spaulding had observed at a black fraternal meeting in Arkansas. In addition to company songs and spirituals, the meeting included prayer and self-improvement exercises in the form of spelling bees and informal debates. Spaulding also brought in outside speakers on a variety of topics, including W. E. B. DuBois, A. Philip Randolph, and Adam Clayton Powell. The Forums were opportunities to stimulate racial pride, cement the ties of the "Mutual family," and provide employees with educational information, all under company auspices.[74]

Events arranged by professional organizations repeated the idea of company outings aimed at a specialized group. Local or national professional organizations sponsored group outings or conventions beginning at least in the 1890s. For example, in June of that year the general agent for Northwestern Mutual Life Insurance, a Mr. Gage, invited the entire Michigan Life Insurance Agents' Association, along with their "wives and lady friends," to his summer home on Grosse Isle. More than fifty partygoers were taken to the island by boat, where they were "made to feel that for the time being he or she owned the grounds."[75] As various managerial groups professionalized between the 1890s and World War I, they increasingly adopted this recreational form of annual meeting. The California Bankers' Association met for three days in May 1909 at the Hotel Del Monte, on the northern California coast. The Del Monte was a magnificently landscaped resort hotel, boasting 1,366 varieties of trees and more than 90 types of roses on its spacious grounds. Special Pullman trains left San Francisco and Los Angeles for the meeting. In addition to speeches and informational programs on topics such as bank advertising, foreign exchange, and preventive legislation, the convention included a golf tournament, tennis, walking tours, automobile trips to local sights, boating, and swimming in the hotel's saltwater bathhouses. The bankers' wives also attended, and they participated in the general festivities as well as in special "ladies'" events, such as tea at the homes of local banking executives and dignitaries. The convention was scheduled on a Memorial Day weekend so that those who attended could extend their stay two more days if they wished to make a complete vacation.[76] Formal professional organizations blurred family and work, intruding corporate concerns into private life.

Within the professional organizations, racial and gender differences emphasized these clubs' exclusivity in part by reinforcing their gendered and racial nature. The National Association of Bank Women, a professional organization with eighty members in 1923, held formal dinners to discuss developments in banking, meet other women, and exchange ideas. Primarily an East Coast organization in the early 1920s, by the early 1930s the organization had a wider representation and had made an effort to associate itself with the much larger white, male professional organization, the American Banking Association. The women's group held their meeting at the same time as the men's group and invited some of the ABA's officers to be guest speakers. The organization was dominated by women who nominally were cashiers and managers but who were concentrated in personnel work and women's departments.[77] These women all were white, and the organization did not include any of the African American women involved in banking in the years before 1930. Nor were women welcome in the black men's insurance organization, the National Negro Insurance Association, begun in 1921, until the 1938 election of Mamie C. Hickerson as the organization's statistician. Black women did not form strictly professional organizations, opting instead for more broadly conceived, community-oriented clubs and associations.[78]

Whites used racial difference in these organizations to create a sense of white solidarity. At the New England Mutual General Agents Association annual meeting in 1931, attendees were given a music sheet for sing-alongs. Songs ranged from straightforward renditions of "Happy Days Are Here Again" and "My Wild Irish Rose" to adaptations of well-known songs. Words sung to the tune of "Old Black Joe" clearly reminded the agents that selling insurance was work but did so through racist humor and self-parody:

> Gone are the days when I lay in bed till nine;
> Gone are the times when I wasted hours so fine;
> Gone, gone for aye, for I've wakened with a jerk;
> I hear the prospects loudly calling, "WORK, WORK, WORK."[79]

The racial element of this song, which invoked a minstrel-era stereotype about "Black Joe" for a commentary on laziness, was typical of the professional meeting's effort to create a sense of solidarity—in this case among white male agents—by emphasizing their exclusivity.

The pattern for events such as the Benjamin Stevens dinner, North Carolina Mutual Life's Forum and excursions, and most managerial gatherings was the homosocial club or fraternal organization rather than the paternal apprentice/master gatherings of the company-wide event. Professional meetings were designed to reinforce differences between executives, managers, and other office workers. They emphasized a class, race, or gender solidarity among the corporate elite, sometimes at the expense of lower-level employees.

Beginning around World War I (and continuing, in some cases, into the present), financial industries also used leisure time to reinforce formal corporate relations among all classes. Similar to efforts exclusively for managers and executives, the events included both on- and off-site opportunities for office employees to get together in interest groups for sports, music, or other leisure activities. On-site employee groups such as choral or band societies or social clubs became common by World War I. Around that time, employees in local offices of the Wells Fargo Company formed Fargo Way clubs. Designed to combine business with pleasure, the clubs varied widely from one place to another, although all were under company auspices. In Arizona, the Douglas-Bisbee Club discussed efficiency and toured industrial plants but also attended a show in the evening. The New York City Fargo Way Club united the company's "commerical men . . . to swap experiences for their mutual advantage." Chicago had two clubs, one for men and one for women, which sponsored activities separately and together. The men's club, for example, included an active orchestra. At the founding of the women's club in late 1916, the men's orchestra was joined by female employees who played the piano or sang. The women's group had a choral society that also entertained at meetings. Joint-club affairs included dances for all members.[80] At Metropolitan Life, employees could choose from a glee club, a choral society, and a band for their musical expression.[81]

Clubs or associations were sponsored by the parent company, but employees organized them and supported them strongly. Female employees began a women's Fargo Way Club, for example. The club had 150 members within months of its founding. Individual clubs came and went, but the impetus behind the corporate leisure association remained strong throughout the 1920s and into the 1930s. The groups provided social continuity throughout the year, bridging the gaps between less frequent company-wide outings. On the one hand, participation in these activities probably was necessary to maintain one's job position or to become "managerial material"; in that sense, participation was an unpaid, extracurricular aspect of work. On the other hand, workers might have their own reasons for joining, only one of which may have been business advancement. Since no one expected participants to be professional athletes or musicians, winning at baseball or executing a flawless solo could be a source of personal satisfaction not directly related to job performance. Personal interest surely helps explain the long-term popularity among workers of these athletic, musical, and social groups.

Off-site activities included company-sponsored team sports and large company outings. In supporting them, management essentially captured the forms of informal organizations in which employees indulged on their own time. In the late nineteenth century, male clerical workers often belonged to baseball or cricket leagues. Baseball in particular seems to have been a popular sport with office workers, perhaps because it replicated many of the job skills necessary for white-collar work: Nineteenth-century sports writers and players alike "linked time, money, and the speed" of baseball together and claimed that the sport reinforced mental and physical clerical skills.[82] The switch to company-affiliated baseball teams at first was very informal: Team members continued to wear the uniforms of their own noncorporate teams, although they formed groups from a pool of fellow employees and represented the company at inter-

New England Mutual employees' baseball team, 1902. Their casual poses and varied uniforms were typical of early corporate sports teams. *Courtesy of* TNE.

mural events. Early team photographs showed groups of individualized men, each with a different costume and each striking a highly personal pose. By World War I, team photographs strove for the sense of interchangeable parts that, if not in uniform, nonetheless communicated a sense of corporate rather than individualized play.[83]

Company-sponsored teams played other teams within or outside the company. Metropolitan Life's men's baseball team participated in company tournaments. In 1923, Metropolitan Life's West Coast track-and-field team competed as members of the San Francisco Business Mens' Athletic Association in the northern California Associated Athletic Federation's Track and Field Meet in Oakland. By World War I, an employee could engage in virtually any sport he or she chose. In 1919, the Wells Fargo Nevada National Bank sponsored baseball, golf, basketball, football, handball, tennis, and hiking. At Provident Mutual Life, men's and women's bowling leagues competed with teams from seven other trust and insurance companies beginning in 1916. The Metropolitan Social and Athletic Association for the West Coast office reported in 1922 on the recent introduction of handball and plans for a future tournament, a bowling match between married and single men, swimming for female employees at the YWCA, as well as volleyball, tennis, and hiking.[84] Generally, athletic teams or events were segregated by gender, but women formed teams in all the major sports. In 1923, for example, the "girls'" basketball team of Metropolitan Life competed in a league that included female office workers at the Standard Oil Company.[85] In the 1922 season, the men's basketball team of Metropolitan Life in San Francisco played against, among others, teams from the San Francisco Boys Club, the First National Bank, Wells Fargo, the Chamber of Commerce, and Mercantile Trust. Such games united a local commercial and financial community through athletics.[86] The clubs did not preclude workers from engaging in sporting events outside company auspices, but they did capture at least a portion of their allegiance.

Large company outings provided intermittent occasions for all the personnel in a company—clericals, managers, and executives—to "break down the barriers, overcome our cold reserve, destroy constraint and indifference, and . . . increase our mutual esteem," as one outing report put it.[87] Sometimes teams were divided according to departments at company sports events, such as the Wells Fargo Nevada National Bank's interdepartment leagues, which pitted Bookkeeping against the Clearing House.[88] More often organizers invented other, more apparently social, criteria. Single men against married men was a common opposition, for example.[89] At the Provident Mutual field day in 1937, men's and women's teams for the potato and wheelbarrow races were given team colors, such as red and yellow, rather than company divisions. Corporate hierarchy remained in the form of team captains, who invariably were officers or supervisors. In a baseball game between various Provident Life company officers in 1937, the highest-ranking among them pitched. In women's sports, female departmental managers captained the baseball teams and usually did the pitching.[90] When officers or managers joined in the general games, then, they joined as privileged players. Class, status, and gender differences between groups thus were reinforced at outings, even as they seemed to bridge those differences.

The use of sports metaphors to describe appropriate behavior in corporate work, particularly sales, compounded the problematic nature of corporate-sponsored leisure. Sports metaphors appeared in every form, from the most simple references to "teamwork" to more complex and extended analogies. Harold P. Cooley, an insurance agency manager for New England Mutual, likened sales to a game in "Play Golf and Be Yourself." The golfer was a life insurance salesman, and the sales prospect a golf ball dangerously hooking into sand traps or resting quietly on the fairway. The proper "club"—sales pitch—would achieve success, and the best life insurance salesmen knew how to think on their feet, maneuver into position for a good "shot," and put the ball in the cup.[91] Most people recognized the function of sports events as managerial training grounds and sites for identifying managerial material, giving these events a strong instrumentalist dimension. Articles in employee newsletters emphasized the energy of participants, their good humor, and their interactions with other players and the audience, all issues related to corporate managerial skills.[92]

Corporate-sponsored leisure also expressed the racial divisions of early-twentieth-century office work. African Americans appear almost nowhere in the photographs of white companies' office outings. Minstrel shows, using blackfaced white performers, were popular entertainments at white conventions and outings.[93] Provident Mutual is the only company that included information about black workers in its company publications or at outings, and that was relatively late, in the 1930s. Provident divided men's baseball teams by race but emphasized their corporate job position as the source of their "rivalry." The contest between the "Mechanics" and the "Porters" was also a competition between white and black men's teams. It brought together on the field two different positions in the male corporate hierarchy, as well as two races. Mechanics clearly followed the artisanal or craft tradition associated with white working-class manhood, while the Porters grew out of African American men's involvement in various forms of personal service.[94] Black employees had a separate field day, on a different date from that of the white employees, and company newsletter reports of their field day were brief—one page, compared to several pages for the white employees. Since a good deal of the impetus behind company-sponsored outings related to corporate advancement, the reports of games and events among white employees were more detailed than those of blacks. Blacks could not expect promotion out of the racial job track, so white management's concern with their activities during field day centered on the employees' alleged gratitude toward the company rather than their interpersonal skills or conduct under pressure.[95]

Company outings, like their less formal predecessors, simultaneously reinforced the corporate ideal of harmonious familial relations and extruded corporate organization into real family and leisure relations. The workplace and its interactions, in other words, were not limited to a specific address in space and time. Management had to maneuver between generating the happy, democratic corporate family and ensuring that traditional social divisions of race, class, and gender were respected. Exactly how these efforts fared is impossible to know; however, workers' activities and attitudes suggest, if not managerial failure, at least compromise. Managerial aims, for example, cannot fully explain the fact that one runner in the African American women's Provident Mutual foot race persisted and "finished the race in her stocking feet" when she lost the heel of her shoe, or the wildly cheering crowd at a Wells Fargo baseball game.[96]

Formalized leisure activities did not exhaust the avenues for company-affiliated social experience. If the social pages of company newsletters are to be believed, male and female workers spent enormous amounts of time with their co-workers off the job, engaging in various kinds of leisure activity or furthering their own social agendas. Some employees were blood kin or met and married co-workers while on the job. Siblings sometimes worked for the same companies and probably helped one another get jobs. For example, Ed McDowell was the supervisor in the personnel division of Metropolitan Life's West Coast office, while his brother Art worked in Auditing.[97] The personal columns of employee newsletters were filled with teasing suggestions regarding the social affairs of employees, often noting the ways proximity in the workplace could lead to romance. The September 1919 issue of the *Wells Fargo Nevadan* recounted in great detail the backgrounds and wedding plans of two couples who had met on the job. One was Clarice Koon and Arthur Durbrow, and the other was Lena Kingsbury and Sam Clarke, who were both clerks for the bank.[98]

Male and female workers generated friendships at work that sometimes became more formalized. Employees created noncompany-sponsored, informal clubs that brought employees together for some specific purpose. Thirteen young men of the Provident Mutual in 1895 formed a "Bachelors' Club." Originally, the club was a facetious support group designed to prevent the engagement of Walter Michener, whom the others feared was "slipping." The only club rule was that the first member to marry had to buy dinner for the entire group. Michener soon was entertaining his fellow club members at "a famous old restaurant." According to one member, "The club was a failure—it should have been called the Benedicts' Club."[99] In 1921, nurses in New York who were employed by industry or insurance firms that catered to industrial workers created an organization for "the improvement of their nursing methods and the exchange of helpful ideas."[100] Clearly, such clubs or organizations had no direct corporate function, even though they were reported in the company newsletter and could conceivably provide indirect benefits to a company. Their main purpose was to further the goals of individual workers.

Employees often got together for planned outings, usually including people of the same status or class within a given company. Male and female workers threw parties for one another, vacationed together, or joined ball teams or dancing groups. An article in the *Pacific Coast News* in 1921 reported a public dance at a local hotel that was attended by so many Metropolitan Life employees that "if all the Metropolitanites were to leave the ballroom there would be very few dancing."[101] Male employees planned hunting parties, which the company newsletters often reported with amusement. A group of Metropolitan Life men, in 1930, spent time at a hunting lodge in Carmel, New York. During their hunt, "one crow, a sparrow, a Holstein and three rabbits met their fate at the hands of this unerring band." Wells Fargo hunters included "Cannonball" Baker, "Fuzzy" Granucci, Fred Miller, "Grunt" Lund, and Norm McKinnon, who, despite their colorful nicknames, among them brought home only four quail. Hunters often reported little result, and the newsletter editors joined them in inventing excuses, such as blank shot and lack of practice. Others clearly knew what they were doing: Hal Wingate of Wells Fargo brought in ten quail from a hunting trip.[102] Young bank messenger boys spent time together swimming, hiking, and fishing; indeed, hiking and fishing seem to have been extremely popular with office workers of both sexes and all ages. Metropolitan Life's West Coast employees organized frequent hiking trips that included both men and women. In 1918, eleven men of the Treasury Department of Provident Life arranged an elaborate weekend fishing trip to New Jersey, which included a spontaneous side trip to Fort Dix.[103] Vacation travel sometimes brought two or three workers together for trips during their annual leave. In 1934, five male employees of Provident Mutual took a cruise together in the Caribbean. Women in particular seem to have traveled together frequently. Sometimes, as in the case of Sue Ransome and Camille Stockstille's trip to Lake Tahoe in 1929, the occasion was a chance to renew a friendship made in the office after one worker had quit.[104] Traveling vacations sometimes extended to the families of employees as well. In the summer of 1921, a Mr. Dudley and Mr. McFarland of Metropolitan Life went with their wives to Yosemite and Tahoe for a camping trip.[105]

Finally, employees celebrated with their office companions their private passages—marriages, birthdays, anniversaries—in and out of the office. Probably because of the large number of young, single women in offices, wedding showers were among the most commonly reported items in company newsletters. Daisy Flint of the Policy Division of Metropolitan Life left her office in March 1922 with "her arms filled with beautiful roses and useful gifts." Her friends at work had given her a luncheon party, and then all attended a shower at the bride's aunt's house. Joining an employee's relatives in celebrating these passages may have been quite common.[106] Her friends at work gave Provident Mutual's Sara W. Mathews, of the Actuarial Department, a wedding shower that included gifts; and when Helen Conlin, of the Accounting Department, married in June, one of her attendants was Irene Hopkins, also an employee of the Accounting Department. While women's engagement parties were reported more often in newsletters, men sometimes were feted as well. In May 1923, the fellow employees of Harry Peters, one of the "young swains" of Metropolitan Life's West Coast office, presented him with "a beautiful metal clock with chimes as a wedding present." In addition, Peters was subjected to a great deal of good-humored tricks "for which all young bridegrooms must stand," thereby bringing the rituals of hazing and stag parties into the office.[107] Sometimes, private parties were purely for enjoyment, without any overtones of special celebration. This was true of Ione Heber's party, at which she treated three other company workers to lunch and a play.[108] Employees maintained these friendships even after leaving an office or a company. Married women returned for a visit with old friends or were given baby showers by former office mates.[109]

Some friendships might have existed before the individuals began to work for the same company, but they were maintained in part by sharing the work experience. Christine Anderson, who documented the boarding arrangements of women clericals in Cincinnati in the 1920s and 1930s, found that rooming house networks often replicated working relationships. Friendships made at work or at the boardinghouse overlapped, blurring the separation of work and friendship relations. Young female roomers (and possibly men in male rooming houses as well) alerted their living companions to jobs with their own companies, held wedding showers for co-workers, or vacationed together.[110] The experience of office work was bound up with the family lives and private rituals of personal life rather than separated from them in clear-cut ways. Companies sought to use some of these connections to personal life and reported them in newsletters and built office leisure around them. However, not all aspects of office friendships were accessible to management's manipulation.

The emphasis on the family, metaphorical and actual, did not obscure the tensions inherent in this family life or stop their expression in corporate leisure and work relations. Many employees, both male and female, hid their marriages or reported them much later, declining to share this transition with other office workers even when married women were an accepted part of the office work force.[111] The employee newsletters themselves, so concerned with creating a pleasant and nurturing attitude, often revealed problems in the corporate family. One issue of the *Wells Fargo Nevadan,* for example, contained an article on the unfortunate side effects of "kidding." It observed that new employees often were submitted to a kind of hazing ritual through the ascription of nicknames, accompanied by unkind comments on personal habits, speech, or movements. Some new workers could even be driven from their jobs by kidding, however well intentioned.[112] Drinking on the job was not commonplace, but it did occur, even during Prohibition. Management seems to have been somewhat tolerant about the use of alcohol while on the job. One company newsletter reported a humorous story about a worker, pseudonymously named "Alex," who disguised his office bottle as ink. Workers in another office sent him a bottle of what appeared to be alcohol, and when Alex and "certain old Cronies" took it to "the back room, glasses in hand, throats dry," they found it *was* ink.[113] Alcohol also appeared on special occasions, such as anniversaries or benedict parties. Drinking in the office seems to have been the exception rather than the rule. Nonetheless, it suggests the presence of an older, preindustrial male work tradition in the rationalized office. Drinking alcohol could cement the bonds between men through clandestine or celebratory behavior, but it also could be disruptive and potentially devastating for those who abused it.

Promotion of the heirs of founders or executives also could have unpleasant consequences. Not every father's son was executive material, and ill-suited heirs could affect business in many ways, from not doing their jobs very well to undermining the political and economic standing of the industry. Probably the most dramatic example of the hazards of nepotism came in the behavior of James Hazen Hyde, the son of Equitable's founder, Henry Baldwin Hyde. On his death in 1899, the senior Hyde left James a controlling interest in the company. James was only twenty-three, and he had entered the family business reluctantly after two successful semesters as a graduate student at Harvard. Although he wanted to continue at college, he bowed to his father's wishes that he join the Equitable. Perhaps because he was aware of his son's youth and alternative interests, Henry Hyde promoted a nonrelative, James Alexander, to the position of president and settled only a vice-presidency on his son. Besides, James's short life had already shown a propensity for extravagance and a lack of sensitivity to the fact that financial industries need at least the appearance of conservatism if they are to hold the public trust. James was a highly visible New York figure, known around town for his love of fine horses, outlandish spending habits, and fancy entertainment, such as the lavish and very expensive Louis XIV Ball he gave in 1905 at Sherry's, a prominent New York City club.[114]

James's public behavior ill became the scion of a life insurance family. His spending sprees suggested either that the company's money was lining its officers' pockets or that life insurance as a product was a scam designed to enrich con men. Neither was a welcome possibility to most people in the industry. In 1905, disagreements over James's behavior split the board of directors, and he resigned. The damage, however, had already been done. Behavior that the public had been willing to overlook became *prima facie* evidence of financial impropriety in the climate of suspicion that hovered over the entire industry by that time. The public and press outcry over young Hyde's irresponsible spending habits while an officer of the largest insurance company in the world, the revelation that other officers and directors of the Equitable may have benefited personally from the company's investments, combined with concerns about the appearance of semi-tontine schemes at the Equitable and in the industry at large, led to the first large-scale investigation of the insurance industry, the 1905 New York state Armstrong investigation.[115] James Hazen Hyde was not personally responsible for the housecleaning and industry-wide shake-up the investigation caused; nevertheless, his behavior was the spark that ignited what otherwise might have died down of its own accord.[116] The Hyde example illustrated that successful passage of a business or a position to an heir depended greatly on that individual's character and abilities.

As in most families, not everyone had the same degree of investment in family solidarity, nor the same attitude towards the benefits of family life. The clearest example of this is the racial segregation of the white financial industries. As in other economic sectors, African Americans who worked for white companies worked as cooks, waiters, janitors, elevator operators, and, in the engineering and printing shops, at the dirtiest and most poorly paid jobs. Racial divisions cut across efforts to create either one big industry or one big family. Sporadic efforts at unionization by various groups also indicate differences between management and workers. The company-sponsored union of Provident Mutual Life's clerks, the House of Delegates, was designed to contain and channel employee grievances. It did its job, but not without revealing tensions among the office staff. At one meeting in 1913, for example, company inequities in vacations led to disagreements between those delegates and managers who were present. A meeting the following year aired employee concerns over the introduction of a time clock. Sometimes there were differences between home-office and branch-office staffs. Complaints surfaced that company officers did not treat agents and managers in the field with respect. Morris P. Capen, New England Mutual's home-office manager, recalled an incident from 1905 when he temporarily managed an agency and received a response from a head office department manager which "had rebuke and sting to it, seasoned seemingly by years of practice."[117]

An exchange in 1938 between the president of Metropolitan Life and some agents of the company revealed some of the differences between levels of management. Earlier in the century, Metropolitan Life agents had been involved in unionization efforts, and the result, the Employees Fidelity Organization (EFO), embodied the conflicted nature of white-collar unions: it simultaneously set employees apart, even as it asserted their fidelity to the company. In April 1938, Samuel L. Roth, then president of the EFO, registered an informal complaint with the president of Metropolitan Life, Leroy A. Lincoln, about "managerial abuses." Roth reported that he had heard many stories from different agents and agencies about managers using "ill considered language" to agents and about managers who had "publicly humiliated and embarrassed Agents in the presence of their fellow-men." Further, Roth noted, "in some Districts, men have been treated more like school children than business men." Roth tempered these accusations by asserting his faith that company executives did not condone this type of behavior. But he reported that rumors claimed the executives knew about such activities and did nothing, thereby sanctioning managerial mistreatment. Roth ended his letter by asserting his loyalty to the company and politely requesting an "open expression" of President Lincoln's disapproval of this behavior.

Roth tried to reconcile conflicting positions in this letter. He spoke as the representative of white-collar professionals not far removed from management, as well as of a union formed to protect and defend employees from management. He was both a peer and a subordinate of the company president. Lincoln's response made that paradox clear. The president's letter forcefully repudiated "misconduct," but phrased possible perpetrators broadly as "Managers, Assistant Managers, or Agents," thereby blurring the distinctions the union's complaint had seen as the crux of the problem. He wanted "specifications," facts: "The Company has in the past removed or demoted Managers on these grounds where the facts have been established and there would be no hesitation about following such a course today." He went on, however, to trivialize Roth's concerns and those of the EFO. He did not want to encourage "mere carping criticism by disgruntled Agents, many of whom may prove to be failures as Agents." Lincoln spent most of his letter complaining about agents: they used high-pressure sales techniques, they grumbled and passed blame instead of shouldering responsibility, they accused others without proof. Those agents who were "unable or unwilling" to sell hard but sell fairly "must be replaced by others who are anxious to secure a position and willing to work in behalf of themselves and their families." Lincoln's letter responded to Roth's concerns, but it also tried to preempt any backlash over his rebuke from district and agency managers. Roth and the union saw legitimate grievances that grew out of the organizational inequities of the corporation and demanded to be treated as men, equal to men at the top. Lincoln, in contrast, saw only a sales staff of problematic employees who whined and complained instead of taking on responsibility.[118] So much for the harmonious "family."

More subtle acknowledgments of the troubles in the workplace family came in the form of a kind of modern *carnivale:* ritual events during which workers turned the hierarchy upside down in controlled settings. Among these were parties staged to mark some aspect of a worker's life course. Often, humorous incidents were recalled and corporate aims and attitudes were ridiculed. A 1932 pamphlet from New England Mutual recounted events in the life of a male manager who was about to be married, including his penchant for hiding alcohol in his desk drawer, as well as his generosity in sharing it with a fellow worker. Generally, a part of "Cape's" job as a manager would have been to control such behavior; however, he neither followed the rules nor expected others to do so during the party. Such events were not unbridled free-for-alls; they made their point much like traditional ritual behavior. At a Provident Mutual company picnic in the 1930s, for example, games and sports events encouraged absurdity but also tried to keep it within bounds. A game called "Trip to California" consisted of opening a bag of prepared clothing, dressing as quickly as possible, and racing to a finish line. The bags included oversized baby clothing, extra-large shoes, and men's and women's attire. Men were given bags of women's clothing, and women received men's. Only managers and supervisors competed, while other employees looked on (no doubt laughing and cheering their "favorites" on to victory). The point of this exercise was

At this Field Day soccer game for Provident Mutual Life, ca. 1932, men and women cross-dressed as part of a game designed to break down corporate status and gender relations. *Courtesy of* HM&L.

to use gender assumptions to ridicule managers in a controlled manner. Other games were more open ended, if no less disruptive of the usual gender and status order. A soccer game among employees (and some of their children) during this 1930s outing was noteworthy for the fact that the men wore dresses and the women wore knickers.[119]

Within companies, disagreements about tone and presentation expressed both class and gender differences.[120] A good example of tensions over status and behavior can be seen in the attitude of Helen Farrar Warren Smith, wife of George Willard Smith, an officer of New England Mutual in the 1920s. Helen Smith's report of the general agents' meeting at Mackinac Island, Michigan, in the early 1920s reveals a complex interplay of gender and class issues. She recalled her first such experience as quite unpleasant, predominantly because of the behavior of the men and of then-president Daniel F. Appel: "At the formal dinner, I was disgusted by the half-drunk men, the risqué stories told by Mr. Appel as toastmaster—everything—and I'm afraid, I showed it. I was so disturbed that the woman next to me, Mrs. Edward Allen, a New York City general agent's wife, whispered to me, 'Relax, darling, relax.'" Appel apparently had a reputation for telling "spicy" stories; however, he did apologize later for his behavior at the convention. Helen Smith's story suggests a glimpse of a much larger phenomenon, when put in the context of the lack of censure on alcohol consumption and the general reputation life insurance and other salesmen had for ribald behavior. We could speculate that what Helen Smith experienced was commonplace at most agents' conventions. Yet, Mrs. Edward Allen apparently took the behavior in stride when she counseled Smith not to register such visible distaste.[121] Mrs. Allen, in fact, was an active general agent's wife. At a later convention in 1927 (when Daniel Appel was still president), Mrs. Allen joined her husband on stage for a series of duets based on popular songs. Mrs. Allen wrote the words, which were verses satirizing and commemorating company individuals and events. She also participated as one of two women in charge of the "ladies'" golf tournament.[122] Clearly, as the wife of an agent, Mrs. Allen threw herself wholeheartedly into the festivities, perhaps garnering her own, individual satisfaction from her efforts.

The wife and children of Metropolitan Life agent John Bayer were not directly connected to his work and no doubt had full, complete lives in the context of their own family. But the Bayers also were inextricably bound up with John Bayer's employer, whether they wanted to be or not. Mrs. Bayer might have attended an agents' convention and been scandalized—or perhaps delighted—by the experience. The children could have been recipients of convention prizes or joined in the sack races at a company outing. Relations with John Bayer's company would not have dominated their lives, but they would have been important, since the work of selling life insurance involved some degree of participation and commitment from the entire family if John Bayer was to be a success.

By the early twentieth century, domestic and corporate life intermingled for workers, managers, and executives. The images of motherhood used as corporate logos and the practices of corporate domesticity privatized the public corporation. The familial rhetoric and structure provided a schematic for work relations. Fictional kinship ties of corporate organization connected the wives and children of white-collar men to the work force. To some extent, corporate leisure activities institutionalized the family relations of the early-nineteenth-century master/apprentice system. Furthermore, as in the early nineteenth-century, kinship ties continued to weave actual family life through the web of corporate organization. These two types of corporate family—the fictive and the actual—were critical to the shape of modern financial industries.

Corporate leisure filled in the interstices of organizational charts and office spaces with ties of consanguinity and competitive play. But beyond efforts to shape workplace leisure, employees themselves generated their own extracorporate ties that built on workplace relations and were perhaps dependent on them. Workers met and married in the office, went on vacations together, celebrated important life transitions with parties and gifts, or, in the alternative, withheld knowledge of important events in their lives from co-workers. Differences of race, class, and gender continued to undermine the "family spirit" of financial companies. The capacity to upset managerial aims was inherent in the different types of group solidarity workers could form. Central to these divisions were those created by and expressed through gender, and it is to the transformative possibilities of gender in the office that we now must turn.

CHAPTER SIX

An "Eve-less Paradise"

The Gender of Self and Work

In 1937, Elizabeth MacGibbon published *Manners in Business,* a book of suggestions for women's office behavior. *Manners* capitalized on the accumulated wisdom of fifty years of advice literature for female office workers. The book's recommendations and admonishments virtually were identical to those of late-nineteenth-century prescriptive works.[1] This literature played on the theme that a business career was a means of personal and economic mobility but also a battleground. The battle consisted of using women's alleged weapons—moral strength, empathy, common sense—to retain a womanly nature in the midst of a male world filled with temptations. Woman's part was to soften and refine business and businessmen. Her reward for fulfilling this female role would be marriage and an honorable retreat from the arena of contention.

This virtually archetypal image of business life as struggle and reward certainly was not unusual. It figured significantly in notions of middle-class manhood in the nineteenth and early twentieth centuries. What is striking, however, is that a female worker's relation to labor was articulated in a similar context of conflict, domination, subordination, and transcendence phrased in gendered terms. The basic question of what it meant to be a worker in the modern office found expression as a tension between manhood and womanhood, a tension resolved by proper gender behavior and relations. The underlying issue of wage labor, for both men and women, was the relative power of workers in the workplace: the nature of dependency and dominance in labor relations. It was phrased, however, in gender metaphors that in turn shaped the economic and organizational development of corporate capitalism.

Male and female workers accepted the same social and corporate definitions of manhood and womanhood to explicate status, to express a commitment (or lack of it) to labor, and to assert a sense of self in relation to others in the workplace. Gendered language provided a way for workers to describe their experiences and understand the meaning of labor within their lives as a whole. Such language conflated the distinctions between an individual's experiences as a worker and as a private person. The experience of corporate work took place in an ideological context that blurred personal and public definitions of gender in the interests of organizational efficiency.

Although economic and demographic factors undergirded the changing nature of labor in financial industries from 1870 to 1930, some managers and office workers held women and womanhood responsible for men's subordination to the new bureaucratic structures. Women were, after all, one of the most visible signs of the changed business environment.[2] Charles Vanse, for one, described the environment at the Equitable as "an ocean of permanent waves."[3] Even those men who supported hiring women attributed to women's presence major changes in men's office behavior and demeanor. A former vice-president of Wells Fargo, John J. Conlon, observed, "the old timers resented the influx of the women as they had always considered the banking business an Eve-less paradise." Male bankers who had no contact with the public were used to "wearing dirty, torn office coats, and the advent of the women . . . was influential in eliminating this practice." Conlon also recalled more than one instance of male workers in the "Eve-less paradise" losing their temper and becoming involved in fights.[4] As if these problems were not enough, some believed that changes in vocabulary and attitude affected not only the experience of work but the behavior of male managers and executives outside the workplace. Vanse thought that the increased popularity of golf among male managers was due to men's need to find an area outside the influence of women, a purpose work had served before women's presence in the workplace brought the social relations of private life into a public environment. But the habits of office life followed men, even òn the golf course. Vanse related a story about a "golfer who was sub-consciously influenced as he addressed the ball and exclaimed 'Tut Tut' to the disgust of his caddy who scornfully remarked 'Gee, Mister! You'll never learn golf wid dem words.'"[5]

Management theorists echoed Vanse's fears. For some, women's presence in offices raised the issue of dependency and the dangers of that dependency for males. In 1932 one management educator, George Frederick, argued that American executives and managers had become "paralyzed" and "petulant" because they had turned so much of their work over to women. Such dependency was an offense not against corporate order but against nature. "After all, there is something a bit silly," Frederick claimed, "in seeing a husky man in an office chair so helpless that there isn't a paper . . . or a utensil he knows how to lay hold upon, without asking a frail little woman on the other side of the room to go get it for him." He likened this businessman to a "spoiled child" whose mother had to pick up after him.[6] The dependency Frederick observed stemmed from the stratification of office work and the job specialization of the corporate structure. The man who could not find his paper clips was the manager who knew nothing of his company's investment practices; lost in the trees, his "job" did not include the right or opportunity to view the forest. Workers and managers participated only in parts of the production process, not in the entire process. Frederick, like Vanse and Conlon, described such fragmentation as the consequence of a relationship between men and women—as the result of gender relations rather than economic or organizational imperatives.

Office rhetoric expressed the fragmentation and subordination of office work in gendered metaphors at least by the 1920s.[7] Female workers' observations about men in offices echoed the image of the infantile business manager or executive, and the image of childlike men was part of the popular picture of male office workers. Many secretaries who responded to the Bureau of Vocational Information's 1925 survey complained about the irrationality of male demands in the workplace. They referred to men as "temperamental," "difficult to work for," moody, and "disagreeable."[8] In 1928 a former secretary, Grace Robinson, lamented, "The man one works for has, more than likely, a healthy, well nourished temper that all its life has been permitted to cavort about naked, untrammeled, and undisciplined."[9] Such complaints grew in part from the demand that all female office workers function as subordinates. Excluded from the decision-making aspects of the production process and asked to identify their self-interest with their position, some women chafed under the impositions of job specialization. Yet women and men, workers and managers alike often described their dissatisfaction with fragmentation and lack of control as a function of gender relationships rather than job, position, or corporate structure.

In these accounts and others, the feminized character of office labor seemed to be a direct result of the feminization of the workplace. According to these constructions, the newly "civilized" worker had lost his manhood in the gendered office.[10] The presence of women altered the social behaviors of the workplace and the association of work with manliness. Office manhood thus took on new, disturbing implications. Descriptions of male office workers as childlike and subservient linked men to stereotyped images of women, suggesting that childlike males were emasculated. This new vision placed men at the same subordinate level as women and threatened to upset the finely balanced power structures of both the gender dichotomy and corporate status. For men, the sense of subordination and vulnerability endemic to corporate work could be overcome by reasserting their position relative to women—by attempting to reinforce a traditional gender hierarchy by separating themselves from women and behaviors ascribed to women. Male workers tried to shape office gender relations in ways that emphasized male dominance. Men commented unfavorably on female workers who asserted themselves; one man, for example, complained about a "cashier, who was rather hard boiled and very much high hat, [who] said she'd show me my desk."[11] A banking executive claimed he preferred good judgment to a college education in his employees and advised college girls to do away with the notion that they were superior just because they went to college. Noncollege women were less sure of themselves and therefore more "malleable."[12] Several former secretaries in the Bureau of Vocational Information survey observed that employers preferred to hire women who did not have college educations because such workers would be less independent and self-assured. One respondent noted, "There is not a little prejudice . . . against the college girl; she's less easily blind folded and men don't like to be 'seen through.'" Another observed, "Some of the men in the concern like to have high school graduates; enjoy the feeling of superiority over their secretaries."[13]

Bosses did seem to prefer employees who were female and who were younger and less educated than themselves. Most female office workers had only a high school education. A federal Women's Bureau report of 1934, for example, indicated that of the 7,501 female office workers who responded to its questionnaire, only 300 had completed college. A 1930 study of 6,057 women office workers in Philadelphia found that only 5.6 percent had had any education above high school.[14] The youth of female office workers was the subject of comment and a demographic fact throughout the period.[15] Photographs of the Metropolitan Life office staff taken in the 1890s suggest a predominantly young, female work force. A respondent to the Bureau of Vocational Information survey noted, "One [employment] agency has said that they find it hard to place a young woman in secretarial work when she attains the age of thirty or thirty-five. . . . The advertisements in the papers seem to bear that statement out. . . . Whereas when I started out I was turned away for lack of experience, today I notice the advertisement calls especially for the inexperienced."[16] So prevalent were young female office workers in financial institutions that the term *girl* became a shorthand for *clerical worker*.[17] Female office workers also tended to be younger than their male counterparts. In 1915, Metropolitan Life reported that the average age of its male clerks was thirty-one, and that of female clerks twenty-seven.[18]

The youthfulness of female office workers stemmed in part from the ideological and economic attractions of the work to young, never-married women. The best-paid and most prestigious of positions open to young women, office jobs also were surrounded by a mythology that emphasized the highly personal, even intimate nature of male–female relations in the office. The "office wife," popular literature claimed, could marry the boss and become a real wife.[19] Age played an important role in this mythology and pointed to its deeper social and sexual meanings. Commonly held notions of appropriate age and gender relations paired an older man with a younger woman in the office. The idea of a young male boss employing an older female secretary upset both the traditional age hierarchy and notions of male dominance; the proper role for an older woman was that of mother. This idea divested the boss–secretary relationship of both its power via marriage imagery (the "wedding" and thus transcendence of two status levels or power levels, the office wife and the corporate family man) and its potent sexual tensions as well.[20]

Corporate executives and managers encouraged the view that all workers, male and female, were dependents in a system of benevolent familial alliances. The ideology of corporate domesticity and the structural paternalism it legitimized stressed the childlike, undisciplined nature of workers, male and female. Corporate domesticity addressed the issue of dependency by lumping men and women together, asserting the commingling of prescribed male and female behavior, and describing an employee who was loyal and obedient regardless of sex, even as gender differences made for different expressions of that loyalty. However, deep-rooted cultural assumptions about male dominance and female subordination could not be overriden so easily. In fact, the implicit challenge to the gender hierarchy posed by corporate domesticity and the feminized images of corporate logos and company personas gave the issue of subordination a highly personal cast.

The evolution of corporate bureaucracy in financial industries associated gender traits with particular jobs, and gender divisions described the hierarchy of positions within a corporation, replicating status differences. People in the lower positions were associated with a wide array of feminine qualities, and those in the upper reaches with masculine qualities. A female manager was expected to adopt masculine business behaviors and beliefs; a male secretary, attributes increasingly defined as feminine. For a woman to display features or attitudes of dominance—age, position, or behavior—undermined the status and gender hierarchies. Men, however, often attributed their own perceived subordination to the presence of women. Crucial components of male self-definition, in other words, hinged on the meanings womanhood assumed in the corporate context. Ironically, this reversal of the hierarchy ascribed to women levels of control and dominance that their definition as subordinates denied.

Patriarchal attitudes and structures in the financial industries applied as much to male as to female workers. Top managers and executives shared the sense that all employees were boys and girls under the care of watchful and protective parents: the executive father and the mother company.[21] Thus, office work involved some degree of subordination and inequality for both men and women. Yet experience bore out the organizational presumption of female inferiority. By 1930, notions of appropriate work for men and women, the promotional hierarchy of corporations, and even company buildings created job segregation by gender and separate promotional tracks, status levels, and pay scales for male and female workers.[22] In clerical industries, women did not enjoy the same opportunities for advancement as men. However, as the role reversal evident in men's sense of dependency illustrates, male workers also experienced powerlessness within the corporation. Descriptions of gender in office work experience increasingly served as descriptions of labor relationships, and gender roles became correspondingly important in ideas about the self.

One of the most important areas of gender differentiation came in efforts by female executives, agents, and managers to distinguish themselves from their male counterparts. The evolution of female brokers, insurance agents, and banking executives reveals the distinction between male and female management roles in business. Women not only entered business, they entered a milieu firmly defined in masculine terms. Federal census reports, which did not begin listing female insurance and real estate agents until 1890, show that from 1890 to 1930 the numbers of women working as insurance agents or brokers increased from 478 to nearly 13,000. Women made up a fairly steady 5 percent of the total number of agents and brokers.[23] Black women were even more common as insurance agents than were women in general. In 1910 and 1930, black women constituted 18 and 17.2 percent, respectively, of African American insurance agents; women in general were only 3 and 5 percent, respectively. North Carolina Mutual Life's Mattie Burke, for example, was the first black female insurance agent in Edenton, North Carolina, in the early twentieth century. Black women's disproportionate representation in this field may have grown out of the prominent role financial industries played in African American communities and the economic importance of black women to their communities and families. In addition, insurance sales was something an individual could do part time or in the evenings—attractive features for women who faced multiple demands on their time.[24] Banking, long known for its fiscal and social conservatism, was among the last of the financial industries to hire women at any level and one of the slowest to admit women to better-paying, more responsible positions. Not until around 1900 did female bookkeepers, cashiers, accountants, managers, and executives appear in banking firms with any frequency, their increasing numbers largely due to the overall growth of the banking industry after 1900.[25]

As products, insurance and banking services aimed predominantly at men. Banking products—trusts, savings accounts, loans—were addressed to men's personal and business needs. As public spaces as well as workplaces, banks were dominated by male workers and customers until around World War I. The life insurance product, as opposed to the producing company, was couched in masculine terms.

Although the financial industries were heavily masculinized, pressure in several areas worked to open a wedge for women. Beyond the contributions of female personnel management advocates to systematic management, female insurance agents exemplified the average woman's role in management. Some of the first female insurance agents began by taking over their husband's debits.[26] Women sometimes worked for their father's agencies or took over after their father's death. By the 1890s the industry was capitalizing on the fact that women and children within the family had persuasive power. Companies recognized the gendered aspects of the consuming public, appealing to men and women as customers in ways that drew on ideals of manhood and womanhood. One way to engage the interest of a potential male client was to convince his wife or children of the need for insurance. Appeals to women as mothers were especially strong. Since it was the widow and her children who would suffer from the death of a male breadwinner, soliciting them could encourage a sale.[27] Companies wishing to maximize their sales began by the 1880s to accept female agents on the grounds that they were uniquely suited, as women, to argue convincingly for the protection and security of women and children. In addition, with the growing numbers of working women in the country, life insurance found a new client in the self-employed woman, the career woman, or the working woman who helped support her family. Female agents and male executives and managers assumed that female agents could best present working women with the need for life insurance.[28] Finally, up to around 1910, companies usually trained their agents. This worked to many women's advantage, since insurance sales could be part time and seasonal; it did not require college or specialized courses, at least in the early period.

During and after World War I similar developments in banking led to the hiring of women. The new-found economic clout of women, a byproduct of their increased earnings during the war years combined with gains in education and literacy among women of all classes, created a new customer base for banks and trust companies. Women's deposits in uptown Manhattan banks in the early 1920s ranged from 50 to 85 percent of all deposits.[29] From about 1915 through the 1930s, many banks created "women's departments," staffed by female executives who catered to the "special needs" of female customers. New York City's first women's department opened in 1916 when the Columbia Trust Company hired a young woman named V. D. H. Furman as the manager of the department. By the early 1920s, nearly every bank in New York City had a women's department. Not confined to the East Coast, women's departments also were created in institutions in Chicago, Kansas City, Dallas, and San Francisco, and in Wyoming, Colorado, Iowa, Kansas, and other states.[30] Aiming at the specific interests of women, in addition to the usual bank or trust products departments also offered instruction in "budget-making and in children's accounts."[31] Banks and trust companies created special "rest rooms" for female customers where they could write letters, meet friends, take a break from shopping, and, of course, prepare to deposit their money or take out a loan. Company journals and professional organization newsletters ran instructional columns on checking accounts, financial advice for widows, and similar issues of interest to female customers. The Old National Bank of Spokane, Washington, for example, created a brochure titled "How Women Bank with the Old National" that doubled as advertising and educational forum. The brochure was designed to make a "special effort to dispel mystery [and] technicalities . . . usually associated with banking by this class of depositors."[32] The most pronounced example of a banking organization that catered to women's interests was Maggie Lena Walker's Saint Luke Penny Savings Bank in Richmond, Virginia, founded in 1903. Walker's intent was to provide financial help to African American women in order to strengthen their broad economic role and their personal financial situation. Washerwomen were among the bank's most important clients.[33]

As a result of the growth of specialized markets for women in insurance, some insurance companies also created women's departments or women's agencies between the 1890s and 1920s. Mutual Life Insurance Company of New York had a women's department by 1893, managed by Louise Starkwather.[34] The Equitable's Boston office began a women's department in 1899. It was headed by Florence Shaal, who later became president of the New England Woman's Life Underwriter's Association, the first female vice-president of the National Association of Life Underwriters, and a nationally known industry figure.[35] From 1899 until 1909, the department had between twenty and sixty employees, all women, including a lawyer and a doctor. In 1896, a woman named Ray Wilner Sundelson acted as an agent and agency manager in an Equitable branch office. In 1915, E. Marie Little was appointed manager of the Little Agency in New York City, which the Equitable home office absorbed in 1916 and renamed the Woman's Department. Little had begun working at the Equitable "in a clerical capacity" twelve years before. In 1915, New England Mutual had at least twelve female agents in various offices around the country. In 1929, the New York Life Insurance Company had both married and single women agents in every geographical division, including one all-female branch office in New York.[36]

As the existence of women's departments suggests, those involved first conceived the female contribution to banking and insurance as a separate division within the industries. Furthermore, female agents, bankers, and brokers normally focused on female clients.[37] Nonetheless, women were involved in traditionally male fields, and some functioned as managers of departments or agencies. In that light, their usurpation of the language of management and sales and their concurrent consciousness of departures from male values make female managers, executives, and agents particularly emblematic of gender role definitions in business. Female insurance sales agents and managers created definitions of their work that simultaneously drew on and undermined masculine and corporate imperatives. They usurped the language of management and sales to describe their work and consciously departed from masculine values. Their expressions reveal the complex relations between the gender of work and the gender of self in life insurance offices.

The meaning of sales work in life insurance was open to interpretation, and sales literature stressed a complicated mixture of behaviors for agents and managers. Sales demanded competitiveness but also cooperation; agents needed to be enthusiastic but rational; they had to be both self-effacing and aggressive servants of society and their company. The life insurance product and customer also were problematic. Clients were recalcitrant enemies and grateful beneficiaries; life insurance was a monetary exchange as well as social stewardship. Above all, life insurance sales was a "manly calling." It is in the context of these contested and masculinized meanings that female sales agents defined their work.

Aware of the gendered basis of their employment, female agents deployed gender relations and imagery to legitimate their work, claiming their superiority to men as workers and arguing for the recognition of "natural" female skills as important components of management. Newsletters printed by women's agencies, for example, used gender to position the agencies within the larger corporate structure. In 1903 Florence Shaal's Equitable agency began publishing a newsletter for agents titled *The Little Sister to the Equitable News,* calling attention to its derivative and gendered relationship to the company's newsletter.[38] Marie Little's agency published the *Little Upstart* from 1916 to 1918, using the manager's name as a pun for the position of her agency within the company (and perhaps to take the menace out of upstart). As their titles imply, the journals borrowed their rationale for existence from the in-house journals for agents published by the Equitable and other companies. Their main purpose, like that of the company journals, was to encourage sales, create solidarity within the agency, and instruct agents on sales technique and attitudes.[39] Annie Russell, the first editor of the *Little Upstart,* declared, "Its purpose is to give helpful suggestions, inspire and cheer agents, and keep each advised of the other's progress and agency standing. Also, we hope it will promote and encourage the very happy spirit that is so manifest in our agency."[40] At the same time, the women's newsletters acknowledged their diminutive, derivative nature; drawing on the analogy of the company as a family, they labeled themselves as childlike, subordinate, and nonthreatening.

The *Little Upstart* consciously tried to set the women's agency apart from male agencies. One early issue asserted feminine qualities against the masculine tradition of the house papers: "We rather glory in our sauciness and impudence and pride ourselves upon the jewel of our inconsistency, and we snap our fingers at precedent and tradition. We want to have a sweetish number [of the newsletter] bubbling over with sentiment and have deliberately planned it."[41] The use of such terms as *sauciness, impudence,* and *inconsistency* and the implication that sentiment was an appropriate management tool cut two ways. On the one hand, the writer recognized common beliefs about women's nature and behavior: women were childish and inconsistent. The late-nineteenth-century middle-class ideal of womanhood allowed young, single women to be emotional, capricious, and even flirtatious, qualities that theoretically disappeared once young women took on the biological and social roles of mothers and wives. Thus, the writer laid claim to an accepted, if arguable, image of womanhood.[42] On the other hand, she inverted the implications of that image by suggesting that these were business strengths rather than womanly weaknesses. *Sauciness* and *impudence* could be translated in the male language of management as *fighting spirit* or *aggressiveness.* The behavior was generic to sales, but it was expressed in a very different way. (Sauciness and impudence were not behaviors prescribed for such female corporate workers as typists, or for managers of either gender.)

Validation of female assertiveness usurped male-centered definitions of aggressive sales behavior. The use of *sauciness* and *impudence* in this context recognized women's minority position in management and sales, but it also accommodated aggression into the canon of feminine business behavior. It turned impudence into an element of a female success ethic, legitimizing it as a womanly version of masculine aggression. The writer set female agents apart from men and other female workers without stepping beyond the bounds of acceptable feminine behavior. At the same time, however, she challenged masculinized definitions of management's role and turned women's perceived weaknesses into work skills commensurate with those of men.

A similar assertion of woman-defined values at the expense of masculine and corporate codes of behavior emerged in the issue of office clothing for agents. Office clothing illustrated female workers' use of alternative avenues of self-definition that undermined official power structures and replaced them with alternative possibilities.[43] Women's office dress emphasized sexuality, suggesting that female workers were not wholly committed to their labor in ways management wanted. Popular women's magazines and company journals and newsletters contributed to this impression by suggesting in words and pictures that the female office worker was dressing to attract a husband.[44] Clothing styles were an aspect of women's office behavior that management consistently found offensive. Business educator and theorist Edward Kilduff expressed it best: "The secretary should realize that a business employer silently criticizes the secretary who wears clothing more suited for social affairs than for office work. . . . Some women secretaries do not seem to realize that it is a business mistake to wear their 'party' clothes to the office, that it is not in keeping with the general scheme of a business office to be 'dressed up.' "[45] This sort of admonition had been common from the time women began to work in offices. In one of the earliest advice books to prospective female office workers, Ruth Ashmore counseled women in 1898 to purchase sensible, dark clothing. Wearing fancy dress at work, she claimed, suggested to employers that a woman was more interested in parties and the social whirl than in earning a living.[46]

Male business clothing had developed by the 1890s into a kind of uniform that middle-class men also wore outside the office. The middle-class man's subdued dark suit asserted his commitment to his job and carried the implication that office work was an essential component of his self-image, in and out of the workplace.[47] Early office clothing for women essentially was a simplified version of middle-class, daytime domestic attire: a dark skirt and a white or dark long-sleeved blouse. Such clothing was not a uniform associated with office work in the same way as a man's dark suit; significantly, however, it was closer symbolically to male office attire than to female dress after about 1915.

Gradually, female workers did develop a "uniform" for office wear, and it was precisely this uniform that managers found so disconcerting. By the 1920s, women's office wear was the same as their leisure wear. Elaborate hair styles, jewelry, perfume, light sandals, and dresses of soft, colorful fabrics told management that female office workers had not sold their entire consciousness to the demands of the typewriter or dictaphone. In addition, such clothing stressed differences between the sexes, accenting femininity and sexuality and reinforcing a gender dichotomy. Leisure clothing underscored female subordination and the perception that women's primary interest lay in marriage rather than in office work, yet, it placed women outside the structure of business: it acted as an assertion of self and womanhood that challenged business values, the divisions of status and dominance, and even manhood. Management certainly looked at women's office attire from both perspectives, seeing clothing as a statement of female distance from the commitments of corporate labor and as a symbol of the feminized office. Women's clothing reminded managers of the explosive potential of sexuality and of management's ultimate inability to control the social construction of a worker's gendered self.

In the *Upstart*'s attention to women's fashion and its admonitions to dress appropriately and sensibly, the newsletter echoed the prescriptions management leveled at clerical workers, secretaries, and other managers. Like male-oriented management journals, the *Upstart* proffered constant advice about dressing for sales work. One article cautioned, "Little Agents should always wear smartly tailored suits," because tailored suits placed the wearers on a businesslike plane and were closer to male office attire. Suits identified female sales agents with male managerial definitions of proper business clothing. Such requests urged female agents to identify themselves with their careers by projecting an image of commitment and serious intent.[48]

The newsletter's comments on dress also alluded to interests at variance with corporate business aims. In keeping with its contrary agenda, clothing columns in the *Upstart* came under headings such as "Flivel and Drivel" and often included mention of the latest fashion or debates over skirt lengths. Unlike advice to male agents, *Upstart* articles focused on fashion as often as on practicality and business image. The columns presumed that women spent a great deal of time purchasing or making their own clothes and noticing those of other women. Columns also indicated that some female agents avoided the tailored suit. Under the title "Who's Who in Bankruptcy," the editor reported, "Marie Smith is sporting a charming new blue crepe de chine frock, all bespangled with beads, most handsome and expensive."[49] Such comments recognized that female sales agents had a distinctive interest in fashion at odds with the practical matters of life insurance sales and suggested that female agents shared something of the perspective of other female office workers.

The political quality of women's language and behavior grew out of a problem of self-definition: How could one remain a woman in a man's world? This question underlay much of women's work experience in offices, and female sales agents and managers addressed it in a variety of ways. Aware of their outsider status, female agents used humor to assert difference and to mask or deflect dissatisfaction and criticism. The language and tone of the *Upstart*, for example, sometimes poked fun at the rituals of life insurance sales, rituals that largely excluded women. One article commented that many items in the *Upstart* might seem "hackneyed to the seasoned agent. . . . [But] we hope our blasé readers will kindly remember that few of our agents have had the educational advantages of the conventions, and of listening to the wiseacres air their knowledge at these assemblies."[50] The newsletter lampooned the pomposity and exclusivity of male management style—an attack on the agents' conventions that was unprecedented in the house journals. While it may have been the unspoken opinion of some agents, it had never appeared in print.

The issue of deviance was particularly important to female agents, since it touched on the intimate relation between individual and social gender. A woman could escape the deadening aspects of office work by adopting male business values and behaviors defined as male—becoming *like* a man. For a woman this meant the surrender of her female self; a man who did so fulfilled his masculine self. Or she could imbue management or sales work with female values. Women sometimes denied their subordinate position at work by asserting their superiority to male workers, using gender awareness to stand the organizational hierarchy on its head and to deny its relevance to their sense of women's role. To avoid the perception that they were out of place, female managers and agents could infuse their work with culturally prescribed feminine values, using assumptions about women's nature to assert female superiority and difference. They spoke and acted as outsiders, flaunting their deviance from the corporate structure; at the same time, they claimed that women's approach to sales and management was superior to that of salesmen and male managers, so that women were more appropriate as insiders than men in this industry. Marie Little, speaking before a class on "Business Today" held at the New York University School of Commerce in 1915, asserted this perceived difference between male and female life insurance agents. A female agent was more suited to the business because life insurance inherently was not "a man's world, . . . for most insurance is for women. Woman is the homemaker, the true instinct of her is home. Who then should be better able to sell insurance [than] women who know the needs of the home? . . . Woman in the insurance field finds her true vocation." Little claimed that women were more committed than men to the higher ideals of life insurance and to the client's welfare because of their intrinsic womanly qualities. Women were "more conscientious than men and, therefore, that very fact will make their statements more conscientious." In contrast, she asserted, male agents were more interested in making a sale than telling the truth. Little thus proposed that women were not bound up in the self-definitions the industry promoted for women or in the male rituals and status of corporate organization; instead, they approached the business on their own terms, as women.[51]

For all their assertions of difference, female agents still faced the fact that sales work required certain generic, male-defined types of behavior. One of the primary attributes of the male sales agent was competitiveness. Both the *Upstart* and the *Little Sister* urged competition among female agents, but the language varied from that of the male-oriented journals, which often used agricultural metaphors to explain the role of male sales agents. Customers were viewed as fertile fields for the right man—the ambitious, energetic, enthusiastic man who worked hard. As an article in the house journal for Equitable, *Items for Agents*, put it in 1909, life insurance "lies as an immense farm before you; every possible implement for working it is furnished by the Society. It is up to you to sow the seed and gather the crop."[52]

A short piece in the *Upstart* titled "Her Garden" implied a smaller, more intimate scope of endeavor. In a larger sense, however, the garden was the "Laboratory of Life." This metaphor echoed the industry's philosophy that life insurance sales was a noble calling of benefit to humanity but stressed its particular suitability as a career for women. The article used the symbolic meanings of various flowers and herbs to describe the qualities agents needed. These characteristics matched those of salesmen generally—ambition, enthu-

siasm, loyalty—but included others foreign to the vocabulary of male management: "Violets for Modesty; and Mignonette to make you sweet. . . . We will
need lots of Red Clover for Industry, and Oh, I pray that my Hollyhocks will
grow for in garden language they mean Ambition. Over here, I shall plant
White Crysanthemums [sic] for Truth and Shamrocks for Loyalty."[53] Striving
for modesty and sweetness were not part of the male canon of management; in
fact, while male managers stressed teamwork and sympathy, male cooperation
and sensitivity had as their ultimate goal a conquered rather than a coaxed
customer. Modesty and sweetness were important components of cultural
womanhood, projected as specifically female elements of business success.

One issue of the *Upstart*, devoted entirely to the career of agency manager
Florence Shaal, made clear the two sexes' different approaches to management
and sales success. One author named Shaal "the good comrade of her women,
ready to give of her very best to help and encourage them; rejoicing in their
successes and sympathizing in their failures and discouragements as though
they were her own."[54] Other encomiums to Shaal in the issue stressed this same
sense of female solidarity and an inherent lack of competitiveness. While male
managers claimed that all leadership involved personalized empathy with subordinates, the female agents whose articles appeared in the *Upstart* added the
notion that personalism was a feminine trait and the mark of a distinctively
female management style.[55]

Female agents distinguished between manly and womanly job attributes in
the different behaviors they ascribed to "business girls" and "businesswomen." After the advent of female professionalism around 1900 and continuing at least to 1930, female office workers stressed the feminine qualities of the
business or office girl and the masculine qualities of the businesswoman. The
heroine of a *Saturday Evening Post* story of 1915 had ambitions to be a
businesswoman, the owner of her own advertising agency.

Unlike the office girls she saw around her, she aspired to a "career." Office
girls were clock watchers, uncommitted laborers, destined forever to be low-
paid subordinates. A businesswoman had to "take hold of [her] work as a man
does, make the sacrifices a man does, economize [her] time as a man does."
Women's "failure" in business came because "they won't go at it as men do and
make the sacrifices men do. They succeed in proportion as they adopt a man's
method."[56] To escape the deadening aspects of corporate work, to step outside
the time and space of wage labor, meant adopting male business values and
behaviors. Such notions were not merely managerial rhetoric. Respondents to
the Bureau of Vocational Information's survey also voiced a distinction between "girls" and "women" in business. One woman, a former secretary,
commented, "I really feel that the business world rubs the bloom from a
woman." Another emphasized that secretarial work "tends to make a business

woman of her, thereby tending to detract sweet feminine qualities."[57] Thus, businesswomen were more like men in their attachment to work and their allegiance to business values.

Upstart writers addressed this issue of gender deviance directly. They emphasized that Florence Shaal, although a manager, had retained her womanhood: "A business woman has been defined by other men besides Shakespeare as 'A woman impudent and mannish grown,' but such a description does not apply to Mrs. Shaal. Dainty, refined, with a magnetic charm of manner, . . . she has had such a brilliantly successful career, and yet has lost nothing of her womanly grace and charm."[58] The writer addressed the issue of the competitive, masculinized "business woman" versus the more selfless, feminine "business girl." In affirming Shaal's essential femininity as a manager, the author denied that management positions necessarily turned women into men. Marie Little addressed the issue of deviance this way: "I think it only fair to remind you that tradition says all life insurance agents are bores. In that case, however, I never found yet a woman agent that was a bore. It seems that that quality is enjoyed by the men alone, and we will let them have it."[59] Little's comment reassured her readers that to become an agent or manager did not mean a woman had to become like a man.

Female life insurance managers and agents attempted to retain social definitions of womanhood and use those attributes as a means of engaging other women's work commitment. One way to accomplish this feat—to be a manager without being manly—was to choose a profession not at odds with cultural definitions of woman's place. Advocates saw life insurance sales, like other evolving "women's professions," such as teaching, nursing, or social work, as uniquely suited to women because it utilized allegedly natural aspects of womanhood. There also was a domestic managerial tradition in middle-class women's role as household managers, employing and directing servants.[60] In the life insurance industry, then, women could become managers and sales agents without having to adopt male business values. Rather, they could emphasize feminine traits, such as modesty and sweetness, and they could draw parallels between masculine characteristics, such as aggression, and feminine ones, such as impudence. In these ways, work could be an expression of the female self rather than a negation of womanhood. By simultaneously presenting themselves as antagonists to corporate norms (as outsiders) and asserting their close match to the industry's rhetoric of social service (as insiders), women redefined the salience of gender in office work.

The issue for both women and men was not so much political and economic equality of opportunity; it was whether an individual chose a position of strength or one of weakness within an economic and social system shaped by

powerful cultural assumptions about the gendered self. Charles Vanse and
Marie Little, among others, used gender analogies to express crucial aspects of
their personal lives in their work. Workers and managers could draw on a
common gendered language and reshape it, defining work in ways that reinforced rather than undermined womanhood or manhood, and at the same time
connecting gender to work in new ways.

Conclusion

The Gender of Business

Alice Peterson's story began this book, and it is fitting that we should return to her here. When she described herself as a "business girl," Alice did not recognize the general history that had made the connection between work and womanhood possible. *Engendering Business* has argued that her fusion of gender and work was not unusual; rather it was typical of the banking and insurance industries. As the financial industries evolved between 1870 and 1930, personal and institutional expressions of gender in the corporate work-place changed. Executives, managers, and workers modified the nineteenth-century ideal of separate gender spheres for men and women in the context of the new world of corporate work.

By 1930 ideas about proper behavior for all employees, including top management and executives, had translated nineteenth-century prescriptions about gender roles into an ideology of labor experience. In this process, notions of private life became an integral part of the public definition of business. The ideal worker under managerial capitalism was a person very much like the ideal nineteenth-century middle-class woman: motivated by duty and loyalty, subservient, and other directed. Domestic architectural imagery, a philosophy of corporate domesticity, and limited job mobility replaced masculine symbols of independence, ambition, and self-made success. The financial industries, in other words, were feminized in more than the simple presence of women. The changing nature of gender in offices created a crisis for management theory, business ideology, architectural solutions to the drive for efficiency, and men's experience as workers. These elements responded by privatizing the public world of business and incorporating gender into the understanding of the nature of corporate work.

At this point, we might well repeat the questions with which this study began: What purposes did gender serve in the office workplace, and for whom? How were corporations gendered? Why did changes occur, and what do they mean in the larger context of late-nineteenth-century business development? I have approached these questions by taking seriously contemporaries' sense of the importance of gender, specifically their obsession with gender as a way to articulate, enforce, or negotiate a sense of legitimacy, privilege, and difference. I have not argued for the exclusivity of gender over material causes, or the centrality of gender to every aspect of society, or even the primacy of gender as a causal agent in economic or technological change. All these factors contributed to the development of office work by the early twentieth century. Cultural change, needless to say, is a multicausal process wherein various social, economic, and individual imperatives and desires interact. I would nonetheless argue for the importance of gender and gendered language to historical change because, as we have seen in the case of corporate development, gender is a powerful explanatory system that allows people to connect their public and private selves, their sense of how society is ordered in its myriad institutional forms, and the disparate causes and consequences of their lives (economic, technological, bureaucratic, and so on). Gendered language encourages people to think and speak about social and individual differences as though they were natural differences; in the process of using and shaping language, historical actors come to terms with the world they are making and remaking.

In the financial industries evolving gender ideals served two purposes of managerial capitalism. First, these ideals encouraged *all* workers, at whatever level, to adopt the efficiency and job commitment needed to meet economic mandates; gender ideals made the needs of the workplace mesh with attitudes about appropriate womanhood and manhood. Focusing on gender, in other words, mediated between corporate economic goals and individuals' sense of who they were as women and men. In the gendered discourse of bureaucratic rationalism, business officials (both black and white) converted middle-class, nineteenth-century social ideals of manhood and womanhood into conservative models for a corporate work ethic. Industry leaders, educators, and professionals used conventional ideals of manhood and womanhood to legitimate financial products, the production process itself, and the relations among companies, the public, and workers. Rather than individualism, they promoted community; in place of paternalism, they offered an expanded image of family relations that blended public and private experience. Particularly in the development of corporate domesticity, financial concerns intermingled notions of protection, nurturance, service, and efficiency. The resulting institutional personalism incorporated nineteenth-century middle-class concepts of women's roles, feminizing business and domesticating corporate experience. In expressions like "office wife," corporate domesticity responded to the increased presence of women in offices and the widely held belief that young women needed protection. In its broader applications, such "domesticity" underscored the dependent and subordinate—the vulnerable—relationship of everyone in the new bureaucracy of corporate capitalism.

Second, the gender ideals of managerial capitalism presented a benevolent, socially responsible face to the public and to employees. Life insurance rhetoric combined a feminized vision of the production process as a nurturing spiritual force with imagery that stressed the familial nature of corporate relations—executives and managers as fathers, and the company itself as a mother to both clients and employees. Gendered images retouched the inherently unstable, threatening picture of unregulated masculine business with a stable, nonthreatening gloss of motherhood and fatherhood, of women and men within the family serving their public children.

Corporate gender metaphors drew their emotive power from nineteenth-century middle-class gender ideals. Financial industries conflated the "separate spheres" of manhood and womanhood, pulling privatized images of home and family into the public world. Much as the woman's task within the middle-class family was to tame the competitive and chaotic urges of men, so the mother company guided and stabilized the public. Just as the middle-class man was supposed to express his manhood through competition harnessed to social service, so male executives and managers ideally served the public by serving their company. From a radical separation between equal socioeconomic roles for men and women, financial corporations used gender to describe an organic institutional relationship.

Race further complicated gender imagery in the financial industries. Gender in African American insurance and banking balanced beliefs about maleness and femaleness differently than did white companies, and yet the goals of public legitimacy and employee allegiance remained the same. In African American companies, ideal male figures contained all the elements of both manhood and womanhood: company rhetoric presented male executives as strong, rational, businesslike, and professional, but also nurturing, tender, and benevolent towards employees and clients. This combination constituted a sort of "benign patriarch," perhaps modeled on the black upper-class notion of patrician race service. Companies were families, but families in which "mother" was subsumed into father. Like white women, black women in offices, such as Susan Gille of North Carolina Mutual Life, embodied the refinement and class status the companies wanted to project. Black women executives (such as Maggie Lena Walker) largely were unsuccessful in their efforts to reformulate the family metaphor. Walker's attempt to construct a corporate family ideal that included equality between men and women—an equality in which black men would protect women and defend the race by supporting black women's right to a fuller role in the business world—represented an important element in middle-class African Americans' definitions of manhood and womanhood.[1] But company rhetoric often emphasized the male father figure rather than corporate motherhood.

The attention given to gender in financial industries partly stemmed from attempts to accommodate ideals of male and female behavior in offices to a production process that menaced those ideals. The insurance and banking industries used gender images to clarify experience because the work force included women as well as men; gender in managerial capitalism thus functioned as a mode of experience as well as a method of discourse. To be a corporate laborer was to be a gendered laborer, and questions of masculinity and femininity were inextricably bound up with what it meant to be a worker.

Gender emerged as a salient factor in corporate development in at least three areas. Various kinds of gendered rhetoric smoothed the assimilation of thousands of women into office work and created new male-defined job categories. Managers, executives, and educators developed new bureaucratic approaches —welfare departments, company-sponsored leisure—and new concepts of social manhood and womanhood to express the institutional meanings of gender. Ideals like corporate domesticity, the office wife, and the benign patriarch of African American companies brought the private world of the family into the public world of business. In the development of African American financial institutions, gendered definitions of community service supported the expression of "race pride": The family metaphor encouraged both self-improvement and hard work, meanings expressed in similar language in white companies.

Gender also helped workers structure their encounters with one another and with managerial aims in the workplace. Male and female workers both participated in and subverted managerial definitions of gender. Male office workers eschewed employee unions in favor of company-sponsored organizations, even as they engaged in tense negotiations over the limits and abuses of managerial prerogatives. Women and men invested emotional energy and wages in parties and treats for office friends, celebrating private passages in the public space of the corporation. Companies oversaw the production of newsletters and promulgated a sense of family spirit, but employee reporters avidly recounted hunting expeditions, vacations, and the latest romantic gossip, turning an official corporate voice to personal, and personalized, uses. The ideological context of the corporate workplace blurred personal and public definitions of gender in the interests of economic and organizational efficiency, public service, racial-solidarity, and personal goals.

Finally, gender had an impact on the corporate production process through the development of spatial and temporal divisions that provided a setting for experience and a language of images, symbols, and spaces. Physical spaces played an extremely important role in company officers' efforts to shape the work experience. In fact, architects and managers strongly believed that office buildings could communicate the structural organization of bureaucratic relations. Systematic managers tried to use the relationship between time and space to modify worker behavior and dubbed that connection "efficiency." As early as the 1890s, architects and executives used the physical boundaries and decorative detail of office space to organize work, generate efficiency, and outline status. As they designed buildings and manipulated furniture, thresholds, and time-space relations to alleviate sexual tensions and to encourage efficient patterns of activity, systematic managers often reinforced notions of gender difference.

The simultaneous evolution of female and male jobs within the corporation and the rationalization of workspaces created a gendered physical world. Clerical workers increasingly were pooled in separate space and time, segregating men from women. The distinction between "manual" and "brain" workers, in part a function of the splitting of the production process, also signified a difference between female and male space and time. Furthermore, symbolically domestic spaces within the corporation, in the form of private offices complete with "husbands" and "wives," fireplaces and carpets, subsumed the familial experience of domesticity within an essentially public realm. Turn-of-the-century business buildings helped segregate the labor force by gender, reinforced the connections between status and gender, and reconstituted the nineteenth-century division of public and private spheres. The physical and temporal aspects of systematic management, however, were not always successful. Workers, sometimes mockingly, reshaped office space and time to suit their own ends. In the process, they subverted managerial aims.

Gendered office spaces contributed to changes in urban public life. Historians have often remarked on the increasing segregation of public and private life in nineteenth-century urban America, and there is no doubt that the movement out of urban areas by both families and manufacturing plants added to the segregation and specialization of city life by 1900. However, segregation was not merely the removal of private life to the suburbs and the concentration of commercial life in urban centers. Rather, as the case of financial industries suggests, the urban landscape experienced new divisions of class and race even as those of gender broke down or were reintegrated. Businesses encouraged middle-class men and women, at both work and leisure, to use various places within the urban environment. For example, corporate executives consciously used office buildings to create a dignified but domestic image in the public mind. As an advertisement for a corporation's reliance on modern technology and old-fashioned family values, corporate architecture brought the patterns of upper-class domestic dwellings into the vernacular language of business streets. Financial office buildings reinforced class solidarity by welcoming middle-class women into the public spaces of business and reinforced nineteenth-century gender distinctions by separating men and women in those public places; in these ways, financial environments undermined the emphasis on separate worlds for middle-class men and women while using the notion of gender difference to commercial advantage.

For all concerned, gender metaphors and images were part of a rich, sometimes ambiguous language that attempted to explain the meaning of labor in a corporate context and the new interpenetrations of public and private life. Gender metaphors had the advantage of being both expandable and mutable, highly specific yet personal. Corporate domesticity, with its symbolic images of womanhood and manhood, masked the hierarchical realities and paternalism of corporate organization. From the broadest managerial perspective, using gender to describe work relations in financial industries suggested that corporate work was based on "natural" hierarchies of gender rather than economic imperatives or class status. The ideological explanation of women's presence in offices, for example, legitimized the goals of corporate economics: If womanhood—the softer, domesticated, selfless half of humanity—gave its imprimatur, surely the general public had nothing to fear. The notion of office wives rounded out the familial metaphor that justified corporate aims to the public and to workers.

Financial industry ideology could subsume workers' discontents into gender discontents by suggesting that the primary business relationship was based on gender rather economic structures or the needs of managerial capitalism. This philosophy absolved male managers of the need to make socially responsible decisions in dealing with workers, to the degree that they relied on the objective rationales of science. Only in African American businesses did the overwhelming need for racial solidarity and an awareness of their leadership role among African Americans temper the rationalism of business manhood. Indeed, black corporate rhetoric valued equally the sound businessman and the charitable patron.

One conclusion that could be drawn from these developments is that not very much changed at all. While women became office workers and, in some instances, even managers in the corporate world, the gender hierarchy that gave men and manhood more privileges, status, and economic value than women and womanhood remained unchanged by objective standards, such as pay differences and job access. Western Europe witnessed a similar continuity in gender inequities, which suggests the intractability in Western culture of unequally valued gender differences. It would seem that this process of gender redefinition in office work was merely another instance of the persistence of unequal structural relations between women and men. Certainly, gender role definition was an important ideological process in offices precisely because it was bound up with questions of status and self-worth at the heart of the corporate system. Corporate bureaucracy built on notions of worker behavior that drew their rationales from cultural ideas about the differences between womanhood and manhood. Gendered definitions of the purpose and experience of work led to multiple layers of status that divided men and women workers into unequal parts. Those inequities were (and are) reflected in different access to position and privilege, pay scales, and opportunity for men and women.[2]

Yet this construction seems to beg several questions. In the first place, it assumes a male standard as the most important. Definitions of status, worth, and power all devolve from a masculinized definition of the world, leaving no room for the individual office workers and managers whose complex use of gendered rhetoric and actions recreated office relations. It does not address the particularity of gender in offices and the ways in which people in the corporate world turned the standard categories of gender difference on their head. Notions of manhood and womanhood drew on one another in the creation of this opposition, generating complex and intertwined interpretations of the relationships among gender, status, and work. Women's presence in what had been defined as a masculine place upset the nineteenth-century dyad of public–private; it broke the ideological boundaries between them and invited inversions and mingling in the social understanding of male and female roles. Male executives and workers saw working women as a challenge to masculine definitions of business, to manhood itself, and to the power structure of corporate organization. Women in business also undermined the assumption that women were wives and mothers first.

In the second place, emphasizing the ultimate structural inequities of a patriarchal system says nothing about where such patriarchal relations came from. The case of the financial industries demonstrates that such relations are constantly in the process of definition by the words and deeds of people (like office workers) who shape those relations, sometimes by affirming and sometimes by challenging the foundations of gender differences. Without denying the material importance of wage and status differences and the persistence of patriarchal inequities, a great deal *did* change: Women had a new workplace and new opportunities; women and men took on new roles in relation to work and to one another. And perhaps most importantly, people at the time saw those changes as important, wrenching, frightening, and exhilarating.[3] It was a new world, even if it reinstitutionalized elements of the old. While patriarchy remains a valid *description* of certain aspects of gender relations, its persistence is not a satisfactory explanation for why the office workplace changed in the particular ways that it did, nor why contemporaries experienced those changes as radical.

Finally, while patriarchal inequities clearly contributed to the gendering of office relations, it does not tell the whole story. The physical and cultural segregation of female workers kept women and female values "in their place" to a certain extent, while the presence of female workers could provide even the lowliest males with a sense of dominance. Nevertheless, the incorporation of perceived female qualities like selflessness and moral purity into the persona of financial industries feminized or domesticated the public face of business, manipulating stereotypes of femaleness but at the same time affirming female-ascribed values. The corporate office in this period was not strictly a male-dominated, public sphere; rather, it was a rich mixture of diverse experiences that mingled home, family, work, and leisure. Thus the construction of gender, spatial, and temporal differences in financial offices speaks to a complex web of intertwined meanings rather than a simple hierarchy of status or a dichotomous struggle over autonomy. What is striking about the uses of gender in corporate offices is, in fact, the degree to which they simultaneously replicated and undermined divergent definitions of work.

Financial industries based a holistic, benign image of business on the dualities of appropriate gender roles. However, they obscured the power relationships inherent in the corporate hierarchy, inviting confusion of the social or biological structures of gender roles with the social and economic mandates of corporate organization. In this process, patriarchy and managerial capitalism reinforced each other. Through pay scales, architectural space, and status prerogatives, corporate organization clearly displayed the subordination of *all* workers to the general business goals of profit and efficiency. In this context, gender operated in the workplace in two ways. On the one hand, women's presence in predominantly clerical or mechanical jobs and men's dominance in managerial positions tied gender to the status hierarchy of corporate labor. Questions of status were tied up with questions of gender and thus with the dynamic process of self-definition in the workplace. On the other hand, the social meanings of womanhood (subordination, dependency, selflessness), translated into the experience of work, described all laborers in managerial capitalism. To be a worker in an office was to be a person like the ideal nineteenth-century woman. This vision of worker dependency and subordination generated strong antinomies in the discussion of male and female roles in the workplace.

The issue of relative domination and subordination among workers in financial industries found articulation as distinctions between male and female roles. However, when executives, managers, or workers spoke of the meaning of corporate labor by referring to a system of dominance and subordination based on gender, they were not simply substituting one description of reality for another in an effort to cloud the issues. In fact, the language of gender constituted a compelling symbolic system for discussing the feeling and character of experience, as well as the institutional structures that shaped it. Gender metaphors provided a deeply personal way for workers to describe their experiences, assert their worth, and understand the meaning of corporate labor in their lives. Yet using gender for these purposes obscured the contribution of factors such as class interests or unequal opportunities to the status divisions in the corporate hierarchy.

Men and women sometimes used gender to articulate different self-definitions and status. Salesmen insisted on the importance of competition, aggression, and work as a "calling." Managers or executives could affirm the masculine nature of their professional, rational expression of scientific economic laws. Reaffirming patriarchal distinctions, male workers could set themselves apart from women and from the subordinate position of labor by linking masculinity to their generally superior position in the corporate structure. Women's interpretations of the work experience denied the hegemony of corporate definitions of status or set women above or on a par with men, in essence reformulating patriarchy. Female clerical workers, secretaries, and managers often shared the assumption that women were more nurturing and other directed than men, and, by insisting on the nonbusiness origins of women's role, female workers supported their domestic position in the corporation. At the same time, some female workers asserted the congruence of female values and industry philosophy, thereby constructing their own sense of the gender of business.

Thinking and speaking about corporate experience in gendered terms highlighted the subordination of all workers. In fact, it is not surprising that, in a work force composed of both women and men, the culturally defined "inferior sex" should become the touchstone for definitions of subordination. Male workers, themselves ultimately subject to the dominance of others, could elevate their position by reference to female workers. If women's presence enabled men to assert their dominance within the system, however, it also highlighted workers' shared dependency. Therefore, defining womanhood as a place both physical and ideological was crucial to the evolution of definitions of maleness. Yet the boundaries remained somewhat fluid. Women could, for example, select positions, such as insurance agent or personnel director, that allowed and even encouraged the assertion of ascribed female talents.

To be a female executive or manager potentially meant to be unwomanly and therefore not a whole person, just as to be a male clerical worker increasingly meant taking on a feminized role. To avoid this difficulty, men could look to promotion into male-defined positions as a way to justify a temporary gender discrepancy. Without this structural outlet, women had to assert a contradictory set of roles in business. Drawing on the nineteenth-century model of womanhood and translating it into the corporate context, women could assert that they were different from men, and from that difference sprang their superiority to men in terms of proper business conduct and values. The evolving rationales of business service and nurturing benevolence in the philosophy of financial industries validated such claims. To maintain that difference and retain womanhood within the business environment, women also could assert that they existed outside male corporate definitions of place, status, and community. It was not so much that women wanted to marry rather than have careers, but that they wanted to retain female values and role definition in both worlds in order to express completely their public and private selves.

But insisting on the distinctiveness of women's commitment to work or management style or on their essential domesticity obscured other sources of inequity in pay and opportunity. The assertion of a set of distinctively feminine values, such as the notion that women are more caring or other directed than men, reinforced belief in women's essential domesticity and lack of business ambition. Women in business found themselves on the horns of a dilemma: To assert uniqueness was to deny what they shared with men as workers, but to insist on similarities to men was to subvert the compelling cultural definitions of gender difference. Cultural prescriptions against women's work, strong social fears that women's ability to earn a living would undermine home and family, and the nineteenth-century tradition of women's moral superiority all informed the supporters of women's presence in the workplace, who argued for women's distinctive contribution to the experience of office labor. The root of tensions over claims for women's difference and very real socioeconomic constraints was the connection that developed between the social and personal meanings of gender and the labor systems of managerial capitalism.

Beneath the surface of discussions about gender in the corporate workplace lurked both apprehension and aspiration. Between 1870 and 1930, the formative period for office work, rationales for women's office labor grew out of nineteenth-century middle-class concepts of woman's essentially domestic role. Femininity and womanhood at work perpetuated those nineteenth-century notions, particularly for clerical workers. For women, brushing against the competition and rationality of male business values threatened to destroy women's uniqueness and make them more like men. For men, nineteenth-century gender and work roles and their social definition as part of the process of public life faced a new work experience that denigrated self-seeking ambition, demanded subservience, and undercut men's ability to master their own destiny. Rationalized management and job specialization shattered nineteenth-century ideals of manhood, undermining the notions of personal will and independence. Dependence on female clerical workers and secretaries to carry forward the record-keeping and paper-processing necessary to build empires and make profits chastened the individualized spirit of manliness. Managerial capitalism's demand for subservience thwarted personal autonomy and threatened to feminize labor—to create a permanent, subordinate status for all workers. Office work, however, seemed to contain for both men and women the potential for social and economic mobility, for an enriched sense of personal worth, and for an expanded participation in public, communal life. To gain the prize without losing the self constituted the basic tension in the restructuring of office gender roles.

The struggle over the work environment had complex and often compromised results, and the uses of gender were multiple and sometimes contradictory. At issue was not so much the mutuality of gender images as their divergent sources and goals. The corporate language of gender conflated the distinctions between an individual's experience as a worker and as a private person. Workers' alternative conceptions of work commitment and efficiency in some ways reinforced corporate gender norms and familial values. The image of women as symbolic housekeepers governing the tempers of messy, childlike men in the workplace or symbolizing the refinement of office work replayed the traditional definition of women as wives, mothers, and homemakers. This image therefore aligned with systematic management's use of womanhood to assuage public fears and structure work relations, but at the same time, it affirmed noncorporate sources of self-satisfaction and personal meaning and denied the importance of corporate privilege. Private offices that expressed manhood as property ownership and company sports as a proving ground for team spirit similarly reinforced particular aspects of manhood at the expense of others. Corporate domesticity co-opted the private meanings of family and manhood for its own purposes. But the records of men's lives also suggest that men expressed their own investment in their families and social life, rather than managerial imperatives. They worked as breadwinners, as careerists, and as members of highly social groups composed of other workers. Conversely, benign domestic imagery failed to completely curtail anger, physical displays of violence, or expressions of male solidarity at odds with management's desire for an obedient, undifferentiated work force.

We are left, finally, with one last issue: the relationship between the changes charted for the financial industries in the United States and those for other economic sectors and at other times and places. Were the changes described here aspects of the growth of international markets, a consumer economy, and an expanding middle-class? How typical were they of other economic sectors at other times? Was there a historical process at work that defied national boundaries? Clearly, one force behind the new office relations was the technological and structural changes of late-nineteenth-century capitalism. Such changes took place at varying speeds throughout the Western world in the nineteenth century, and it could be argued that they demonstrated a transnational economic phenomenon. New economic relations that relied increasingly on national and international consumer markets and an expanding middle class drove companies to economies of scale. In turn, the demand arose for new technologies and new divisions of labor, leading ultimately to deskilling, the demographic feminization of the work force, and job specialization. These changes developed in the financial industries in the United States quite early, at least by the 1870s. At the same time, the managerial revolution and the widespread introduction of bureaucratic relations created a rationalized workplace vastly different from the precorporate model. Certainly, such economic and technological changes played a major role in the development of corporate organization at the turn of the century.

The history of gender in insurance and banking suggests that we need to continue to raise questions about causation and ask in particular why so much of this adaptation took on gendered forms or was expressed in gendered language. The invisible hand of the marketplace belonged to a gendered corporate body and existed in a gendered world. Explanations that purport to be based on neutral laws of economic supply and demand actually share roots in the development of masculinized concepts of management in the late nineteenth century: They are historical artifacts meant to be interrogated. Workers and markets were not neutral economic entities but women and men who were workers and consumers. The fact that workers and markets were made up of gendered people clearly provided both opportunities and problems to be resolved.

Images and expectations about gender in the office workplace reinforced and delineated each other. This process was based on the symbols, images, and metaphors available to connect the abstract qualities of status and power relationships to the specific experiences of managing people, selling insurance, or typing reports. Discussions about manhood and womanhood, concern with gender deviance, and gendered uses of space and bodily expression all attempted to fuse the economic and social concerns of the corporation with the individual concerns of workers. The social constructions of gender expressed in financial industries informed both the experience of work and the underlying economic and organizational structures of the corporate work system. On the one hand, workers used gendered language alternately to subvert or reinforce managerial definitions of corporate work. On the other hand, managerial philosophy offered explanations of corporate work that undermined certain gender behaviors and affirmed others. For all concerned, the gendered work ethic represented a slippery, potentially explosive accommodation to the most intimate aspects of the labor force. The result, for people at all levels of the corporate structure, was a precarious balance between personal, corporate, and social visions of the working self. Women and men in offices acted out these tensions from a variety of perspectives. The outcome was the gendering of business—the permeation of corporate ideology, status, and experience with power relationships that took their strength from cultural notions of manhood and womanhood.

U.S. Life Insurance Company Offices, 1850–1941

The three main companies used here as examples of the life insurance industry inhabited a series of home offices. The Appendix shows the changes of address and ownership of the various home offices.

Equitable Life Assurance Society (New York City)

1859	98 Broadway (rented)
1859	92 Broadway (rented)
1870	Broadway & Cedar (enlarged 1886–87)
1912	Broadway & Cedar (destroyed by fire)
1915	120 Broadway
1924	393 Seventh Avenue

Metropolitan Life Insurance Company (New York City)

1868	243 Broadway (rented)
1870	319 Broadway (rented)
1876	Park Place & Church Street
1890–93	One Madison Avenue
1893–1905	Expanded to 24th and 25th Streets, and to 4th Avenue

| 1909 | Tower built at Park Place |
| 1909–26 | Expansion at Madison Avenue |

New England Mutual Life Insurance Company (Boston)

1844–55	Merchants Bank Building, 28 State Street (rented)
1856–58	14 State Street (rented)
1858–75	State and Congress Streets
1875–1941	87 Milk Street

The home offices have gone through numerous periods of expansion since the last dates listed. Only Metropolitan Life is still housed in the same area as it was in 1876. Its original offices at One Madison Avenue were demolished to make room for modernization in the mid-1930s. However, the boardroom was moved, intact, into the rebuilt structure.

ABBREVIATIONS

Archives and Manuscript Collection	*Abbreviation*
Mutual Benefit Life Insurance Company, Agency Procedures Book, ca. 1850. Baker Library, Harvard Graduate School of Business Administration, Cambridge, Massachusetts	BL
Bureau of Vocational Information Papers. Schlesinger Library, Cambridge, Massachusetts	BVI

Special Collections Department, William R. Perkins Library, Duke University, Durham, North Carolina
    Rencher Harris Papers
    Seth Kendall Papers
    Fannie B. Rosser Papers
    James H. Southgate, Sr. Papers
	DUL

Equitable Life Assurance Society of the United States Archives. The Equitable Life Insurance Company, New York, New York	ELASA

Hagley Museum and Library, Wilmington, Delaware
    E. I. DuPont de Nemours Papers
    Pamphlet Collection
    Pennsylvania Railroad Collection
    Philadelphia National Bank Papers
    Provident Mutual Life Insurance Company Papers,
    Remington Rand Papers
    Trade Catalogue Collection
	HM&L
	
	PML

Metropolitan Life Insurance Company Archives. The Metropolitan Life Insurance Company, New York, New York.	MLICA
The New England Historical Collection. Corporate Library, Boston, Massachusetts	TNE

Abbreviations

North Carolina Mutual Life Insurance Company
Heritage Papers. Durham, North Carolina   NCM

Wells Fargo Corporate Archives. Wells Fargo Company,
San Francisco, California   WFCA

Widener Library. Harvard University Libraries,
Cambridge, Massachusetts   WL
  Equitable Life Assurance Society, Boston. *Plans and
  Descriptions of the Equitable Building, Corner of
  Milk & Devonshire Streets.* New York: New York
  Graphic Co., 1874.
  Life Office Management Association. *Life Insurance
  Home Office Buildings: A Study of the Problems of
  Building Construction.* Fort Wayne, Indiana: The
  Association, 1933.

NOTES

Introduction: The Business of Gender

1. Interview with the author, May 1984. At the informant's request, I have used a pseudonym throughout.

2. Michelle Z. Rosaldo, "The Use and Abuse of Anthropology: Reflections on Feminism and Cross-Cultural Understanding," *Signs* 5, no. 3 (Spring 1980): 389–417; Judith Gerson and Kathy Peiss, "Boundaries, Negotiation, Consciousness: Reconceptualizing Gender Relations," *Social Problems* 32, no. 4 (Apr. 1985): 317–31.

3. My use of the term *industry* to describe financial institutions follows the broad meaning of the term, which denotes a complex of economic institutions clustered around a particular product. See, for example, Robert H. Wiebe, *The Search for Order, 1877–1920* (New York: Hill & Wang, 1967), 23.

4. Alan Trachtenberg, *The Incorporation of America: Culture and Society in the Gilded Age* (New York: Hill & Wang, 1982).

5. Rosabeth Moss Kanter, *Men and Women of the Corporation* (New York: Basic Books, 1977); Thomas C. Cochran, *Business in American Life: A History* (New York: McGraw-Hill, 1972), esp. chap. 16 and 20; and JoAnne Yates, *Control through Communication: The Rise of System in American Management* (Baltimore: Johns Hopkins University Press, 1989). On the use of managerial and corporate organization in the industrial sector, see David E. Nye, *Image Worlds: Corporate Identities at General Electric, 1890–1930* (Cambridge: MIT Press, 1985). By *corporate culture* I mean the formal and informal rules and understandings that make corporations distinct institutions. These rules and understandings include both organizational charts, which outline job hierarchies and pay scales, and the sort of informal knowledge about how to "get things done" that are part of any large, bureaucratic system.

6. "Service" occupations have been narrowly defined as those in which a worker provides some form of personal attention, such as waitressing, nursing, or retail clerking. See, for example, Dorothy Sue Cobble, *Dishing It Out: Waitresses and Their Unions in the Twentieth Century* (Urbana: University of Illinois Press, 1991); and Susan Porter Benson, *Counter Cultures: Saleswomen, Managers, and Customers in American Department Stores, 1890–1940* (Urbana: University of Illinois Press, 1988). I am using the phrase "clerical-service" occupations or industries to describe financial organizations, for two reasons. First, many workers in these industries served the public directly, such as bank tellers or cashiers. Second, their often genuine (and fiscally sound) concern with the health and welfare of clients

and employees led to widespread efforts at community education and outreach that made service a self-defined characteristic.

7. Daniel J. Walkowitz, "The Making of a Feminine Professional Identity: Social Workers in the 1920s," *American Historical Review* 95, no. 4. (Oct. 1990): 1051–75; and Ava Baron, "An 'Other' Side of Gender Antagonism at Work: Men, Boys, and the Remasculinization of Printers' Work, 1830–1920," in *Work Engendered: Toward a New History of American Labor,* ed. Ava Baron (Ithaca: Cornell University Press, 1990), 1–46.

8. Carole Srole, "'A Position that God Has Not Particularly Assigned to Men': The Feminization of Clerical Work, Boston, 1860–1915" (Ph.D. diss., University of California, Los Angeles, 1984), 29–30; Elyce Rotella, *From Home to Office: U.S. Women at Work, 1870–1930* (Ann Arbor: UMI Research Press, 1981), 80–83.

9. See, for example, Mary Ryan, *Cradle of the Middle Class: The Family in Oneida County, New York, 1790–1865* (New York: Cambridge University Press, 1984); and Leonore Davidoff and Catherine Hall, *Family Fortunes: Men and Women of the English Middle Class, 1750–1850* (Chicago: University of Chicago Press, 1987).

10. Lee Holcomb, *Victorian Ladies at Work* (London: Hamden, 1973), 141–48; Jürgen Kocka, *White Collar Workers in the United States, 1890–1940* (Beverly Hills: Sage, 1980); Miriam Gluckman, *Women Assemble: Women Workers and the New Industries in Inter-War Britain* (New York: Routledge, 1990); Judith Wishnia, *The Proletarianizing of the* Fonctionnaires: *Civil Service Workers and the Labor Movement under the Third Republic* (Baton Rouge: Louisiana State University Press, 1990), 33, 94.

11. Meta Zimmeck, "Jobs for the Girls: The Expansion of Clerical Work for Women, 1850–1914," in *Unequal Opportunities: Women's Employment in England, 1800–1918,* ed. Angela John (London: Basil Blackwell, 1986), 153–77.

12. Wishnia, *Proletarianizing,* 33.

13. Alfred D. Chandler, *The Visible Hand: The Managerial Revolution in American Business* (Cambridge: Harvard University Press, 1977).

14. Sociologists have been more sensitive to this issue in the contemporary workplace. See, for example, Kanter, *Men and Women of the Corporation.*

15. Wilma J. Pesavento, "Sport and Recreation in the Pullman Experiment, 1880–1900," *Journal of Sport History* 9, no. 2 (Summer 1982): 38–62.

16. M. S. Stuart, *An Economic Detour: A History of Insurance in the Lives of American Negroes* (1940; reprint ed., New York: Johnson Reprint Corporation, 1970).

17. Robert A. Padgug, "Sexual Matters: On Conceptualizing Sexuality in History," *Radical History Review* 20 (Spring/Summer 1979): 8–9. It is also possible to argue that biology is not a given but a social creation; see, for example, Thomas Laqueur, *Making Sex: Body and Gender from the Greeks to Freud* (Cambridge: Harvard University Press, 1990).

18. Joan W. Scott, *Gender and the Politics of History* (New York: Columbia University Press, 1988), 28–50.

19. Gerda Lerner, *The Creation of Patriarchy* (New York: Oxford University Press, 1986), 8–9.

20. For an analysis of the pervasiveness of gender images and their dualistic nature see Gayle Rubin, "The Traffic in Women: Notes on the 'Political Economy' of Sex," in *Toward an Anthropology of Women,* ed. Rayna R. Reiter (New York: Monthly Review Press, 1975), 157–210; and Scott, *Gender and the Politics of History.*

21. Sherry B. Ortner and Harriet Whitehead, *Sexual Meanings: The Cultural Construction of Gender and Sexuality* (New York: Cambridge University Press, 1981).

22. Michel Foucault, *The History of Sexuality,* Vol. 1, *An Introduction* (New York: Vintage Books, 1980).

23. Rosaldo, "Use and Abuse of Anthropology," 405.

24. Foucault, *History of Sexuality,* 17–49.

25. Cynthia Eagle Russett, *Sexual Science: The Victorian Construction of Womanhood* (Cambridge: Harvard University Press, 1989).

26. See, for example, Robert K. Merton, *Sociological Ambivalence and Other Essays* (New York: Free Press, 1976), esp. part 1.

27. On the social functions of space, see Erving Goffman, *The Presentation of Self in Everyday Life* (Garden City, N.Y.: Doubleday, 1959); Michel Foucault, *Discipline and Punish: The Birth of the Prison* (New York: Pantheon Books, 1977); Sara M. Evans and Harry C. Boyte, *Free Spaces: The Sources of Democratic Change in America* (New York: Harper & Row, 1986); and Leslie K. Weisman, *Discrimination by Design: A Feminist Critique of the Man-Made Environment* (Urbana: University of Illinois Press, 1992).

28. Stuart M. Blumin, "Black Coats to White Collars: Economic Change, Non-manual Work, and the Social Structure of Industrializing America," in *Small Business in American Life,* ed. Stuart W. Bruchey (New York: Columbia University Press, 1980), 100–121; Stuart M. Blumin, "The Hypothesis of Middle-Class Formation in Nineteenth-Century America: A Critique and Some Proposals," *American Historical Review* 90, no. 2 (Apr. 1985): 299–338; Stuart Blumin, *The Emergence of the Middle Class: Social Experience in the American City, 1760–1900* (New York: Cambridge University Press, 1989); and Ryan *Cradle of the Middle Class.* For the English case, see Davidoff and Hall, *Family Fortunes.* Determining the class status of office workers and managers is fraught with conceptual pitfalls—so many, in fact, that there is no complete agreement about what constitutes middle-class status. See Kathleen Canning, "Gender and the Politics of Class Formation: Rethinking German Labor History," *American Historical Review* 97, no. 3 (June 1992): 736–68.

29. Kathleen Canning discusses the notion of class as social identity in "Gender and the Politics of Class Formation."

30. James Oliver Horton, "Freedom's Yoke: Gender Conventions among Antebellum Free Blacks," *Feminist Studies* 12, no. 1 (Spring 1986): 51–75.

31. My discussion of the black middle class is based on Stephanie Jo Shaw,

"Black Women in White Collars: A Social History of Lower-Level Professional Black Women Workers, 1870–1954" (Ph.D. diss., Ohio State University, 1986), 61–79. See also Willard B. Gatewood, *Aristocrats of Color: The Black Elite, 1880–1920* (Bloomington: Indiana University Press, 1990). On race, gender, and sexuality, see Darlene Clark Hine, "Rape and the Inner Lives of Black Women in the Middle West: Preliminary Thoughts on the Culture of Dissemblance," in *Unequal Sisters: A Multi-Cultural Reader in U.S. Women's History*, ed. Ellen Carol DuBois and Vicki L. Ruiz (New York: Routledge, 1990), 292–97.

32. Shaw, "Black Women," 67.

33. Ibid., 63.

Chapter One: From Six to Forty Thousand

1. *A Family of 40,000: How Health and Happiness are Provided for its Members* (New York: Metropolitan Life Insurance Company, 1926), MLICA; *All in the Days Work* (New York: Metropolitan Life Insurance Company, 1929), 29–40, MLICA; Morton Keller, *The Life Insurance Enterprise 1885–1910: A Study in the Limits of Corporate Power* (Cambridge: Belknap Press, 1963), 37.

2. Typewritten note, V.F. Employees, 1867–1960 I, MLICA; *The Metropolitan Life Insurance Company: Its History, Its Present Position in the Insurance World, Its Home Office Building, and Its Work Carried on Therein* (New York: Metropolitan Life Insurance Company, 1908), MLICA; Marquis James, *The Metropolitan Life: A Study in Business Growth* (New York: Viking Press, 1947), 174.

3. Alan Trachtenberg, *The Incorporation of America: Culture & Society in the Gilded Age* (New York: Hill & Wang, 1982); Alfred D. Chandler, *The Visible Hand: The Managerial Revolution in American Business* (Cambridge: Harvard University Press, 1977).

4. Anita Rapone, *The Guardian Life Insurance Company, 1860–1920: A History of a German-American Enterprise* (New York: New York University Press, 1987), 5; J. Owen Stalson, *Marketing Life Insurance: Its History in America* (Cambridge: Harvard University Press, 1941), 32–35.

5. The mutual aid society has continued, in various forms, up to the present. See Mary Ann Clawson, *Constructing Brotherhood: Class, Gender, and Fraternalism* (Princeton: Princeton University Press, 1989).

6. Anglo-American life insurance relied on British regulations and companies until the late eighteenth century. Until about 1860, Britain dominated European life insurance. See Stalson, *Marketing*, 32–46.

7. In Britain the word *assurance* was used for life companies, while *insurance* was reserved for fire and marine insurance. In the United States, some early life insurance companies used the word *assurance* in their name and spoke of *life assurance*. By 1900 the two words had become interchangeable, and the former has gradually fallen out of favor.

8. Cited in Walter B. Weare, *Black Business in the New South: A Social History of the North Carolina Mutual Life Insurance Company* (Chicago: University of

Illinois Press, 1973), 5. The Free African Society soon folded but was important to black and national history. From it came the African Methodist Episcopal Church, black abolitionist organizations, and groups opposed to the colonization of former slaves. The earliest known free African American mutual aid society was the African Union Society, begun in 1780 in Newport, Rhode Island; see Alexa B. Henderson, *Atlanta Life Insurance Company: Guardian of Black Economic Dignity* (Tuscaloosa: University of Alabama Press, 1990), 3. On the Independent Order of Saint Luke, see Elsa Barkley Brown, "Womanist Consciousness: Maggie Lena Walker and the Independent Order of Saint Luke," *Signs* 14 (Spring 1989): 616.

9. Clawson, *Constructing Brotherhood*, chap. 4; Weare, *Black Business*, 11–12.

10. Stalson, *Marketing*, xxxix. *The Insurance Monitor and Wall Street Review*, for example, began publication in 1853.

11. Ibid., 53–103, 107.

12. Ibid., 360–63; Paul B. Trescott, *Financing American Enterprise: The Story of Commercial Banking* (New York: Harper & Row, 1963), 90.

13. Numerous instances of this type of women's business have not yet surfaced; however, we do know women often were involved in investment as family members. See Naomi Lamoreaux, *Insider Lending: Banks, Personal Connections, and Economic Development in Industrial New England, 1784–1900* (New York: Cambridge University Press, 1994), chap. 1.

14. In his history of The New England, Abram T. Collier points out that, as mutual companies, New England Mutual Life and Mutual of New York "set the standard" for our current life insurance industry, in which mutual companies hold most of the industry assets and have the highest net worth. Abram T. Collier, *A Capital Ship, New England Life: A History of America's First Chartered Mutual Life Insurance Company, 1835–1985* (Boston: The New England, 1985), 1–3.

15. *Corporation* can be a confusing term. It refers to an economic and legal form—the chartered joint-stock company—that courts have treated as a legal entity since the late eighteenth century. It is also an organizational form that links a board of directors who represent stockholders to the bureaucratic hierarchy. I am emphasizing the widespread appearance, by the late nineteenth century, of companies composed of both the legal and bureaucratic corporate forms. On the history of the corporation as an entity, see Oscar Handlin and Mary Handlin, "Origins of the American Business Corporation," *Journal of Economic History* 5, no. 1 (May 1945): 1–23.

16. Doyce B. Nunis, Jr., *The Past Is Prologue: A Centennial Profile of Pacific Mutual Life Insurance Company* (San Francisco: Pacific Mutual Life Insurance Company, 1968), 8–23.

17. Stalson, *Marketing*, 160–177, 327–356.

18. The distinction between an "agent" and a "broker" was a fine one, and sometimes the terms were used interchangeably. Generally, by the early twentieth century an agent sold premiums to clients and represented one company. A broker was not licensed to sell insurance and referred customers to agents. Brokers, like agents, made commissions on the resulting sale. Brokers were self-employed; agents were contractors of a company.

19. On early female agents, see Stalson, *Marketing*, 359. A typical example of educational newsletters for agents is Metropolitan Life's *The Metropolitan of New York*, MLICA.

20. This is not to suggest that insurance companies or banks sold an unnecessary product. In fact, given the economic transformations of the nineteenth century, these financial industries filled a critical need not adequately met by older forms of financial security such as family partnerships or land or workers' associations. On the life insurance "product," see Collier, *Capital Ship*, 47–48.

21. Until the twentieth century, the advantages of banks, trusts, and unions generally were available only to specific classes of people. Life insurance, particularly after the specialization of the post–Civil War decades, had a product for everyone. See Alan L. Olmstead, "New York Savings Banks in the Antebellum Era," in *Papers of the 15th Annual Meeting of the Business History Conference*, ed. Fred Bateman and James D. Foust (Indianapolis: Graduate School of Business, Indiana University, 1968), 128–30.

22. James, *Metropolitan Life*, 43; M. S. Stuart, *An Economic Detour: A History of Insurance in the Lives of American Negroes* (1940; reprint ed., New York: Johnson Reprint Corporation, 1970), 9, 33, 35; Henderson, *Atlanta Life*, 8.

23. Brown, "Womanist Consciousness," 615–16.

24. Jeremy Atack, "Firm Size and Industrial Structure in the United States during the Nineteenth Century," *Journal of Economic History* 46 (June 1986): 463–75.

25. The numbers of employees are approximations. Census reports did not separate those employed in fire, marine, and life insurance. Department of the Interior, *Preliminary Report on the Eighth Census, 1860* (Washington: Government Printing Office, 1862), 78–79; Department of the Interior, *The Statistics of the Wealth and Industry of the United States, 1870* (Washington: Government Printing Office, 1873), 3:812–23; *The [Spectator] Insurance Year Book, 1920–1921: Life, Casualty, and Miscellaneous*, vol. 48 (New York: The Company, 1920), 110–86; William Alexander, *The Equitable Life Assurance Society of the United States: 65 Years of Progress and Public Service, 1859–1924* (New York: The Equitable Life Assurance Society of the United States, 1924), 27–28.

26. Twelve of the banks in existence in 1800 have been operating continuously ever since. See Benjamin J. Klebaner, *Commercial Banking in the United States* (Hinsdale, Ill.: Dryden Press, 1974), 3.

27. Trescott, *Financing American Enterprise*, 69.

28. Klebaner, *Commercial Banking*, 82; Thomas Cochran, *Business in American Life: A History* (New York: McGraw-Hill, 1972), 156.

29. Burton Hendrick, *The Story of Life Insurance* (London: William Heinemann, 1907); Keller, *Life Insurance*; James, *Metropolitan Life*, 94; R. Carlyle Buley, *The Equitable Life Assurance Society of the United States 1859–1959* (New York: Appleton-Century-Crofts, 1959). The name of the Germania was changed to the Guardian Life Insurance Company in 1917 due to the anti-German sentiment of World War I; see Rapone, *The Guardian*, 1, 151; Henderson, *Atlanta Life*.

30. Of the major carriers, only Metropolitan Life continued to insure black clients. Weare, *Black Business*, 38, 64.

31. Ibid., 8–11, 14–24; Robert E. Weems, Jr., "The History of the Chicago Metropolitan Mutual Assurance Company: An Examination of Business as a Black Community Institution" (Ph.D. diss., University of Wisconsin-Madison, 1987), 11; Robert C. Puth, "The Origins, Development, and Current Situation of the Negro Life Insurance Industry," in Bateman and Foust, *Papers*, 134–37.

32. My discussion of the phenomenal growth of the life insurance industry in the 1840s and 1850s is based in part on Viviana Zelizer's perceptive analysis of its cultural and ideological context in *Morals and Markets: The Development of Life Insurance in the United States* (New York: Columbia University Press, 1979); Boston Tontine Association, "The Constitution of the Boston Tontine Association," Boston, Massachusetts, 1791, Pamphlet Collection, HM&L.

33. Hendrick, *Story of Life Insurance*, 36–41. Clients sometimes took advantage of loopholes in insurance policies. For example, instances of "carrying" among black fraternal organizations occurred up to World War I. This was the practice of misrepresenting one's relationship to an insured person and taking out a policy on his or her life. Usually, the insured party was elderly or ill, and the policyholder clearly hoped to make money on a timely, if natural, death. See Stuart, *Economic Detour*, 18.

34. Mary Ann Clawson has observed that the emphasis on commodification of human life in the life insurance industry led to the enormous growth of fraternal insurance in the 1890s, when it outsold the commercial product; see *Constructing Brotherhood*, 222. The major remaining barrier in the industry by the late nineteenth century was that between "race business" and white establishments; see Stuart, *Economic Detour*, xvii–xix.

35. Olmstead, "New York Savings Banks," 128–29.

36. Stuart, *Economic Detour*, xvii–xxv; "Women in Insurance," *The Equitable News* 42 (June 1903), 11, ELASA; Wendell Buck, *From Quill Pens to Computers: An Account of the First One Hundred and Twenty-five Years of The Manhattan Life Insurance Company of New York, New York* (Manhattan Life Insurance of New York, ca. 1974), 8; Nunis, *Past is Prologue*, 9–11; "The Best is Yet to Be," advertising brochure, ca. 1920, PML.

37. Zelizer, *Morals and Markets*, 43.

38. Thomas E. Mertes, "Dissertation Research Proposal," 1988, 2 (unpublished ms.).

39. William Worthington Fowler, *Ten Years in Wall Street* (Hartford, Conn.: J. D. Denison, 1870), 100–110.

40. Stalson, *Marketing*, 360–63.

41. Buck, *From Quill Pens*, 18, 28; Margery Davies, *Woman's Place is at the Typewriter, 1870–1930* (Philadelphia: Temple University Press, 1982), 9; David Lockwood, *The Black-Coated Worker: A Study in Class Consciousness* (London: George Allen & Unwin, 1958), 20.

42. Harry Braverman, *Labor and Monopoly Capital: The Degradation of Work*

in the 20th Century (New York: Monthly Review Press, 1974), 295.

43. Asa S. Wing, "Reminiscence," *Between Ourselves* 3, no. 1 (Mar. 1915): 6, PML.

44. Jordan was hired in 1860. "When the Equitable Was an Infant Enterprise," *The Equitable News* (26 Jul. 1909), 7, ELASA.

45. Equitable Veteran Legion, *The Equitable Spirit* 1, no. 1 (26 Jul. 1933), n.p., ELASA.

46. Stuart M. Blumin, *The Emergence of the Middle Class: Social Experience in the American City, 1760–1900* (New York: Cambridge University Press, 1989), 76–77.

47. B. G. Orchard, cited in Lockwood, *Black-Coated Worker,* 21.

48. Quoted in "How Well Do I Remember?" *The Equitable Spirit* 1, no. 1 (26 Jul. 1933), n.p., ELASA.

49. Janice Weiss, "Educating for Clerical Work: The Nineteenth-Century Private Commercial School," *Journal of Social History* 14 (Spring 1981): 405–23.

50. Priscilla Murolo, "White-Collar Women: The Feminization of The Aetna Life Insurance Company, 1910–1930," paper presented at the annual meeting of the American Historical Association, New York City, Dec. 1985, 5; "50 Years Ago . . . A Look Back by Three Who Were There," *Equinews* (Jul.–Aug. 1967), 13, ELASA; "Reminiscences," typewritten manuscript, ca. 1945, 2, WFCA. As late as 1930, the U.S. Census report showed 691 boys and girls between the ages of ten and fourteen employed as "messengers, errand, or office boys and girls." See Alba M. Edwards, *Population: Comparative Occupation Statistics for the United States, 1870–1940, 16th Census of the United States, 1940* (Washington: Government Printing Office, 1943), 78.

51. See, for example, the category of "office boy" in Department of Interior, *Census Reports,* Vol. 2, *Twelfth Census of the United States, 1900: Population,* Part 2 (Washington: Government Printing Office, 1902), 505. The ad was quoted in Zora Putnam Wilkins, *Letters of a Business Woman to Her Daughter and Letters of a Business Girl to Her Mother* (Boston: Marshall Jones, 1923), 40. "Our Promising Office Boy," *The Equitable News* 73 (Aug.–Sept. 1906), 11 ELASA; "Salary Breakdown at Prudential Insurance Company," interoffice communication, Nov. 10, 1919, V.F. Personal Haley Fiske, #1, 1911–1929, MLICA.

52. R. A. Proctor, "Typewriter," *Knowledge* 2 (1882): 402–3; Weiss, "Educating," 415; Stalson, *Marketing,* 578–80, 585, 590, 595.

53. Lockwood, *Black-Coated Worker,* 21; Herbert Rudd recalled his start in 1888 as an office boy and his subsequent training and promotion in "How Well Do I Remember?," n.p. For more recent corporate training and mentoring patterns, see Rosabeth Moss Kanter, *Men and Women of the Corporation* (New York: Basic Books, 1977). Several employees of the Equitable observed that even by the 1920s and 1930s, the company still hired young men with a grammar-school education, trained them in the business, and left them to further their formal education in night school. "50 Years Ago," 13.

54. The term *clerical workers* is based on Braverman's classification. It includes bookkeepers, secretaries, stenographers, cashiers, file clerks, telephone operators,

office machine operators, payroll clerks, receptionists, stock clerks, and typists. It is distinct from the term *clerk*, even though *clerk* was used into the twentieth century to describe clerical workers. Braverman, *Labor*, 295–96.

55. Stalson, *Marketing*, 119.

56. Nunis, *Past Is Prologue*, 8–9; Advertisement, *The Insurance Monitor* 19, no. 217 (Jan. 1871): 78, HM&L.

57. Thomas E. Mertes, "Introduction" (unpublished ms.); Amos Fiske, *The Modern Bank: A Description of Its Functions and Methods and a Brief Account of the Development and Present System of Banking* (New York: D. Appleton & Company, 1923), 50–53.

58. James, *Metropolitan Life*, 70; JoAnne Yates, *Control through Communication: The Rise of System in American Management* (Baltimore: Johns Hopkins University Press, 1989), 21.

59. Braverman, *Labor*, 300.

60. *System* (1910), quoted in Lisa M. Fine, *The Souls of the Skyscraper: Female Clerical Workers in Chicago, 1870–1930* (Philadelphia: Temple University Press, 1990), 91.

61. Srole, "'A Position,'" 116–19.

62. Figures on female clerical figures in 1900 are from Weiss, "Educating," 413; Cindy Aron, *Ladies and Gentlemen of the Civil Service: Middle-Class Workers in Victorian America* (New York: Oxford University Press, 1987), chap. 4; Carole Srole, "'A Position that God has not Particularly Assigned to Men': The Feminization of Clerical Work, Boston, 1860–1915" (Ph.D. diss., University of California, Los Angeles, 1984), 8; Sara Alpern, "Women in Banking: Early Years," *Encyclopedia of American Business History and Biography* (New York: Facts on File, 1990), 468–71.

63. James, *Metropolitan Life*, 70; Srole, "'A Position,'" 29. The figures were computed from "Home Office Veterans in Service . . . April 23, 1893," V.F. H.O. 1876–1893 and "Home Office Staff: Duration of Service," V.F. Employees 1867–1960 (I), MLICA. The increase in female clerical workers was duplicated in western Europe, although more slowly. See Meta Zimmeck, "Jobs for the Girls: The Expansion of Clerical Work for Women, 1850–1914," in *Unequal Opportunities: Women's Employment in England, 1800–1918*, ed. Angela John (London: Basil Blackwell, 1986), 153–55; and Judith Wishnia, *The Proletarianizing of the Fonctionnaires: Civil Service Workers and the Labor Movement under the Third Republic* (Baton Rouge: Louisiana State University Press, 1990), 33.

64. Carole Srole has found that in late-nineteenth-century Boston, male clerical workers had a particularly high death rate from tuberculosis. She suggests this was less the result of working conditions in offices than of the type of men who chose clerical work. Less physically demanding work may have appealed to less healthy men. See Srole, "'A position,'" 177–78. See also *North American Review* 97, no. 201 (Oct. 1863): 324 for contemporary observations on clerks' short life expectancy. Textile factories and offices were among the few gender-integrated workplaces in the nineteenth century. For that reason they make a better comparison than artisan workplaces, which were closer to offices in bureaucratic structures and personnel

relations. Daphne Spain, *Gendered Spaces* (Chapel Hill: University of North Carolina Press, 1992), 183–96.

65. Srole, "'A Position,'" 110–12, 131.

66. Zimmeck, "Jobs for Girls," 154–55.

67. Erickson, *Employment of Women*, 92; Henderson, *Atlanta Life*, 142–44.

68. Aron, *Ladies and Gentlemen;* Anita Rapone, "Clerical Labor Force Formation: The Office Woman in Albany, 1870–1930" (Ph.D. diss., New York University, 1981), tables 5.4 and 5.7, and 130. See also Ileen DeVault's discussion of the problematic nature of the "collar line" in her *Sons and Daughters of Labor: Class and Clerical Work in Turn-of-the-Century Pittsburgh* (Ithaca: Cornell University Press, 1990), 1–7; Srole, "'A Position,'" 139, 181, 231. The quotation is from the abstract of Ileen DeVault's "Sons and Daughters of Labor: Class and Clerical Work in Pittsburgh, 1870s–1910s" (Ph.D. diss., Yale University, 1985), n.p.

69. Lee Holcomb, *Victorian Ladies at Work* (London: Hamden, 1973); Wishnia, *Proletarianizing*, 94; Jürgen Kocka, *White Collar Workers in the United States, 1890–1940* (Beverly Hills: Sage, 1980), 134–37.

70. Jacqueline Jones, *Labor of Love, Labor of Sorrow: Black Women, Work and the Family from Reconstruction to the Present* (New York: Vintage Books, 1985), 154, 161, 180–81.

71. See *Fifteenth Census of the United States: 1930, Population*, Vol. 5, *General Report on Occupations* (Washington: Government Printing Office, 1933), table 3.

72. Photograph, Home Office Personnel, 1909, NCM; Henderson, *Atlanta Life*, 142–44.

73. Ethel Erickson, *The Employment of Women in Offices*, Bulletin of the Women's Bureau, No. 120 (Washington: Government Printing Office, 1934), 92.

74. Stuart, *Economic Detour*, 36–37; "Mass Meeting of 500 Urges Punishment of Insurance Collector," *Baltimore Afro-American* (February 4, 1921), Charles N. Hunter Papers, DUL.

75. Erickson, *Employment of Women*, 92. For an analysis of the impact of black insurance on Chicago, see Weems, "Chicago Metropolitan Mutual." On African American banks in Chicago in the 1920s, see Madrue Chavers-Wright, *The Guarantee* (New York: Wright-Armstead Associates, 1985).

76. Chandler, *Visible Hand*.

77. Sidney Pollard, "The Genesis of the Managerial Profession: The Experience of the Industrial Revolution in Great Britain," *Studies in Romanticism* 4, no. 2 (Winter 1965): 57–80; Susan Porter Benson, *Counter Cultures: Saleswomen, Managers, and Customers in American Department Stores, 1890–1940* (Urbana: University of Illinois Press, 1986).

78. Braverman noted the similarities between precorporate clerkship and corporate managers in *Labor*, 293; Chandler, *Visible Hand*, 1–10. On the development of managerial stratification and conflicting priorities, see M. Christine Anderson, "Gender, Class, and Culture: Women Secretarial and Clerical Workers in the United States, 1925–1955 (Ph.D. diss., Ohio State University, 1986), 17–74; and Robert K. Merton, "Functions of the Professional Association," *American Journal of Nursing* 58, No. 1 (Jan. 1958): 50–54.

79. Stuart D. Brandes, *American Welfare Capitalism, 1880–1940* (Chicago: University of Chicago Press, 1976).

80. Wilma J. Pesavento, "Sport and Recreation in the Pullman Experiment, 1880–1900," *Journal of Sport History* 9, no. 2 (Summer 1982): 38–62.

81. Management theorist Joseph Litterer coined *systematic management* in the 1960s. It broadens the definition of scientific management to suggest the general trend, at the turn of the twentieth century, toward efficiency and standardization. See Yates, *Control through Communication,* 2.

82. Collier, *Capital Ship,* 59–60; Farmers and Mechanics' Bank of Philadelphia, "Instructions to Employees, 1871–1905," Philadelphia National Bank Papers, HM&L.

83. On scientific management, see Frederick Winslow Taylor, *The Principles of Scientific Management* (1911; reprinted, New York: Norton, 1967); R. H. Goodell, "Saving 42% on Routine Office Work," *System* 37 (June 1920): 1184–86, 1306, 1309; and Hinton Gilmore, "Gingering up Office Work: Methods by Which the Office Manager of a Michigan Concern Obtained Better Work," *System* 28 (June 1915): 185–89.

84. Gilmore, "Gingering Up," 187; George F. Card, "Charting Each Stenographers' Work," *System* 23 (Jan. 1913): 435.

85. Goodell, "Saving 42%," 1309–10; Gilmore, "Gingering Up," 186.

86. See, for example, Anderson, "Gender, Class, and Culture," 17–74; and Murolo, "White-Collar Women," 14–28. For the situation in manufacturing industries, see Daniel Nelson, *Managers and Workers: Origins of the New Factory System in the United States, 1880–1920* (Madison: University of Wisconsin Press, 1975), 75.

87. Anderson, "Gender, Class, and Culture," 35–63; Sharon Strom, *Beyond the Typewriter: Gender, Class, and the Origins of Modern Office Work, 1900–1930* (Urbana: University of Illinois Press, 1992), 128.

88. Farmers and Mechanics' Bank, "Instructions to Employees, 1871–1905."

89. Buck, *From Quill Pens,* 4–5, 21; Rapone, *The Guardian,* 173; Stalson, *Marketing,* 360–63; "When the Equitable Was an Infant Enterprise," 6.

90. Mertes, "Introduction"; Keller, *Life Insurance,* 1. The New York Stock Exchange in the mid-nineteenth century was, in effect, a social club. See Deborah Gardner, "The Architecture of Commercial Capitalism: John Kellum and the Development of New York, 1840–1875" (Ph.D. diss., Columbia University, 1979), 128.

91. Buck, *From Quill Pens,* 29.

92. Srole, "'A Position'," 96–104; Aron, *Ladies and Gentlemen,* 146–47.

Chapter Two: A "Nation of Silk Knees"

1. "Women in Business: II" *Fortune* 12 (Aug. 1935): 50. The gender of this author is unknown; however, the article's general tone suggests that it was written by a man.

2. Stuart M. Blumin *The Emergence of the Middle Class: Social Experience in the American City, 1760–1900* (New York: Cambridge University Press, 1989), sees this division beginning in the 1820s and argues that it is an important aspect of emerging definitions of the middle class.

3. The classic explication of patriarchy and office work remains Margery Davies, *Woman's Place is at the Typewriter, 1879–1930* (Philadelphia: Temple University Press, 1982). See also Sharon Strom, *Beyond the Typewriter: Gender, Class, and the Origins of Modern Office Work, 1900–1930* (Urbana: University of Illinois Press, 1992). On the relations among gender, skill, and labor-market segmentation, see Ruth Milkman, *Gender at Work: The Dynamics of Job Segregation by Sex During World War II* (Urbana: University of Illinois Press, 1987).

4. Mary Ryan, *Cradle of the Middle Class: The Family in Oneida County, New York, 1790–1865* (New York: Cambridge University Press, 1984), 165–76; Blumin, *Emergence*, 76–78.

5. See, for example, Lori D. Ginzberg, *Women and the Work of Benevolence: Morality, Politics, and Class in the 19th Century United States* (New Haven: Yale University Press, 1990).

6. Margaret Marsh has called this role "masculine domesticity." Margaret Marsh, "Suburban Men and Masculine Domesticity, 1870–1915," in *Meanings for Manhood: Constructions of Masculinity in Victorian America,* ed. Mark C. Carnes and Clyde Griffen (Chicago: University of Chicago Press, 1990), 112; Joan M. Seidl, "Consumer's Choices: A Study of Household Furnishing, 1880–1920," *Minnesota History* (Spring 1983): 183–197. For men's advice on domestic arrangements, see also James H. Southgate, Sr. to Mrs. Southgate, 12 Sept., 1883, James H. Southgate Papers, and Rencher Harris to Plassie Harris, 6 March 1926, Rencher Harris Papers, both in DUL.

7. Angel Kwolek-Folland, "Discoveries in the Meaning of Domesticity: Middle-class Women and Cultural Change in the United States, 1870–1900" (M.A. thesis, Kansas State University, 1982), 75.

8. Mary Blewett, *Men, Women and Work: Gender, Class and Protest in the New England Shoe Industry, 1780–1910* (Urbana: University of Illinois Press, 1988), 120–41.

9. Blumin, *Emergence*, chap. 3; Joe L. Dubbert, *A Man's Place: Masculinity in Transition* (Englewood Cliffs: Prentice-Hall, 1979), 28.

10. Madison C. Peters, *The Strenuous Career, or Short Steps to Success* (Chicago: Laird & Lee, 1908), 22.

11. "An Old Agent's Letters to His Son," *The Equitable News* 50 (Feb. 19, 1904), n.p., ELASA; James Hopper, "The Love Pirate," *Cosmopolitan,* part I, 58 (December 1914), 5.

12. E. Dwight Kendall to Seth H. Kendall, 20 Nov. 1853 and 25 Mar. 1854, Seth H. Kendall Papers, DUL.

13. E. Dwight Kendall to his mother, 16 Sept. 1875, Seth H. Kendall Papers, DUL.

14. Southgate's symptoms suggest a stomach ulcer, probably aggravated by treatments that included mercury and other toxins. James Southgate, Sr. to James

Southgate, Jr., 28 Apr. 1883; 21 Jul. 1883; and 20 Sept. 1883, James H. Southgate, Sr. Papers, DUL.

15. James Southgate, Sr. to James Southgate, Jr., 21 Jul. 1883 and 20 Sept. 1883; James Southgate, Sr. to Mrs. Southgate, 12 Sept. 1883, James H. Southgate, Sr. Papers, DUL.

16. Peter Filene, *Him/Her/Self: Sex Roles in Modern America,* 2d ed. (Baltimore: Johns Hopkins University Press, 1986), 70–72; Dubbert, *A Man's Place,* 99–124.

17. Anthony Rotundo, *American Manhood: Transformations in Masculinity from the Revolution to the Modern Era* (New York: Basic Books, 1993).

18. Irvin Wyllie, *The Self-Made Man in America: The Myth of Rags to Riches* (New Brunswick: Rutgers University Press, 1954), 86–87. On the connections between manhood and violence, see Carroll Smith-Rosenberg, *Disorderly Conduct: Visions of Gender in Victorian America* (New York: Alfred Knopf, 1985), 90–108.

19. James Platt, *Business* (New York: G. P. Putnam's Sons, 1889), vii.

20. Orison Swett Marden, *Power of Personality* (1899; reprint ed., New York: Thomas Y. Crowell Co., 1906), 7; *Who Was Who in America* (Chicago: Marquis, 1966), s.v. "Marden, Orison Swett."

21. James Southgate, Sr. to James Southgate, Jr., 1 May 1883, James H. Southgate, Sr. Papers, DUL.

22. E. Dwight Kendall to Seth H. Kendall, 12 Apr. 1854, Seth H. Kendall Papers, DUL.

23. Wyllie notes that the first recorded reference to a "self-made man" is Henry Clay's attribution of the term to a group of American manufacturers in 1823. Wyllie, *Self-Made Man,* 19.

24. Anthony Rotundo, "Manhood in America: The Northern Middle Class, 1770–1920" (Ph.D. diss., Brandeis University, 1982), esp. pp. 15–17; Orison Swett Marden, *Character: The Greatest Thing in the World* (New York: Thomas Y. Crowell, 1899), 21, 25.

25. Rotundo, "Manhood in America," 149–59; John Cawelti, *Apostles of the Self-Made Man* (Chicago: University of Chicago Press, 1968), 4, 47–50, 170; Peters, *Strenuous Career,* 11.

26. Albert Shaw, *The Outlook for the Average Man* (New York: Macmillan, 1907), 153.

27. Ibid., 149.

28. Orison Swett Marden, *The Young Man Entering Business* (1899; reprinted, New York: Thomas Y. Crowell Co., 1903), 81, 97.

29. Marden, *Character,* 10.

30. Marden, *Young Man,* 130, 146, emphasis in the original.

31. Peters, *Strenuous Career,* 103.

32. Warren I. Susman, *Culture as History: The Transformation of American Society in the 20th Century* (New York: Pantheon, 1984), 271–85; Dubbert, *A Man's Place,* 34; Marden, *Character;* Filene, *Him/Her/Self,* 70.

33. Marden, *Character,* 48.

34. Quoted in ibid., 6.

35. Peters, *Strenuous Career*, 30–31.

36. Ibid., 32. Quotation from J. E. West, "The Real Boy Scout," *Leslie's Weekly* (1912): 448, cited in Jeffrey P. Hantover, "The Boy Scouts and the Validation of Masculinity," in *The American Man*, ed. Elizabeth H. and Joseph H. Pleck (Englewood Cliffs, Prentice-Hall, 1980), 295–96.

37. Ryan, *Cradle*; Blumin, *Emergence*, 77; "How a Young Man Without Capital Can Make His Fortune," *The Equitable News* 23 (Nov. 1901), n.p., ELASA.

38. The quote is from Alan R. Raucher, "Dime Store Chains: The Making of Organization Men, 1880–1940," *Business History Review* 65 (Spring 1991): 132. For examples of this phenomenon among the working class, see Ava Baron, "Questions of Gender: Deskilling and Demasculinization in the U.S. Printing Trade, 1830–1915," *Gender and History* 1 (Summer 1989): 178–99; and Mary Blewett, "Manhood and the Market: The Politics of Gender and Class among the Textile Workers of Fall River, Massachusetts, 1870–1880," in *Work Engendered: Toward a New History of American Labor*, ed. Ava Baron (Ithaca: Cornell University Press, 1991), 92–113.

39. Peters, *Strenuous Career*, 22. On gender and professionalization, see Regina Morantz-Sanchez, *Sympathy and Science: Women Physicians in American Medicine* (New York: Oxford University Press, 1985); and Michael Grossberg, "Institutionalizing Masculinity: The Law as a Masculine Profession," in Carnes and Griffen, *Meanings for Manhood*, 133–51.

40. Edward W. Bok, "Young Man in Business," *Cosmopolitan* 16 (1894): 334–35.

41. Marden, *Young Man*, 96, 101; Rev. F. E. Clarke, "Our Business Boys," in *Our Business Boys and Girls* (1884; reprint ed., Chicago: Werner Co., 1895), 38; "When the Equitable Was an Infant Enterprise," *The Equitable News* (26 Jul. 1909), 3, ELASA.

42. Clarke, "Our Business Boys," 40. Hastings was quoted in Thomas J. Watson, ed., *Personality in Business* (New York: A. W. Shaw, 1917), 30.

43. Bok, "Young Man in Business," 336; "A Message from Edward Bok," *Remington Notes* 3, no. 8 (Oct. 1914): n.p., Remington Rand Papers, HM&L; *Who's Who in America* (Chicago: Marquis, 1928), s.v. "Bok, Edward W."

44. Bok, "Young Man in Business," 336, 337, 339.

45. Ibid., 332.

46. Frances Maule, *She Strives to Conquer: Business Behavior, Opportunities and Job Requirements for Women* (New York: Funk & Wagnalls, 1936), 15, 67.

47. Edward Hines, "What Personality Means in Business," in Watson, *Personality*, 9; James Truslow Adams, *Our Business Civilization: Some Aspects of American Culture* (New York: A. C. Boni, 1929), 18. Adams was the recipient of several college degrees (some honorary); the author of numerous books, including one that won the Pulitzer Prize in 1922; and a captain in the U.S. Army Intelligence in World War I. Prior to these illustrious (and, in his mind, apparently less venal) pursuits he had been a member of the New York Stock Exchange. *Who's Who in America* (Chicago: Marquis, 1928), s.v. "Adams, James Truslow."

48. Priscilla Murolo, "White-Collar Women: The Feminization of The Aetna Life Insurance Company, 1910–1930," paper presented at the annual meeting of the American Historical Association, New York City, Dec. 1985, 5–6.

49. Frances White, "Dr. Van de Warker on 'The Relations of Women to the Professions and Skilled Labor,'" *The Penn Monthly* 6 (Jul. 1875): 522.

50. Miss Snow, typewritten manuscript, "Women in Business," Folder 7, BVI.

51. Edith Johnson, *To Women of the Business World* (Philadelphia: J. B. Lippincott, 1923), 6.

52. For a related discussion, see Lisa M. Fine, *The Souls of the Skyscraper: Female Clerical Workers in Chicago, 1870–1930* (Philadelphia: Temple University Press, 1990), 51–75.

53. Cited in Blumin, *Emergence,* 78.

54. Johnson, *To Women,* 8.

55. See Zora Putnam Wilkins, *Letters of a Business Woman to Her Daughter and Letters of a Business Girl to Her Mother* (Boston: Marshall Jones, 1923); Johnson, *To Women;* Ruth Ashmore, *The Business Girl in Every Phase of Her Life* (New York: Doubleday & McClure Co, 1898); Maude Redford Warren, "Green Timber," *Saturday Evening Post* 188 (27 Nov. 1915): 19–29, 53–54; Caroline A. Huling, *Letters of a Business Woman to Her Niece* (New York: R. F. Fenno, ca. 1906). For an analysis of the theme of office women "marrying the boss," see Donald Robin Makosky, "The Portrayal of Women in Wide Circulation Magazine Short Stories" (Ph.D. diss., University of Pennsylvania, 1966); and Fine, *Souls,* 69–70.

56. Edward Jones Kilduff, *The Private Secretary: The Duties and Opportunities of the Position,* rev. ed. (New York: Century, 1924), 7–8.

57. No. 1781, Box 33, Folder 384, BVI. Except for public speeches such as Miss Snow's, no names will be used from this survey, because the respondents were promised anonymity.

58. Filene, *Him/Her/Self,* 83–86.

59. Types ms., Box 37, Volume 6a, BVI.

60. Edward Jones Kilduff, *The Private Secretary: His Duties and Opportunities* (New York: Century, 1919); Kilduff, *Private Secretary* (1924).

61. Kilduff, *Private Secretary* (1924), 53.

62. Clara Lanza, "Women Clerks in New York," *Cosmopolitan* 10 (1891): 490.

63. Kilduff, *Private Secretary* (1924), 54.

64. R. LeClerc Phillips, "The Temperamental Typist," *North American Review* 227 (1929): 12.

65. Ibid., 12–13.

66. W. W. Charters and Isadore B. Whitley, *Summary of Report on Analysis of Secretarial Duties and Traits* (New York: National Junior Personnel Service, 1924), 173–75; Alice Harriet Grady, "Secretary Work in the Business Office," in *Vocations for the Trained Woman: Opportunities Other than Teaching,* ed. Agnes F. Perkins (Boston: Women's Educational and Industrial Union, 1910), 210–11.

67. No. 1335, Box 32, Folder 376, BVI.

68. No. 1436, Box 33, Folder 384, BVI.

69. Henry Horwood, "The Big Man's Other Self," *Van Norden, the World Mirror* 4 (Jan. 1909): 457, 460.

70. Kilduff, *Private Secretary* (1924), 17.

71. No. 1308, Box 32, Folder 376; No. 1156, Box 32, Folder 376; No. 1778, Box 33, Folder 384, BVI.

72. No. 1226, Box 32, Folder 376; No. 1753, Box 33, Folder 384; No. 2009, Box 33, Folder 383; No. 2027, Box 33, Folder 383, BVI.

73. No. 1308, Box 32, Folder 376; No. 982, Folder 371, BVI.

74. No. 2034, Box 33, Folder 383, BVI.

75. Kilduff, *Private Secretary* (1924), 24.

76. Ibid., 25, emphasis added.

77. Edward T. Hall, *The Hidden Dimension* (Garden City: Doubleday, 1966), 2, 107–22.

78. Elyce Rotella cites a 1927 survey on the gender preferences of office managers for workers filling specific jobs. Women's trades included file clerk, secretarial stenographer, stenographer, dictating machine operator, bookkeeping machine operator, calculating machine operator, and typist. Men's trades included correspondent, receiving clerk, shipping clerk, timekeeper, and stock clerk. See *From Home to Office: U.S. Women at Work, 1870–1930* (Ann Arbor: UMI Research Press, 1981), 167.

79. Grace Hazard, "A Feather Duster," *Scribner's Magazine* 85 (Feb. 1929): 180.

80. Organizational chart of Mailing Department, June 1921, E. I. duPont de Nemours Papers, HM&L.

81. Makosky, "Portrayal of Women," 25. "Typewriter" was a term applied to both the machine and the people who operated it.

82. The image shows up in corporate humor. See, for example, "President Presents 25-Year Medal to Miss Thiele," *The Intelligencer* 20, no. 6 (Apr. 1929): 40, MLICA.

83. Makosky, "Portrayal of Women," 34.

84. Ellen Ada Smith, "The Typewriting Clerk," *Longman's Magazine* 31 (1897–98): 431–46.

85. "The Typewritten Letter," *McClure's Magazine* 2 (1883–84): 446. The reference here to the piano may have been twofold. Lisa Fine has found that typewriter companies advertised for young women who could play the piano to sell their wares, assuming that such manual skills would transfer and that only girls of a "refined" class would know how to play. Fine argues that typewriters were not "gender-neutral" machines and that employers consciously selected women because of their alleged manual dexterity. *Souls,* 21–22.

86. Smith, "Typewriting Clerk," 431–46; Fine, *Souls,* 69.

87. "Typewritten Letter," 450.

88. Elaine Tyler May, *Great Expectations: Marriage & Divorce in Post-Victorian America* (Chicago: University of Chicago Press, 1980); Kenneth A. Yellis, "Prosperity's Child: Some Thoughts on the Flapper," *American Quarterly* 21

(Spring 1969): 44–64; Christina Simmons, "Companionate Marriage and the Lesbian Threat," *Frontiers* 4 (1979): 54–59.

89. Hopper, "The Love Pirate," 3–9; James Hopper, "The Love Pirate," part II, 58 (Jan. 1915): 215–24. This plot outline is very similar to that of *The Office Wife,* a popular film made in 1930, discussed in Fine, *Souls,* 143–44.

90. Grace Robinson, "The Rocky Road to Secretarial Success," *Liberty* (21 Apr. 1928): 21–22, 24, 26, 28; Mildred Harrington, "Too Much Dictation," *American Magazine* 110 (Sept. 1930): 57, 137–39; Lauretta Fancher, "His Secretary Speaking," *Collier's* 83 (13 Apr. 1929): 28, 40; Loire Brophy, *If Women Must Work* (New York: Appleton-Century, 1936), 120.

91. Harrington, "Too Much Dictation," 57.

92. Justine Mansfield, "Business Girls as 'Office Housekeepers,'" *Office Economist* 8 (May 1926): 7.

93. Ibid., 13–14.

94. Robinson, "Rocky Road," 21.

95. "Women in Business, II," 55.

96. No. 1767, Folder 384b, BVI.

Chapter Three: Science and Sensibility

1. Theodore Dreiser, *Sister Carrie,* ed. Donald Pizer (New York: W. W. Norton, 1970), 3–4.

2. Frederick Nichols, *The Personal Secretary: Differentiating Duties and Essential Personal Traits* (Cambridge: Harvard University Press, 1934), 30.

3. "Have You a Little 'Deception' Clerk in Your Business?" *Literary Digest* 64 (6 Mar. 1920): 131; Ellen Lane Spencer, *The Efficient Secretary* (New York: Frederick A. Stokes, 1917), 175–84; Frances Avery Faunce with Frederick G. Nichols, *Secretarial Efficiency* (New York: McGraw-Hill, 1939), 515–69; W. W. Charters and Isadore B. Whitley, *Summary of Report on Analysis of Secretarial Duties and Traits* (New York: National Junior Personnel Service, 1924), 173–77; Margery Davies, *Woman's Place Is at the Typewriter, 1870–1930* (Philadelphia: Temple University Press, 1982), 51–53; Lisa M. Fine *The Souls of the Skyscraper: Female Clerical Workers in Chicago, 1870–1930* (Philadelphia: Temple University Press, 1990), 83–84.

4. H. G. Kenagy, "He Makes His Agents Egotists!" *Manager's Magazine* 4, no. 2 (Mar.–Apr. 1929): 9–12; Merle Crowell, "If You Ask Me . . . ," *American Magazine* 108 (Nov. 1929): 35; Edward A. Woods, "Retaining Agents: A Responsibility of the Manager," *Manager's Magazine* 2, no. 1 (Jan. 1927): 3–7; Orison Swett Marden, *Power of Personality* (New York: Thomas Y. Crowell, 1906); Magner White, "The Race Is Not Always to the Swift Nor the Hard-Boiled," *American Magazine* 108 (Nov. 1929): 52, 174–78; James Logan, "Men—The Biggest Problem in Business," *System* 30 (Dec. 1916): 559–66.

5. A. Meynard, "Ode to the Boss," *Remington Notes* 4, no. 3 (Jan. 1917): 6, Remington Rand Papers, HM&L.

6. Frederick A. Savage, "Life Insurance: The Business and the Man," *The New England Pilot* 1, no. 10 (Apr. 1916): 139, TNE; Robert Wiebe, *The Search for Order, 1877–1920* (New York: Hill & Wang, 1967).

7. American Kardex Company, *A Proposal of Kardex: Cards in Sight,* Tonawanda, N.Y., ca. 1925; Office Equipment Catalogue, Inc., *Office Equipment Catalogue,* ca. 1920; Horder's Stationery Stores, Inc., *Everything for the Office,* Chicago, 1919; Addressograph Catalogue, ca. 1915; Art Metal Construction Company, *The Book of Better Business,* Jamestown, N.Y., 1917, 11; and Shaw-Walker Steel Equipment, Co., *Built Like a Skyscraper,* 1927; all in Trade Catalogue Collection, HM&L. On gender in the printing industry, see Ava Baron, "An 'Other' Side of Gender Antagonism at Work: Men, Boys, and the Remasculinization of Printers' Work, 1830–1920," in *Work Engendered: Toward a New History of American Labor,* ed. Ava Baron (Ithaca: Cornell University Press, 1991), 47–69.

8. David F. Noble, *America by Design: Science, Technology & the Rise of Corporate Capitalism* (New York: Oxford University Press, 1979), 40–41; Robert K. Bain, "The Process of Professionalization: Life Insurance Selling" (Ph.D. diss., University of Chicago, 1953), 130.

9. JoAnne Yates, *Control through Communication: The Rise of System in American Management* (Baltimore: Johns Hopkins University Press, 1989), 2; Barbara Ehrenreich and John Ehrenreich, "The Professional-Managerial Class," in *Between Labor and Capital,* ed. Pat Walker (Boston: South End Press, 1979), 4–45. They define the professional-managerial class "as consisting of salaried mental workers who do not own the means of production and whose major function in the social division of labor may be described broadly as the reproduction of capitalist culture and capitalist class relations" (12). See also Margaret Hedstrom, "Automating the Office: Technology and Skill in Women's Clerical Work, 1940–1970" (Ph.D. diss., University of Wisconsin, 1988), 22. Hedstrom uses the term *systematizers* to refer to the pre-Taylorism movement.

10. Irvin Wyllie, *The Self-Made Man in America: The Myth of Rags to Riches* (New Brunswick: Rutgers University Press, 1954), 40. See also Alan Trachtenberg, *The Incorporation of America: Culture and Society in the Gilded Age* (New York: Hill & Wang, 1982), 45–63; and E. Anthony Rotundo, *American Manhood: Transformations in Masculinity from the Revolution to the Modern Era* (New York: Basic Books, 1993), 195.

11. Trachtenberg, *Incorporation,* 107–8.

12. On the hegemonic relationship between "science" and "objectivity," see Michel Foucault, *The Order of Things: An Archaeology of the Human Sciences* (New York: Vintage, 1973). On the relationship between science and cultural definitions of maleness, see Evelyn Fox Keller, *Reflections on Gender and Science* (New Haven: Yale University Press, 1985). Even female personnel managers, who shared the scientific assumptions of their male peers, often entered management because of their belief in the special needs of female workers. I discuss female managers and the "female management style" in more detail in chapter 6.

13. Olivier Zunz has argued the opposite: that "scientific sales" was concerned with moral or ethical principles. Zunz, however, does not distinguish between the

various types of sales schools and the different historical roots of "scientific" and "impressionistic" sales. As a result, he obscures the implications of sales ideology for masculinity and for the gender division of labor in management. See *Making America Corporate, 1870–1920* (Chicago: University of Chicago Press, 1990), chap. 7.

14. Susan Hartman Strom, *Beyond the Typewriter: Gender, Class, and the Origins of Modern American Office Work, 1900–1930* (Urbana: University of Illinois Press, 1992), 129–35.

15. This combination of humanistic and rationalized concerns is clear, for example, in Marie Louise Wright, "City Cruel Only to Girls who Are Not Efficient, Says Guardian of 2,000," *The Evening Mail* [New York] (8 May 1913), n.p., MLICA.

16. The two most important scholars of the history of management and professionalization essentially ignored the sales area. See, generally, Wiebe, *The Search for Order*; Robert Wiebe, *Businessmen and Reform: A Study of the Progressive Movement* (Cambridge: Harvard University Press, 1962); and Alfred Chandler, *The Visible Hand: The Managerial Revolution in American Business* (Cambridge: Harvard University Press, 1977).

17. M. Christine Anderson, "Gender, Class and Culture: Women Secretarial and Clerical Workers in the United States, 1925–1955" (Ph.D. diss., Ohio State University, 1986), 97–98, 175–86. On social psychology and management, see also F. J. Roethlisberger and William J. Dickson, *Management and the Worker* (Cambridge: Harvard University Press, 1939); and Elton Mayo, *The Social Problems of an Industrial Civilization* (Cambridge: Graduate School of Business Administration, Harvard University, 1945).

18. In the widest sense of the term, *management* referred to controlling and directing the affairs of a company to maximize financial gain. The railroads probably made the earliest systematic efforts to create a management tier that would coordinate disparate workplaces and work functions. See, for example, Walter Licht, *Working for the Railroad: The Organization of Work in the Nineteenth Century* (Princeton: Princeton University Press, 1983). As in financial industries, a bureaucracy probably was created, in the first instance, because of the difficulties of coordinating geographically dispersed work forces and job sites.

19. *Impressionistic management* is my term for a cluster of ideas that developed around insurance sales.

20. "Life Insurance Management," *The Insurance Monitor and Wall Street Review* 15, no. 6 (June 1867): 355, HM&L.

21. Henry C. Fish, *Agent's Manual of Life Assurance* (New York: 1867), 49–62, HM&L.

22. "From Missouri?" *The Intelligencer* 16, no. 5 (Apr. 15, 1922), 8, MLICA.

23. "Three Tools," *New England Pilot* 14, no. 5 (Nov. 1928): 82, emphasis in original, TNE.

24. W. F. Winterble, "Securing and Developing College Men," *Manager's Magazine* 3, no. 3 (Jul. 1928): 13.

25. On women in sales work and gendered definitions of skill, see Susan Porter

Benson, *Counter Cultures: Saleswomen, Managers, and Customers in American Department Stores, 1890–1940* (Urbana: University of Illinois Press, 1986), 130–35.

26. Peter Filene, *Him/Her/Self: Sex Roles in Modern America*, 2d. ed. (Baltimore: Johns Hopkins University Press, 1986), 140.

27. *Twenty-second Annual Report of the Directors of the New England Mutual Life Insurance Company* (Boston: Nathan Sawyer & Son, 1865) and *Twenty-Fourth Annual Report of the Directors of The New England Mutual Life Insurance Company* (Boston: Nathan Sawyer & Son, 1867), TNE. R. Carlyle Buley, *The Equitable Life Assurance Society of the United States, 1859–1959* (New York: Appleton-Century-Crofts, 1959), 68.

28. Woods, "Retaining Agents," 6. Usually, agents were not technically employees of a company, since they worked on a commission rather than salary basis. However, companies' concerns with public image and accountability (particularly after the 1905 Armstrong investigation and the resulting legislation), meant that agents were treated as direct representatives.

29. Advertisement, *The Weekly Underwriter* 22, no. 16 (8 May 1880): 312.

30. Advertisement, *The Weekly Underwriter* 42, no. 8 (22 Feb. 1890): 28.

31. On agents as "apprentices," see William Alexander, "How to Be an Agent," *The Equitable News* 11 (Nov. 1900), 5, ELASA; Burton Hendrick, *The Story of Life Insurance* (London: William Heinemann, 1907), 110–14; Marquis James, *The Metropolitan Life: A Study in Business Growth* (New York: Viking Press, 1947), 31.

32. Magazine abstract, Dec. 1939, V.F. Employees 1867–1960(I), MLICA; "Outline of Discussion on Method in Recruiting and Training Men Conducted by Earle W. Brailey, Assistant Superintendent of Agencies," 1 Mar. 1929, 2–3, TNE.

33. Karen Halttunen, *Confidence Men and Painted Women: A Study of Middle-class Culture in America, 1830–1870* (New Haven: Yale University Press, 1982).

34. Dreiser, *Sister Carrie*, 3–5. *Sister Carrie* was first published in 1900; the story takes place in the 1880s and 1890s.

35. Harvey J. Clermont, *Organizing the Insurance Worker: A History of Labor Unions of Insurance Employees* (Washington: Catholic University of America Press, 1960), 1.

36. Sinclair Lewis, *Babbitt* (New York: Grosset & Dunlap, 1922); Bruce Barton, *The Man Nobody Knows* (New York: Grosset & Dunlap, 1925), i–v.

37. Bain, "Process," 43–44.

38. James, *Metropolitan Life*, 79–81.

39. Bain, "Process," chap. 4.

40. Quote is in Clermont, *Organizing*, 1–3. See also Samuel L. Roth, president of Employees Fidelity Organization, to Leroy A. Lincoln, president of Metropolitan Life Insurance Company, 18 Apr. 1938, V.F. Managers to 1939 (I), MLICA.

41. Bain, "Process," 130–31.

42. Woods's voice carried a great deal of weight in the insurance world. He became general agent of his father's Equitable agency in Pittsburgh at the age of twenty-five, and he turned it into one of the largest and most prestigious agencies in

the country. Woods was by 1915 a very wealthy man. See Bain, "Process," 127–32; *The Intelligencer* (31 Dec. 1921): n.p., MLICA.

43. Kenagy, "He Makes His Agents Egotists!," 9–12; Willis Hatfield Hazard, "The Art of Personal Selling," *Manager's Magazine* 1, no. 3 (Jul. 1926): 20–23. For a somewhat earlier description of selling as an art, see "Loyalty," *The New England Pilot* 1, no. 6 (Dec. 1915): 75, TNE.

44. "Securing and Developing College Men," *Manager's Magazine* 3, no. 3 (Jul. 1928): 13–14. On the debates over employing college men in retail sales, see Alan R. Raucher, "Dime Store Chains: The Making of Organization Men, 1880–1940," *Business History Review* 65 (Spring 1991): 140–41.

45. Woods, "Retaining Agents," 3–4.

46. James, *Metropolitan Life,* 50; *The Metropolitan* 19, no. 3 (1895): 2; 19, no. 8 (1895): 2, MLICA.

47. "The Agent," *The Metropolitan* 18, no. 8 (1894), 2, MLICA.

48. Mary Ryan, *Cradle of the Middle Class: The Family in Oneida County, New York, 1790–1865* (New York: Cambridge University Press, 1981), 141; Halttunen, *Confidence Men,* 50; Rotundo, *American Manhood,* 196–205.

49. Rencher Harris to Plassie Harris, 12 Mar. 1926, Rencher Harris Papers, DUL.

50. *North American Review* 97, no. 201 (Oct. 1863): 306, 302; quote from Bain, "Process," 141.

51. Darwin P. Kingsley, cited in Morton Keller, *The Life Insurance Enterprise, 1885–1910: A Study in the Limits of Corporate Power* (Cambridge: Harvard University Press, 1963), 29; Haley Fiske, "Mother Metropolitan," *Life Insurance Addresses and Papers,* vol. 3 (Privately printed, ca. 1920), 1, MLICA.

52. *The Equitable Record* 62 (1890): 2, ELASA.

53. Hazard, "Art of Personal Selling," 23, emphasis in original. Hazard also was the editor of *The New England Pilot,* a journal produced by the home office of New England Mutual for agents and clearly oriented to the managerial view. See 2, no. 14 (Aug. 1928): 1–30, TNE.

54. Hazard, "The Art," 23.

55. *The New England Pilot* 7, no. 12 (June 1922): 184, TNE.

56. Quote from Elizur Wright in typewritten ms. notes for lecture by Glover S. Hastings, 1924, Home Office Training School file, TNE.

57. Ibid.

58. "How a Young Man without Capital can Make His Fortune," advertisement reproduced in *The Equitable News* 23 (Nov. 1901), n.p., ELASA. Emphasis in original.

59. "Self-Supervision," *The New England Pilot* 14, no. 3 (Sept. 1928): 43, TNE.

60. "A Man Who Wins," *The Pointer* (1907), newsletter of the Rhode Island and Connecticut General Agency, TNE.

61. "The Science of Salesmanship," reproduced in *The New England Pilot* 1, no. 12 (1 Dec. 1908): 11, TNE.

62. *Items for Agents* 64 (14 Jan. 1909): 5, ELASA. Emphasis in original.

63. Albert H. Curtis, "Methods for Keeping up Enthusiasm and Securing Pros-

pects through Policy Holders," in *Papers Read at the Fourth Annual Meeting, General Agents' Association of the New England Mutual Life Insurance Company, New York City, 26–28 July 1904* (Boston: New England Mutual Life Insurance Co., 1904), 38–42, TNE.

64. *Items for Agents* 65 (21 Jan. 1909): 1–2, ELASA. Emphasis in original.

65. Orison Swett Marden, *Masterful Personality* (New York: Thomas Y. Crowell, 1921), 46–47.

66. Bain, "Process," 52–55.

67. Rotundo, *American Manhood,* 245. Rotundo argues that competitiveness developed as a masculine virtue in the 1880s and 1890s, but he does not link this change to the growth of a consumer economy.

68. "Pointers on How to Secure the Application," *The New England Pilot* 1, no. 12 (1 Dec. 1908): 1, TNE. This newsletter was produced by the Thomas & Kaye General Agency in Louisville. It was produced independently, without home-office approval. Phyllis Steele, archivist of The New England, has noted that since this was an agency publication it could be more forthright in its discussion of sales techniques. Personal communication to author.

69. Ibid.

70. Insurance Research and Review Service, *The Principles of Advanced Salesmanship* (Indianapolis: The Insurance Research and Review Service, 1941), 5.

71. Louis F. Paret, "Agency Spirit," *Manager's Magazine* 1, no. 1 (Jan. 1926): 5.

72. Clarence N. Anderson, "Secret of Success is Self-Control," *The New England Pilot* 13, no. 7 (Jan. 1928): 135, TNE.

73. "The Benefits of Rivalry," *The New England Pilot* 7, no. 8 (Feb. 1922), 121; Glover S. Hastings, "The Advantages of an Information Bureau, A General Agents' Exchange, and a Regular Company Publication, to be conducted by the Home Office," in *Papers Read at the Fourth Annual Meeting,* 32–37; "Personal Items," *The New England Pilot* 14, no. 6 (Dec. 1928): 99; all in TNE. "The Saratoga Convention," *The Equitable News* 10 (Oct. 1900), 7, ELASA.

74. Quote from Elizur Wright, Hastings lecture, TNE.

75. Mary Ryan has noted that the Oneida, New York, Sons of Temperance stopped collecting sick benefits from members in the 1840s and "contracted instead with an insurance company"; Ryan, *Cradle,* 142. On life insurance executives' membership in fraternal organizations, see *Nosahogan News,* Waterbury, Conn. (Sept. 1947), n.p., Vertical Files, Biography Section, TNE. "NEL Directors' Life Sketches," undated typescript, post-1937, entry for Percival Lowell Everett, Vertical Files, Biography Section, TNE. See also "Dr. Harold M. Frost, Physician with Two Full Careers, Died Saturday," *The Courier-Gazette,* Rockland, Me. (5 Mar. 1968), n.p., Vertical Files, Biography Section, TNE. On black fraternal organizations, see William J. Kennedy, *The North Carolina Mutual Story: A Symbol of Progress, 1898–1970* (Durham: North Carolina Mutual Life Insurance Company, 1970), 20.

76. Mary Ann Clawson, *Constructing Brotherhood: Class, Gender, and Fraternalism* (Princeton: Princeton University Press, 1989); Charles F. Marden, *Rotary and Its Brothers: An Analysis and Interpretation of the Men's Service Club* (Prince-

ton: Princeton University Press, 1935). On fraternal organizations, see also Mark C. Carnes, *Secret Ritual and Manhood in Victorian America* (New Haven: Yale University Press, 1989).

77. William May, "Significance of the Job of the Manager," *Manager's Magazine* 1, no. 4 (Oct. 1926): 21.

78. Paret, "Agency Spirit," 4.

Chapter Four: The Domestic Office

1. Charles G. Loring, "Office Buildings Now and Then," *Architectural Forum* 52 (June 1930): 821.

2. Susan Porter Benson, *Counter Cultures: Saleswomen, Managers, and Customers in American Department Stores, 1890–1940* (Urbana: University of Illinois Press, 1986).

3. Robert Sommer, *Personal Space: The Behavioral Basis of Design* (Englewood Cliffs: Prentice-Hall, 1969).

4. Ibid., 19.

5. Richard Edwards's *Contested Terrain: The Transformation of the Workplace in the Twentieth Century* (New York: Basic Books, 1979) conceptualizes the efforts of scientific management to "control" the work force as, in part, a function of changing work spaces. His use of the word *terrain* is more metaphorical than analytical.

6. Daniel Bluestone, "Landscape and Culture in 19th Century Chicago," (Ph.D. diss., University of Chicago, 1984), 245–47.

7. John Burchard and Albert Bush-Brown, *The Architecture of America: A Social and Cultural History* (Boston: Little, Brown, 1961), 152.

8. *The Metropolitan Life Insurance Company: Its History, Its Present Position in the Insurance World, Its Home Office Building, and Its Work Carried on Therein* (New York: n.p., 1908), 31, MLICA.

9. R. Carlyle Buley, *The Equitable, 1859–1959* (New York: Appleton-Century-Crofts, 1959), 20; Photographs, ELASA; William Alexander, "Far Away and Long Ago," *The Equitable Spirit* 2, no. 1 (26 Jul. 1933): n.p.; "When the Equitable Was an Infant Enterprise," *The Equitable News* (26 Jul. 1909), 7, ELASA.

10. In his study of the precorporate office in England, David Lockwood noted that nineteenth-century partnerships did not generate very much paperwork, since records were used primarily as legal documents rather than as funds of information from which to make business decisions. This practice limited the functional needs of office size to work spaces for copyists and executives and a small amount of storage space. See *The Blackcoated Worker: A Study in Class Consciousness* (London: George Allen & Unwin, 1958), 19–20.

11. Marquis James, *The Metropolitan Life: A Study in Business Growth* (New York: Viking Press, 1947), 45.

12. Bluestone, "Landscape and Culture," 251. On banks, see William H. Birkmire, *Planning and Construction of High Office Buildings* (New York: John Wiley,

1898), 13, 81–97; and "Northwestern Bank Architecture," *Coast Banker* 2, no. 5 (May 1909): 225, WFCA.

13. Bluestone, "Landscape and Culture," 251; Sam Bass Warner, *The Urban Wilderness: A History of the American City* (New York: Harper & Row, 1972), 85–112.

14. *1500 Walnut Street Building: A Modern Bank and Office Building of Twenty-two Stories in the New Financial Center of Philadelphia* (Philadelphia, 1918), pamphlet collection, HM&L. This brochure used the building's proximity to "leading hotels and clubs" as a selling point. Beginning in the early nineteenth century, the work of middle-class men moved out of a family setting and into a physically separate workplace. Many leisure activities also removed from the family residence. Middle-class men joined fraternal organizations, or by the late nineteenth century, social or business clubs. The advent of specific class-oriented leisure areas came in the late nineteenth century with the growth of places such as Coney Island and, for the middle and upper classes, vacation resorts. Bluestone, "Landscape and Culture," 234–35, 245–47; Mary P. Ryan, *The Cradle of the Middle Class: The Family in Oneida County, New York, 1790–1865* (New York: Cambridge University Press, 1984); Stuart M. Blumin, *The Emergence of the Middle Class: Social Experience in the American City, 1760–1900* (New York: Cambridge University Press, 1989); Mary Ann Clawson, *Constructing Brotherhood: Class, Gender and Fraternalism* (Princeton: Princeton University Press, 1989); Kathy Peiss, *Cheap Amusements: Working Women and Leisure in Turn-of-the-Century New York* (Philadelphia: Temple University Press, 1986); Perry R. Duis, *The Saloon: Public Drinking in Chicago & Boston, 1880–1920* (Urbana: University of Illinois Press, 1983). Theodore Dreiser, in *An American Tragedy* (New York: H. Liveright, 1929), gives a vivid image of the class-conscious social life of turn-of-the-century resorts.

15. Randolph Sexton, *The Logic of Modern Architecture: Exteriors and Interiors of Modern American Buildings* (New York: Architectural Books Publishing Company, 1929).

16. Birkmire, *Planning and Construction;* Carl W. Condit, *American Building: Materials and Techniques,* 2d ed. (Chicago: University of Chicago Press, 1982).

17. Kenneth T. Gibbs, *Business Architectural Imagery in America, 1870–1930* (Ann Arbor: UMI Research Press, 1984), 14.

18. Henry B. Fuller, *The Cliff Dwellers: A Novel* (1893; reprinted, New York: Irvington, 1981).

19. Gibbs, *Business Architectural Imagery;* Bluestone, "Landscape and Culture."

20. See, for example, advertisements for the Berkshire Life Insurance Company and the Security Insurance Company, *The Insurance Monitor* 19, no. 217 (Jan. 1871): 22, 24. Contemporaries fully recognized the communicative function of tall office buildings. Critics saw skyscraper cities as a metaphor for the unpredictability and social irresponsibility of American capitalism. See Fuller, *Cliff Dwellers,* for an especially caustic treatment of the destructive aspects of business. Fuller uses the uneven skyline of the skyscraper city and its cold, imposing façades as metaphors

for the economic cycle (see 1–4). Owners and promoters hoped the buildings would communicate stability and security in a period of economic "booms" and "busts." They heralded the appearance of a new building through advertising, publishing information in newspapers, hosting building tours, and distributing informational pamphlets. This sort of publicity program was typical of life insurance and banking, both of which sold no visible product and dealt primarily with money and service. See *Plans and Descriptions of the Equitable Building, Corner of Milk & Devonshire Streets* (New York: New York Graphic, 1874), 5–7, WL; E. M. Bacon, *King's Dictionary of Boston* (Cambridge: Moses King, 1883), 253.

21. The insurance industry was a leader in reworking architectural imagery to communicate business values to the general public. Gibbs, *Business Architectural Imagery,* 93–124.

22. *Home Office Building, New England Mutual Life Insurance Company,* TNE. For illustrations and commentary on the northern Baroque, see Julius S. Held and Donald Posner, *Seventeenth and Eighteenth Century Art: Baroque Painting, Sculpture, and Architecture* (Englewood Cliffs: Prentice-Hall, 1977), 133–34, 138, 286–88.

23. Deborah Gardner, "The Architecture of Commercial Capitalism: John Kellum and the Development of New York, 1840–1875" (Ph.D. diss., Columbia University, 1979), 134.

24. Abram T. Collier, *A Capital Ship: New England Life* (Boston: The New England, 1985), 70–71; *Metropolitan Life Insurance Company,* 23. MLICA; "Wells Fargo Nevada National Bank," *Coast Banker* 7, no. 2 (Aug. 1911): 89, WFCA. As late as 1928, Provident Mutual Life's new office building in Philadelphia used Renaissance styling and included a tall clock tower; see "New Home Occupied by Provident Mutual," press release (9 Apr. 1928), PML.

25. *A Bank for Fredericksburg: Two Centuries of Banking in Virginia,* National Bank of Fredericksburg, Fredericksburg, Virginia, company brochure, ca. 1989, author's collection.

26. Elizabeth C. Cromley, *Alone Together: A History of New York's Early Apartments* (Ithaca: Cornell University Press, 1990), 15–20.

27. The mixture of references to the public, civic architecture of Italian city-states, the monarchies of predemocratic Europe, and domestic palatial architecture served several purposes. The Italian inference suggested a public-spirited business with ties to the American past and uniquely American values. Early-nineteenth-century public and domestic architecture revived Greek and Roman classicism in the neoclassical or "Federal" style, identifying buildings such as state capitols and banks with notions of republican virtue. This style remained popular for banks well into the twentieth century. See Lillian B. Miller, *Patrons and Patriotism: The Encouragement of the Fine Arts, 1790–1860* (Chicago: University of Chicago Press, 1966), 40–44; Samuel M. Green, *American Art, A Historical Survey* (New York: The Ronald Press, 1966), 125–31. On the symbolic significance of the "American-Roman style," see Yi-Fu Tuan, *Topophilia: A Study of Environmental Perception, Attitudes, and Values* (New York: Prentice-Hall, 1974), 198–99. For an example of

early-twentieth-century banking architecture, see "Building of American Bank & Trust, Co., New Haven, Conn.," *The American Architect* 63, no. 2193 (Jan. 2, 1918): plate 8.

The Baroque detailing on the mansard roofs of Metropolitan Life, the Equitable, New England Mutual, and others, along with their ornate columns and windows, recalled the opulence of a predemocratic era and communicated "high culture" and elevated status. Peter Thornton has referred to the upper-class domestic architecture of the period 1870 to 1900 as "American urban palace." This style drew on Baroque, Gothic, Renaissance, and classical architectural motifs in an eclectic but recognizable mixture. See Thornton's *Authentic Decor: The Domestic Interior, 1620–1920* (London: Weidenfeld & Nicholson, 1984), 308. See also Cromley *Alone Together,* 2.

28. In this interpretation I disagree with Kenneth Gibbs's assertion that insurance buildings constructed after 1870 moved away from domestic imagery. Gibbs, *Business Architectural Imagery,* 21–24; Cromley, *Alone Together,* 140.

29. Robert W. Rydell, "The Culture of Imperial Abundance: World's Fairs in the Making of American Culture," in *Consuming Visions: Accumulation and Display of Goods in America, 1880–1920,* ed. Simon J. Bronner (New York: W. W. Norton, 1989), 201. On the economic and cultural history of amusement parks, see Judith A. Adams, *The American Amusement Park: A History of Technology and Thrills* (Boston: Twayne, 1991), 19–56.

30. Gibbs, *Business Architectural Imagery,* 93.

31. For the links among progress, spirituality, and technology, see Leo Marx, *The Machine in the Garden: Technology and the Pastoral Ideal in America* (New York: Oxford University Press, 1980).

32. Within five years there were so many visitors that the company added four more elevators. See James, *Metropolitan Life,* 30; *Plans and Descriptions of the Equitable Building,* 5–7. On roof gardens, see Cromley, *Alone Together,* 154. Cromley finds the roots of roof gardens and viewing platforms in New York City nightlife in the early 1880s. My study of commercial architecture suggests both an earlier date and a more immediate source in business buildings. The main point here is that such diverse public spaces—entertainment, living, and working— usually have been seen as widely divergent experiences, but they shared many of the same assumptions and stylistic conventions.

33. *Metropolitan Life Insurance Company's Building,* company brochure, New York, 1893, MLICA.

34. Reproduction of 1910 advertisement, in *Tower 75* (New York: Metropolitan Life Insurance Company [1984]) MLICA.

35. Ibid.

36. *The Home Office,* 75th Anniversary Number (1943), V.F., H.O. General, 29–32, MLICA.

37. "Wells Fargo Nevada National Bank," *Coast Banker* 7, no. 2 (Aug. 1911): 88–92, WFCA; Sinclair Lewis, *Babbitt* (New York: Grosset & Dunlap, 1922), 52.

38. Randolph Sexton, *American Commercial Buildings of Today,* part I (New York: Architectural Books, 1929), 14. Sexton saw skyscrapers as an excellent

expression of American nationalism. See also Gibbs, *Business Architectural Imagery*, 1–2.

39. "Bank Utilities and Construction," *Coast Banker* 2, no. 5 (May 1909): 205, WFCA.

40. Benson, *Counter Cultures*, esp. 82–91.

41. *First Madison Avenue Building*, ca. 1910, V.F. H.O. General, MLICA.

42. "Home Office Building, Victor Talking Machine Co., Camden, New Jersey," *The American Architect* 111 (28 Mar. 1917): 197.

43. "Wells Fargo Nevada National Bank," *Coast Banker* 7, no. 2 (Aug. 1911): 90, WFCA.

44. On the articulation of status in early-nineteenth-century office buildings, see Frank Duffy, "Office Buildings and Organisational Change," in *Buildings and Society: Essays on the Social Development of the Built Environment*, ed. Anthony P. King (London: Routledge & Kegan Press, 1980), 255. The emphasis on luxury and the division of public and private spaces also were typical of department stores during the period. In both instances, the purpose was the same: to present and sell a "product." See, for example, Benson, *Counter Cultures*, 38–47.

45. For the relationship between female shoppers and feminized urban space, see William Leach, "Transformations in a Culture of Consumption: Women and Department Stores, 1890–1925" *Journal of American History* 71 (Sept. 1984): 319–42; Benson, *Counter Cultures*, 76; and Bluestone, "Landscape and Culture," 260. On banking, see, for example, R. M. Waters, "Business Building Department," *Coast Banker* 11, no. 1 (Jan. 1915): 28, WFCA.

46. Henry W. Cook and Edwin H. Brown, "The New Life Insurance Home Office," *Proceedings of the American Life Convention*, 18th Annual Meeting of the American Life Insurance Convention, Oct. 1923 (n.p., 1923), 125.

47. Harry Braverman, *Labor and Monopoly Capital: The Degradation of Work in the Twentieth Century* (New York: Monthly Review Press, 1974), 305.

48. Cited in Priscilla Murolo, "White-Collar Women: The Feminization of the Aetna Life Insurance Company, 1910–1930," paper presented at the annual meeting of the American Historical Association, New York City, Dec. 1985, 8.

49. Photographs, NCM.

50. The earliest use of the term *efficiency* I have found in the life insurance industry is in remarks made in 1865 by Benjamin F. Stevens, the Secretary of New England Mutual. Cited in Collier, *A Capital Ship*, 59–60.

51. For the development of scientific management, see Samuel Haber, *Efficiency and Uplift: Scientific Management in the Progressive Era, 1890–1920* (Chicago: University of Chicago Press, 1964); Daniel Nelson, *Frederick W. Taylor and the Rise of Scientific Management* (Madison: University of Wisconsin Press, 1980); and Stephen Kern, *The Culture of Time and Space, 1880–1918* (Cambridge: Harvard University Press, 1983), 115–17. On the impact of these ideas on architectural design, see George Hill, "Some Practical Limiting Conditions in the Design of the Modern Office Building," *Architectural Record* 2 (Jul. 1892–Jul. 1893): 445; George Hill, "The Economy of the Office Building," *Architectural Record* 15 (Apr. 1904): 313; Adolph M. Schwartz, "An Artistic Office Cuts Our Payroll," *System* 42

(1922): 251–52; and John Taylor Boyd, Jr., "Office Interiors," *Architectural Forum* 41 (Sept. 1924): 145.

52. *Metropolitan Life Insurance Company,* 12–48, MLICA; Photographs, Mechanics-American National Bank, St. Louis, *Remington Notes* 2, no. 5 (ca. 1910): 7; Continental National Bank, Chicago, *Remington Notes* 2, no. 4 (ca. 1910): 15, both in Remington Rand Papers, HM&L.

53. Martha Davis, "Movement as Patterns of Process," *Main Currents in Modern Thought* 31, no. 1 (Sept.–Oct. 1974): 3–16. Michel Foucault details the increasing connection in the nineteenth century between the body and social control in *Discipline and Punish: The Birth of the Prison* (New York: Pantheon Books, 1977). See also Robert Sklar, *Movie-Made America: A Cultural History of American Movies* (New York: Random House, 1975), 5–13, 48–49.

54. Charles E. Myers, "Interior Woodwork," *Coast Banker* 2, no. 5 (May 1909): 205, WFCA.

55. "Victor Talking Machine Co.," 196.

56. Adrian Forty, *Objects of Desire* (New York: Pantheon Books, 1986), 124; Lance Knobel, *Office Furniture: 20th Century Design* (New York: E. P. Dutton, 1987), 11. For the history of the roll-top desk, see Kenneth L. Ames, *Wooton Patent Desks: A Place for Everything and Everything in Its Place,* Exhibition Catalogue (Indianapolis: Indiana State Museum, 1983).

57. Entry dated Nov. 22, 1880, "Instructions to Employees, 1871–1905," handwritten notebook, Farmers and Mechanics' Bank, Philadelphia National Bank Papers, HM&L.

58. R. H. Goodell, "Saving 42% on Routine Work," *System* 37 (June 1920): 1184. This function of spatial arrangements was explicitly stated in Life Office Management Association, *Life Insurance Home Office Buildings: A Study in the Problems of Building Construction* (Fort Wayne: Life Office Management Association, 1933), 3–5. See also "The Ideal Arrangement of a Stenographer's Desk," *Remington Notes* 4, no. 6 (Sept. 1917): 10, HM&L.

59. *The Executive's Workshop: A Booklet on Efficient Office Arrangement* (Rochester: Yawman Erbe Manufacturing, ca. 1922), 6–7, Trade Catalogue Collection, HM&L.

60. Life Office Management Association, *Life Insurance,* 3–5. For another example of organization by room and division, see "Organization of the New England Mutual" (1 Oct. 1931), Home Office Training School File, TNE.

61. This was a fairly typical allowance for office space. E. I. duPont's home office, built in 1911, allowed 167 square feet for each employee, which included space for filing and support services; see Memo to H. G. Haskell from Irenée duPont dated Feb. 9, 1911, duPont Building (1911–12), I. E. duPont de Nemours Papers, HM&L. Life Office Management Association, *Life Insurance,* 8–24.

62. The committee took the specifics on desk space, distances, and orientation from a Metropolitan Life office planning and layout guide.

63. See *Instructions to Employees, 1871–1905* Farmers and Mechanics' Bank, Philadelphia National Bank Papers, HM&L.

64. Thomas Schlereth, *Cultural History and Material Culture: Everyday Life, Landscapes, Museums* (Ann Arbor: UMI Research Press, 1990), 167. See also advertisement for "Series 160 Master Clock" (New York: International Business Machines, 1926), 20, Trade Catalogue Collection, HM&L.

65. E. P. Thompson, "Time, Work-Discipline, and Industrial Capitalism," *Past & Present* 38 (Dec. 1967): 56–97; *The Board Room of Metropolitan Life* (New York: Metropolitan Life Insurance Company, 1970s), 1, MLICA. This clock was in use from the 1890s. Another reference to the symbolic importance of managerial or company clocks can be found in Doyce B. Nunis, Jr., *Past Is Prologue: A Centennial Profile of Pacific Mutual Life Insurance Company* (San Francisco: Pacific Mutual Life Insurance Company, 1968), 17.

66. See, for example, the trade catalogues *Hoskins Office Stationery* (Philadelphia: William H. Hoskins, ca. 1910), 79–80; *You Can Never Forget with the Universal Desk Set* (Camden, N.J.: C. Howard Hunt Pen Company, 1912; *Everything for the Office,* (Chicago: Horder's Stationery Stores, 1919); all in Trade Catalogue Collection, HM&L.

67. For an early example of the social difficulties of a gender-integrated office workplace, see Cindy S. Aron, *Ladies and Gentlemen of the Civil Service: Middle-Class Workers in Victorian America* (New York: Oxford University Press, 1987), 164–65. Contemporaries recognized the problems of male–female interaction in the business office. See, for example, Ruth Ashmore, *The Business Girl in Every Phase of Her Life* (Philadelphia: Curtis, 1898), 15–16, 19–20; and Caroline A. Huling, *Letters of a Business Woman to Her Niece* (New York: R. F. Fenno, ca. 1906), 39. These two "advice" books were typical of a genre that developed in the late nineteenth century to provide guidelines for behavior for women working in offices.

68. Charles H. Vanse, "How Well Do I Remember," *The Equitable Spirit* 1, no. 4 (23 Apr. 1934): n.p., ELASA.

69. Advertisement for Heyer Duplicator Co., Inc., Chicago, in *Office Equipment Catalogue* 3rd ed. (Chicago: Office Equipment Catalogue, 1926), 88, Trade Catalogue Collection, HM&L. On masculinity and printers, see Ava Baron, "Acquiring Manly Competence: The Demise of Apprenticeship and the Remasculinization of Printers' Work," in *Meanings for Manhood: Constructions of Masculinity in Victorian America,* ed. Mark C. Carnes and Clyde Griffen (Chicago: University of Chicago Press, 1990), 152–63.

70. See, for example, Maude Radford Warren, "Green Timber," part I, *Saturday Evening Post* 188 (10 Nov. 1915): 3–5, 38–39, 41–42; and part II, 188 (27 Nov. 1915): 19–20.

71. Harry A. Hopf, *Modern Office Planning with Special Reference to New Building Construction* (New York: H. A. Hopf, 1922), 6–7.

72. *Plans of the New Building of the Metropolitan Life Insurance Company, Corner of Park Place and Church Street, New York City* (1876); and *Plans of the Main Offices of the Metropolitan Life Insurance Company,* V.F. H.O. (1876–1893), MLICA.

73. See, for example, Photographs, Continental National Bank, Chicago, and Mechanics-American National Bank, St. Louis, HM&L.

74. *Metropolitan Life Insurance Company,* 33, 36, 71–72.

75. *Mailing Department* (June 1921), E. I. duPont de Nemours Papers, HM&L.

76. *Metropolitan Life Insurance Company,* 33, 36, 71.

77. "Victor Talking Machine Co.," 200.

78. Life Office Management Association, *Life Insurance,* 29–30.

79. Like many of the more public aspects of corporate buildings, the boardroom was a point of company pride and a symbol of corporate stability. When the company tore down its older building in 1958, the boardroom was moved intact into the new building. See *The Board Room of Metropolitan Life,* MLICA. For a similar use of domestic interiors in British concerns, see Forty, *Objects of Desire,* 144.

80. Angel Kwolek-Folland, "The Elegant Dugout: Domesticity and Moveable Culture in the United States, 1870–1900," *American Studies* 25, no. 2 (Fall 1984): 21–37; Angel Kwolek-Folland, "The Useful What-not and the Ideal of 'Domestic Decoration,'" *Helicon Nine* 8 (1983): 72–83. "Dens" even could be found on the late-nineteenth-century frontier. See Angel Kwolek-Folland, "Discoveries in the Meaning of Domesticity: Middle-Class Women and Cultural Change in the United States, 1870–1900" (M.A. thesis, Kansas State University, 1982), esp. fig. 35. On the notion of "gentlemen" executives, see Forty, *Objects of Desire,* 144.

81. *Golden Anniversary* (Lebanon, Pa.: First National Bank of Lebanon, 1906), Pamphlet Collection, HM&L.

82. *Living Room, Bedroom, and Office Chairs* (Wayland, N.Y.: W. H. Gunlocke Chair, 1922); *Derby Roll-top Desk and Fine Office Furniture* (Boston: Derby & Kilmer Desk, ca. 1880); *Steel Office Equipment* Catalogue No. 825 (Cincinnati: Globe-Wernicke, 1926), 2; *Office, Dining, Bedroom, Library & Rocking Chairs* (Gardner, Mass.: S. K. Pierce & Son, 1925); *Office Desks, Tables & Accessories, Radio Cabinets* (Whitesboro, N.Y.: Quigley Furniture, ca. 1925), all in Trade Catalogue Collection, HM&L.

83. Cheryl Robertson, "From Cult to Professional: Domestic Women in Search of Equality," in *The Material Culture of Gender/The Gender of Material Culture,* ed. Kenneth L. Ames and Katharine Martinez (New York: W. W. Norton, forthcoming).

84. Knobel, *Office Furniture,* 6.

85. "Victor Talking Machine Co.," 196: Aymar Embury II, "Business Offices from a Decorative View-Point," *The House Beautiful* 34 (Oct. 1913): 148–51; Horace G. Simpson, "The Architectural Treatment of Business Offices," *The Architect* 17 (1919): 37; Schwartz, "Artistic Office" 251–52; Sidney deBrie, "Decorating the Eight-Hour Home," *Country Life* 48 (Oct. 1925): 16–20.

86. Sexton, *Logic of Modern Architecture,* 11–12.

87. Irenée duPont to Alfred duPont, 27 Feb. 1911, duPont Building (1911–12), E. I. duPont de Nemours Papers, HM&L.

88. A survey of office workers done in 1978 noted that workers considered

physical and conversational privacy the most critical determinants of job satisfaction; not surprisingly, people who had private offices were more satisfied with their surroundings and work space than other workers. Louis Harris & Associates, *The Steelcase National Study of Office Environments: Do They Work?* (Grand Rapids, Mich.: Steelcase, 1978), iv–v.

89. Blumin, *Emergence*, 149, 158.

90. *Plan of Treasurer's Office,* Blueprints, Broad Street Office (Philadelphia: Pennsylvania Railroad, 1929), Pennsylvania Railroad Papers; and Blueprints, 4 Feb. 1911, DuPont Building (1911–12), E. I. duPont de Nemours Papers; both in HM&L.

91. On plumbing, see *Plans and Descriptions of the Equitable Building, Corner of Milk & Devonshire Streets* (New York: New York Graphic Co., 1874), plate V, ELASA; *Plan of the Main Offices of the Metropolitan Life Insurance Company,* MLICA; *Plans for New England Mutual Life Insurance Company,* 24 May 1935 (additions and changes to existing building), TNE; "The Metropolitan Tower," *The American Architect* 96 (6 Oct. 1909): 126, V.F., Tower, MLICA; *Metropolitan Life Insurance Company's Building,* 1893, MLICA; *Home Office Guide* (1937), 19, TNE.

92. "Victor Talking Machine Co.," First Floor plan, plate no. 2153.

93. *Home Office Guide,* 19; "Interview with Mr. Good," 8 Dec. 1953, V.F., H.O. General, MLICA; *Rules and Regulations Governing the Office Employes of the Metropolitan Life Insurance Company of New York* (1895), 4–5, MLICA; *Rules Governing Home Office Clerical Employees* (1921), MLICA; Murolo, "White-Collar Women"; Memorandum from J. V. E. Westfall to departments, 5, Nov. 1920, TNE.

94. *A Wonderful Village: Activities of the Metropolitan Life Insurance Company in the Big Building Fronting Madison Square* (6 Nov. 1911), 3, MLICA; "Rest and Tea Rooms for Our Girl Employees" and "Boys Enjoy the Luncheon and Lounge Rooms," *The Wells Fargo Nevadan* 1, no. 1 (Aug. 1919): 4, 6, WFCA; *Home Office Guide,* 16.

95. Norman F. Cushman, *Reminiscences of an Audit Clerk of the Home Office at Park Place during 1892–1893* V.F., H.O. 1876–1893 (Park Place), MLICA. For the absence of women's lunchrooms in New York City prior to the 1880s, see *Trow's New York City Directory* (New York: Trow City Directory, 1876). Corporate lunchrooms still exist at Metropolitan Life, the Equitable, The New England, and many other companies. Although no longer segregated by gender, they continue the familial tradition of the earlier lunchrooms by providing inexpensive meals that serve the dual purpose of keeping the employees on the premises and reinforcing the notion of corporate concern for employees' welfare.

96. Cushman *Reminiscences,* 1.

97. Murolo, "White-Collar Women," 9.

98. *Union National Bank of Wilmington: Its History and New Building* (Wilmington: Union National Bank, (1908?), Pamphlet Collection, HM&L. Bob Pacini notes that the Union Trust Company of San Francisco's new building in 1910 contained a "ladies' waiting room" as well as oriental rugs and indoor plants; see

"Union Trust Company," *Banker* (Oct. 1979): 11. On separate hotel entrances, see Huling, *Letters*, 172. For the gender segregation of department stores, see Leach, "Transformations in a Culture of Consumption," 331.

99. *Rules Governing Employees*, 4.

100. This stricture appears for the first time in the 1915 edition of *Rules Governing Home Office Clerical Employes*, 13. It makes its last recorded appearance in the 1933 edition, titled *A Manual of Information, Rules & Suggestions for the Guidance of Home Office Employees*, 21, MLICA.

101. Anonymous, *Mutual Forty Years Ago*, MONY Vertical Files, 12. Cited in Gardner, "Architecture of Commercial Capitalism, 119.

102. "The Romance of 32 Park Place," typewritten ms., n.d., V.F., H.O., 1876–1893, 11, MLICA; C. W. Borton, "The Get Together Movement," *Between Ourselves* 4, no. 1 (Dec. 1915): 7–8, PML; *Instructions to Employees*, Farmers and Mechanics' Bank, see esp. entries for 14 Apr. 1887 and 7 Jan. 1888.

103. Sinclair Lewis, *The Job* (New York: Harper & Bros., 1917), 42–43.

104. "Romance of 32 Park Place," 10. For another example of a raised platform for officers, see Gardner, "Architecture of Commercial Capitalism" 118.

105. Lewis, *The Job*, 43.

106. "Personals," *Between Ourselves* 6, no. 4 (Sept. 1918): 168, PML; "Take it From Me," *Pacific Coast News* 1, no. 13 (26 Aug. 1921): 2; "Ye Office Prattle," *Pacific Coast News* 1, no. 7 (19 Feb. 1921): 4, MLICA; "Marriages," *New England Pilot* 1, no. 1 (Jul. 1915): 12, TNE.

107. "Cupid's Darts," *Wells Fargo Nevadan* 1, no. 2 (Sept. 1919): 9, WFCA.

108. Leach, "Transformations," 331.

Chapter Five: The Family Way

1. "Family Records of Agent John P. Bayer," *The Intelligencer* 4, no. 1 (Feb. 5, 1910): cover, MLICA.

2. On the continuing importance of the extended family in business, see Clyde Griffen and Sally Griffen, "Family and Business in a Small City: Poughkeepsie, New York, 1850–1880," *Journal of Urban History* 1, no. 3 (May 1975): 316–38.

3. In a similar way, the early aviation industry used female pilots to demonstrate the simplicity and safety of mechanical flight. See Joseph J. Corn, "Making Flying 'Thinkable': Women Pilots and the Selling of Aviation, 1927–1940," *American Quarterly* 31 (1979): 556–71. I am grateful to Patrick Nolan for calling my attention to this article.

4. Mary P. Ryan, *Women in Public: Between Banners and Ballots, 1825–1880* (Baltimore: Johns Hopkins University Press, 1990), 26.

5. "Proposals and Rates of the Pennsylvania Company for Insurance on Lives and Granting Annuities" (Philadelphia: The Pennsylvania Company, 1859), Scrapbook, 1857–1919, HM&L. A search of trade papers and company advertisements in the late nineteenth century turned up only two departures from this pattern of female figures. One was the Hercules Mutual Life Assurance Society of the United

States, a short-lived New York company that used pictures of the Greek strongman in its advertising. Although a classical allusion, Hercules possessed none of the refinement of the female images. He was half-clad in an animal skin and leaned on an enormous wooden club as he contemplated a wormy apple. The pose was loosely based on the famous Farnese Hercules. The second variation was the logo of the Mutual Benefit Life Insurance Company of Newark, N.J. This company, in the late 1860s, used an image of a pelican—whether male or female is unclear—feeding its young, with the caption, "I live and die for those I love." While not a human figure, the pelican shared the notion of parental protection with other insurance advertising imagery. Advertisements, *The Insurance Monitor* 19, no. 217 (Jan. 1871): 77; and 15, no. 12 (Dec. 1867): 150, HM&L.

6. On the use of female imagery by ethnic and working-class mutual benefit societies, see Ryan, *Women in Public,* 35.

7. Advertisements, *The Insurance Monitor and Wall Street Review* 15, no. 10 (Oct. 1867): 641, 684, HM&L.

8. Advertising insert, *The Insurance Monitor* 19, no. 218 (Feb. 1871), HM&L.

9. John Quincy Adams Ward executed a statue for the Equitable in 1871, based on an emblem designed for use on the company's policies in 1860. Lewis I. Sharp, *John Quincy Adams Ward: Dean of American Sculpture* (Newark: University of Delaware Press, 1985), 184; and R. Carlyle Buley, *The Equitable Life Assurance Society of the United States 1859–1959* (New York: Appleton-Century-Crofts, 1959), 106–7.

10. Phyllis E. Steele, Special Collections Coordinator, *Uses of Company Symbols,* 28 Jul. 1988, TNE.

11. Advertising mock-ups, Provident Mutual Series IV, Advertising and Sales Promotion, PML.

12. "The Old Way and the New," *Remington Notes* 4, no. 8 (Sept. 1918): 8–9, HM&L; *Business System,* 11th ed., catalogue 5 (Grand Rapids: Fred Macey, 1901), Trade Catalogue Collection, HM&L.

13. Interview with W. J. Kennedy, Jr., 19 Jan. 1968, cited in Walter B. Weare, *Black Business in the New South: A Social History of the North Carolina Mutual Life Insurance Company* (Chicago: University of Illinois Press, 1973), 76.

14. James Mann, former archivist of the Metropolitan Life Insurance Company, called my attention to Fiske's theory of worker/employer relations. Haley Fiske, "Mother Metropolitan," *Life Insurance Addresses & Papers,* vol. II (Privately printed, n.d.), 25–26, MLICA.

15. Fiske, "Mother Metropolitan," 1–29. For a similar development of paternalism, see Wing, "Reminiscences," 11.

16. *The Intelligencer: In Memoriam—Haley Fiske 1852–1929* 20, no. 7 (6 Mar. 1929): 17, MLICA.

17. Reprinted from *Western Climber* in *Pacific Coast News* 3, no. 5 (Jan. 1925): 2, MLICA; Buley, *The Equitable,* vol. 1, 404, 544–45. For another nineteenth-century example of the feminine gender ascribed to organizations, see Barbara Franco, "The Ritualization of Male Friendship and Virtue in Nineteenth-Century Fraternal Organizations," in *The Material Culture of Gender/The Gender of Mate-*

rial Culture, ed. Kenneth L. Ames and Katharine Martinez (New York: W. W. Norton, forthcoming); and Mark C. Carnes, *Secret Ritual and Manhood in Victorian America* (New Haven: Yale University Press, 1989).

18. Priscilla Murolo, "White-Collar Women: The Feminization of The Aetna Life Insurance Company, 1910–1930," paper presented at the annual meeting of the American Historical Association, New York City, Dec. 1985, 6–8.

19. See, for example, *A Family of 40,000: How Health and Happiness are Provided for its Members* (New York: Metropolitan Life, ca. 1926), MLICA; "Family Affairs," *New England Pilot* 1, no. 11 (May 1916): 165, TNE; "One Big Family," *New England Pilot* 13, no. 2 (Aug. 1927): 1, TNE; and Buley, *The Equitable,* 160. "Romance Scores another Inning in Family Circle," *Wells Fargo Nevadan* 1, no. 8 (March 1920): 6; "The Second Generation," *Wells Fargo Nevadan* 1, no. 5 (Dec. 1919): 10, both in WFCA.

20. "The Main Equitable Question," *The Nation* 80, no. 2075 (6 April 1905): 262; and remarks made in 1899 by R. A. McCurdy, president of Mutual of New York, reprinted in Buley, *The Equitable,* 544. I am grateful to Thomas Mertes for calling my attention to these two sources. See also Wendell Buck, *From Quill Pens to Computers: An Account of the First One Hundred and Twenty-Five Years of The Manhattan Life Insurance Company of New York, NY* (New York: Manhattan Life Insurance Company, ca. 1974), 21, 28–29; Anita Rapone, *The Guardian Life Insurance Company, 1860–1920: A History of a German-American Enterprise* (New York: New York University Press, 1987), 18; Asa Wing, "Reminiscences," *Between Ourselves* 3, no. 1 (Mar. 1915): 11, PML; and Weare, *Black Business,* 139.

21. M. Christine Anderson suggests that the advent of the "human relations" school in offices grew out of the financial crisis of the Great Depression, when employers and managers perceived a need for a more cooperative approach to worker control. The implementation in offices of human relations plans in the late 1930s clearly was a conscious shift in terminology and rationale, but I would argue that the principles of human relations already were present by the 1910s in life insurance. See M. Christine Anderson, "Gender, Class, and Culture: Women Secretarial and Clerical Workers in the United States, 1925–1955" (Ph.D. diss., Ohio State University, 1986), 75–108.

22. For a general summary of the social motherhood movement, see Mary P. Ryan, *Womanhood in America: From Colonial Times to the Present,* 2d ed. (New York: New Viewpoints, 1979), 118–50.

23. For early-twentieth-century welfare capitalism in industry, see Richard Edwards, *Contested Terrain: The Transformation of the Workplace in the Twentieth Century* (New York: Basic Books, 1979), 90–97.

24. *Metropolitan Life Insurance Company Highlights, 1868–1983,* 2, MLICA; A. R. Horr, Vice-President, "Memorandum for heads of Departments," 18 Feb. 1921, TNE. Emphasis added.

25. *Office Outing, New England Life Insurance Company,* New Ocean House, Swampscott, Mass. (9 June 1921), souvenir pamphlet, TNE; *New England Mutual Life Insurance Company, Office Outing,* New Ocean House, Swampscott, Mass. (12 June 1923), souvenir pamphlet, TNE; "The Athletic Association Smoker," *The*

Home Office 5, no. 6 (Nov. 1923): 1–2, MLICA; "Annual Outing Attracts 750," *Pacific Coaster* 11, no. 1 (June 1929): 1, 15, MLICA; *Items for Agents* 2 (1909), 2, ELASA; Murolo, "White-Collar Women," 6. On nineteenth-century employees' sports organizations, see Buley, *The Equitable,* 65.

26. Marie Louis Wright, "City Cruel Only to Girls Who Are Not Efficient, Says Guardian of 2,000," *Evening Mail* (8 May 1913): n.p., MLICA.

27. Ibid.

28. Circular, Special No. 2-A, p. 12, BVI.

29. See, for example, *Wells Fargo Nevadan* 1, no. 2 (Sept. 1919), WFCA.

30. Daniel Nelson, *Managers and Workers: Origins of the New Factory System in the United States, 1880–1920* (Madison: University of Wisconsin Press, 1975), 118; Daniel Nelson, *Frederick W. Taylor and the Rise of Scientific Management* (Madison: University of Wisconsin Press, 1980), 118.

31. Agnes L. Peterson to Alice Standish-Buell, 13 April 1918; *List of Firms Doing Some Form of Welfare Work* (n.d.); *Women as Labor Managers,* ca. 1921; BVI.

32. Metropolitan Life, in fact, was the first life insurance company to institute a visiting nurse service for its clientele. *Metropolitan Life Insurance Company Highlights, 1868–1983,* MLICA; Lucy C. Conrad, "Distribution of Christmas Baskets," *Between Ourselves* 25, no. 1 (Jan. 1937): 7–9, PML.

33. *Rules Governing Home Office Clerical Employes* (New York: Metropolitan Life Insurance Company, 1921), 20, MLICA.

34. *Sewing Room,* 23 Aug. 1915, V.F. Employees, 1867–1960, MLICA.

35. Abram T. Collier, *A Capital Ship: New England Life* (Boston: The Company, 1985), 226; "There Must Be a Reason," *The Pilot's Log* 1, no. 2 (Dec. 1973), 2–12, TNE; William J. Kennedy, *The North Carolina Mutual Story: A Symbol of Progress, 1898–1970* (Durham: North Carolina Mutual Life Insurance, 1970).

36. *Insurance Opinion* [New York] 3, no. 3 (Aug. 1895): 40, HM&L; announcement in *The Weekly Underwriter* 22, no. 5 (Feb. 21, 1880): 94, HM&L; BULEY, *The Equitable* 540.

37. "J. Stinson Scott General Agent at Rochester," *Provident Notes* (Oct. 25, 1931): 273, PML; "Major John R. Hegeman," *The Home Office* 5, no. 6 (Nov. 1923): 9, MLICA. The younger Hegeman died in 1923; see Collier, *A Capital Ship,* 78, 232.

38. The other two families were the Dows and the Wrights. See Collier, *A Capital Ship,* 45, 69–81; and personnel directories, TNE. Personal communication to author from Howard Clement III, June 1991.

39. Buley, *The Equitable,* plate p. 164a.

40. Announcement in *The Indicator* 9, no. 8 (Aug. 1890): 394, HM&L.

41. Appendices D and E, Collier, *A Capital Ship,* 307, 310; entry for George Willard Smith, *National Cyclopedia of American Biography,* vol. 54, Vertical Files, Biography Section, TNE; *New England Life 1982 Annual Report to Policyholders,* 16 Mar. 1982, 3, TNE. Helen Farrar Warren Smith, *That's The Way It Was* (Boston, Mass.: Privately printed, 1984), 24, notes that Alison Warren Smith was born 27 Oct. 1922.

42. *The Union National Bank of Wilmington: Its History and New Building* (Wilmington: Union National Bank, 1908), n.p., Pamphlet Collection, HM&L.

43. Kennedy, *North Carolina Mutual,* 12, 19.

44. "Personals," *Between Ourselves* 21, no. 7 (Jul. 1934): 115, PML; Photographs, home office staff, ca. 1921, NCM.

45. Announcement in *The Weekly Underwriter* 23, no. 18 (Nov. 20, 1880): 300. This is the earliest reference I have found to a female insurance agent. Announcement in *The Indicator* 9, no. 4 (Apr. 1890): 167. Both in HM&L. I have not discovered any references to women leaving their daughters agencies or encouraging their daughters to follow them into the insurance business.

46. Unfortunately, Lucy Wright died in 1866 at the age of twenty-five. One of her ten surviving brothers and sisters, Walter C. Wright, became the first actuary of New England Mutual in 1866 and served as such until 1900. See "Lucy Jane Wright, Late Actuary of the Union Mutual Life Insurance Company," *The Insurance Monitor and Wall Street Review* 15, no. 6 (June 1867); 337, HM&L; *The Cyclopedia of American Biographies,* 1903 ed., s.v. "Wright, Elizur"; Collier, *A Capital Ship,* 45. Collier claims that "a daughter [of Elizur Wright] first served as an actuary for NEL and then later for Union Mutual in Maine." According to Phyllis Steele, currently the historical collection coordinator of The New England, this probably refers to Lucy Jane. Personal communication to author, 25 Nov. 1991.

47. I am grateful to James Mann, former archivist of the Metropolitan Life Insurance Company, for providing information on this life insurance tradition. See also Marquis James, *The Metropolitan Life: A Study in Business Growth* (New York: Viking Press, 1947), 81. Mary Ryan, *The Cradle of the Middle Class: The Family in Oneida County, New York, 1790–1865* (New York: Cambridge University Press, 1984), 138, note patterns of family inheritance regardless of gender in the early nineteenth century. Naomi Lamoreaux found female family members appointed to the board of directors of the Eagle Bank of Bristol, Rhode Island, in 1848 or 1849; personal communication to author, 29 Dec. 1991. See also advertisement for female insurance agents in *The Indicator* 9, no. 9 (Sept. 1890): 421, HM&L.

48. *The National Cyclopedia of American Biography,* 1950 ed., s.v. "Pedder, Alice Pratt Berdell"; *Golden Anniversary of the First National Bank of Lebanon, Pennsylvania, 1856–1906* (Lebanon, Pa: First National Bank of Lebanon, 1906), n.p., Pamphlet Collection, HM&L; announcement, *The Weekly Underwriter* 22, no. 7 (Mar. 6, 1880): 138, HM&L. On Jessie Herndon, see Alexa B. Henderson, *Atlanta Life Insurance Company: Guardian of Black Economic Dignity* (Tuscaloosa: University of Alabama Press, 1990), 131.

49. Henderson, *Atlanta,* 32; "Pedder," *National Cyclopedia,* 324. On the economic functions of female sociability, see Leonore Davidoff and Catherine Hall, *Family Fortunes: Men and Women of the English Middle Class, 1780–1850* (Chicago: University of Chicago Press, 1987).

50. *The Indicator* 9, no. 3 (Mar. 1890): 139; 9, no. 2 (Feb. 1890): 191; 9, no. 1 (Jan. 1890): 33, all HM&L.

51. Ibid., 9, no. 5 (May 1890): 250, HM&L.

52. Ibid., 9, no. 3 (Mar. 1890): 139, HM&L.

53. "Corporate wives" is Rosabeth Moss Kanter's term. See her *Men and Women of the Corporation* (New York: Basic Books, 1977), esp. chap. 5. See also Hilary Callan and Shirley Ardener, eds. *The Incorporated Wife* (Dover, N.H.: Croom Helm, 1984).

54. Louis F. Paret, "Agency Spirit," *Manager's Magazine* 1, no. 1 (Jan. 1926): 5; W. F. Winterble, "Securing and Developing College Men," *Manager's Magazine* 3, no. 3 (Jul. 1928): 14.

55. See, for example, *New England Pilot* 13, no. 3 (Sept. 1927): 50; *New England Pilot* 13, no. 2 (Aug. 1927): 21–27, TNE; "When the E.M.B.A. Convened," *Wells Fargo Messenger* 3, no. 1. (Sept. 1914): 11; "Special Convention Section . . . California Banker's Association," *Coast Banker* 2, no. 7 (June 1909): n.p., WFCA; and "Women and Insurance," *Provident Notes* 6, no. 2 (Feb. 10, 1923): 19, PML.

56. Paul E. Johnson, *A Shopkeeper's Millennium: Society and Revivals in Rochester, New York, 1815–1837* (New York: Hill & Wang, 1978), 46.

57. *The Indicator* 9, no. 1 (Jan. 1890): 32, HM&L; *Wells Fargo Messenger* 5, no. 5 (Jan. 1917): 84, WFCA.

58. Souvenir menu dated 9 Apr. 1897, Invitations, Menus and Dinners, 1897–1929, TNE.

59. Photograph, 1 Aug. 1923, Fannie B. Rosser Papers, DUL.

60. "Love Feast at Des Moines," *The Equitable News* 50 (Feb. 1904), 14, ELASA.

61. Wilma J. Pesavento, "Sport and Recreation in the Pullman Experiment, 1880–1900," *Journal of Sport History* 9, no. 2 (Summer 1982): 38–62. On female industrial workers and sports in the twentieth century, see Monys Hagen, "Industrial Harmony through Sports: The Industrial Recreation Movement and Women's Sports" (Ph.D. diss. University of Wisconsin, Madison, 1990).

62. John R. Schleppi, " 'It Pays': John H. Paterson and Industrial Recreation at the National Cash Register Company," *Journal of Sport History* 6, no. 3 (Winter 1979): 24; Stuart Brandes, *American Welfare Capitalism, 1880–1940* (Chicago: University of Chicago Press, 1976), 16.

63. Louis Ashbrook, "Reminiscence: Purpose of the Get Together Meeting," *Between Ourselves* 1, no. 2 (Mar. 1913): 1; Asa S. Wing, "Closing Remarks: The Get Together Dinner," *Between Ourselves* 1, no. 2 (Mar. 1913): 25, PML; dinner program, 16 Nov. 1917, WFCA.

64. See, for example, "Chicago's Big Picnic at Dellwood Park," *Wells Fargo Messenger* 6, no. 1 (Sept. 1917): 14, WFCA; *Office Outing: New England Mutual Life Insurance Company, New Ocean House, Swampscott, Mass., Thursday, June Ninth, 1921* and *New England Mutual Life Insurance Company Office Outing, New Ocean House, Swampscott, Mass., Tuesday, June 12, 1923*, Invitations, Menus, and Programs, 1897–1929, TNE; "Annual Outing Attracts 750," *Pacific Coaster* 11, no. 1 (June 1929): 1, 15, MLICA.

65. "Annual Outing," 1, 15.

66. "How Many Can You Recognize," *The Spinning Wheel* (Aug. 1949): 2–3, TNE. The photograph from the 1923 outing probably did not include all the attendees.

67. Spouses were included in some of the earliest outings, but substantial evidence of children at these events appears for the first time in the mid-1930s. Children are visible in photographs from company events of the Provident Mutual Life, for example, in 1935, and are mentioned in a Wells Fargo report of a company picnic in 1935. *Between Ourselves* 25, no. 6 (June 1937): 85, PML; *Wells Fargo Messenger* 7, no. 1 (Jan. 1935): 63, WFCA. Children appear much earlier in records of general agents' meetings. In a group photograph from the New England's 1923 office outing, one child appears in the front row. It is not clear whether she is an anomaly or merely the only child who could be captured for the photograph. "How Many," 2–3.

68. "Provident Field Day," *Between Ourselves* 25, no. 6 (June 1937): 86–93, PML.

69. Leonard C. Ashton, "The Great Athletic Meet in Orianna," *Between Ourselves* 5, no. 2 (Mar. 1917): 52, PML.

70. The New England, for example, did not put general agents' annual meetings under home-office sponsorship until 1930, when the annual meeting was held in Biloxi. Collier, *A Capital Ship*, 60, 96.

71. "One Big Family," *The New England Pilot* 13, no. 2 (Aug. 1927): 21–27, TNE.

72. Weare, *Black Business*, 11. White companies also promoted community outreach, but for different reasons; see my chap. 4.

73. Rencher Harris to Plassie Harris, 6 and 12 Mar. 1926, Rencher Harris Papers, DUL.

74. Weare, *Black Business*, 133–35.

75. *The Indicator* 9, no. 6 (June 1890): 332, HM&L.

76. "California Bankers' Association Convention," *Coast Banker* 2, no. 5 (May 1909): 216d–f; and "Special Convention Section," *Coast Banker* 2, no. 7 (June 1909): n.p., WFCA. See also *Scrapbook* (Philadelphia: Insurance Society of Philadelphia, 1901), HM&L.

77. Anne Seward, "Forging Ahead—The Women in Banking," *Clearing House* (Sept. 1923): 15; "Association of Bank Women," *Pacific Banker* (Oct. 1932): 176, WFCA. See also Genevieve N. Gildersleeve, *Women in Banking: A History of the National Association of Bank Women* (Washington, D.C.: Public Affairs Press, 1959).

78. In addition, one prominent Chinese-American female bank manager, Chang Ho Gee, apparently was not included in female professional organizations. "Can Fill Any Job Says Miss Gee," *Coast Banker* 59 (June 1937): 455, WFCA; see also Judy Yung, *Chinese Women of America: A Pictorial History* (San Francisco: Chinese Culture Foundation, 1986), 53. On African American organizations, see M. S. Stuart, *An Economic Detour: A History of Insurance in the Lives of American Negroes* (1940; reprinted, New York: Johnson Reprint Corporation, 1970), 323–27; and Elsa Barkley Brown, "Womanist Consciousness: Maggie Lena Walker and the Independent Order of Saint Luke," *Signs* 14, no. 3 (Spring 1989): 610–33.

79. From *Book of Songs: Swampscott [Mass.] Convention, September 9, 10, 11,*

1931, General Agents' Association, Records of Annual Meetings, 1904–present, TNE.

80. "A Douglas-Bisbee Club" and "New York Now Has a Fargo Way Club" *Wells Fargo Messenger* 5, no. 12 (Aug. 1917): 213; "Our Chicago Girls Form a Fargo Way Club," *Wells Fargo Messenger* 5, no. 6 (Feb. 1917): 98, WFCA.

81. "Coming Metropolitan Events," *The Home Office* 11, no. 10 (Mar. 1930): n.p., MLICA.

82. Steven Gelber, "'Their Hands Are All Out Playing': Business and Amateur Baseball, 1845–1917," *Journal of Sport History* 2, no. 1 (Spring 1984): 5–27 (the quote appears on 9); Steven Gelber, "Working at Playing: The Culture of the Workplace and the Rise of Baseball," *Journal of Social History* 6, no. 3–4 (June 1983): 3–22.

83. For a perceptive discussion of shifts in corporate photographs of General Electric workers, see David E. Nye, *Image Worlds: Corporate Identities at General Electric, 1890–1930* (Cambridge: MIT Press, 1985), esp. chap. 5.

84. "In the Realm of Sports," *The Wells Fargo Nevadan* 1, no. 1 (Aug. 1919): 12–13, WFCA; S. A. Tatnall, "Bowling," *Between Ourselves* 5, no. 1 (Dec. 1916): 23; "M.S.A.A." and "Sports," *Pacific Coast News* 2, no. 6 (Apr. 28, 1922): 2–3, MLICA.

85. *Pacific Coast News* 4, no. 9 (May–June 1923): 6, MLICA.

86. "A Retrospect," *Pacific Coast News* 2, no. 6 (Apr. 28, 1922): 2, MLICA.

87. *The Spirit of the Home Office, Office Outing, New England Mutual Life Insurance Company, New Orleans House, Swampscott, Mass., Tuesday, June Thirteenth, 1922*, Invitations, Menus, and Programs, 1897–1929, TNE.

88. "Realm of Sports," 12.

89. See, for example, *Office Outing, New England Mutual 1922*: and "Bowling," *Pacific Coast News* 2, no. 6 (Apr. 28, 1922): 2, MLICA.

90. *Between Ourselves* 25, no. 6 (June 1937): 90, PML.

91. Harold P. Cooley, "Play Golf and Be Yourself," *The New England Pilot* 14, no. 10 (Apr. 1929): 188–89, TNE. See also James Logan, "Men—the Biggest Problem in Business," *System* 30, no. 6 (Dec. 1916): 561; and Winterble, "Securing and Developing College Men," 16.

92. David Nye observes that company sports events had three functions: to recruit, to create universal criteria for advancement, and to expand the sense of a corporation from a specific office or site to a larger existence. He notes that Kurt Vonnegut, Jr.'s novel *Player Piano* parodies the all-male camps General Electric held on Association Island. *Image Worlds*, 93–111.

93. See, for example, *Office Outing, New England Mutual, 1921*.

94. Mary Blewett, *Men, Women and Work: Gender, Class and Protest in the New England Shoe Industry, 1781–1910* (Urbana: University of Illinois Press, 1988): Jacqueline Jones, *Labor of Love, Labor of Sorrow: Black Women, Work, and the Family from Reconstruction to the Present* (New York: Vintage Books, 1985).

95. George Connelly, "Mechanics vs. Porters," *Between Ourselves* 21, no. 7

(Jul. 1934): 110–11; Elijah Dennis et al., "Another Field Day," *Between Ourselves* 25, no. 6 (June 1937): 104–5, PML.

96. Dennis, "Another Field Day;" "Chicago's Big Picnic," 14.

97. "Who's Who Regarding Vacations," *Pacific Coast News*, 1, no. 13 (Aug. 26, 1921): 2, MLICA. See also "Personals," *Between Ourselves* 6, no. 2 (Mar. 1918): 91, PML.

98. "Cupid's Darts" and "Clarke-Kingsbury," *Wells Fargo Nevadan* 1, no. 2 (Sept. 1919): 9–10, WFCA. See also "Personals," *Between Ourselves* 6, no. 4 (Sept. 1918): 168; *Between Ourselves* 25, no. 4 (Apr. 1937): 64; "Personals," *Between Ourselves* 24, no. 12 (Dec. 1936): 219, all PML; and "Personals," *Pacific Coast News*, 1, no. 3 (Nov. 12, 1920): 4, MLICA.

99. "Bachelors' Club," *Between Ourselves* 22, no. 5 (May 1934): 64, PML. Another bachelors' club is mentioned in "The Band Wagon," *The Home Office* 11, no. 10 (Mar. 1930): 31, MLICA.

100. "Mrs. Brockway Honored by Industrial Nurses Club," *The Home Office* 11, no. 10 (Mar. 1930): 9, MLICA.

101. "Just Wait!" *Pacific Coast News* 1, no. 9 (Apr. 22, 1921): 4, MLICA.

102. H. R. S., "Agency and Audit," *The Home Office* 11, no. 10 (Mar. 1930): 33, MLICA; "Hunting," *Wells Fargo Nevadan* 1, no. 1 (Aug. 1919): 12, WFCA; "Sports: Quail Hunters," *Wells Fargo Messenger* 5, no. 1 (Nov. 1932): 5, WFCA.

103. "Hiking," *Pacific Coast News* 4, no. 8 (Apr. 1923): 8, MLICA; "Broad Street Pier Fishing Rendezvous," *Wells Fargo Nevadan* 1, no. 2 (Sept. 1919): 11, WFCA; "A Healthy Hike," *Between Ourselves* 5, no. 3 (June 1917): 87, PML; S. H. Troth, "The Treasury Tea-Party," *Between Ourselves* 6, no. 3 (June 1918): 104, PML.

104. See, for example, "Personals," *Between Ourselves* 5, no. 4 (Sept. 1917): 133, PML; "Personals," *Between Ourselves* 21, no. 7 (Jul. 1934): 115, PML; and "Miss Sue Ransome" and "Vacation in South," *The Pacific Coaster* 11, no. 3 (Aug. 1929): 6, 11, MLICA.

105. "Who's Who Regarding Vacations," *Pacific Coast News* 1, no. 13 (Aug. 26, 1921): 2, MLICA.

106. For another example, see "Personals," *Pacific Coast News* 1, no. 9 (Apr. 22, 1921): 4, MLICA.

107. *Between Ourselves* 22, no. 6 (June 1934): 98, PML; "Personals," *Pacific Coast News* 1, no. 9 (Apr. 22, 1921): 4, MLICA; and "Society News" *Pacific Coast News* 4, no. 9 (May–June, 1923): 12, MLICA. A cartoon from the New York *Tribune*, reprinted in *The Home Office* and the *Pacific Coast News*, suggested that not only were both men and women treated to gifts and parties, but that the need to contribute to these affairs could become onerous. See "There's At Least One in Every Office," *The Home Office* 5, no. 6 (Nov. 1923): 26; and *Pacific Coast News* 5, no. 1 (Dec. 1923): 11, MLICA.

108. "Entertains Index Girls," *Pacific Coaster* 11, no. 3 (Aug. 1929): 10, MLICA.

109. See, for example, "Personals," *Between Ourselves* 24, no. 12 (Dec. 1936): 218, PML; and "Social Notes," *Pacific Coaster* 11, no. 3 (Aug. 1929): 10, MLICA.

110. Anderson, "Gender, Class and Culture," 199–225.

111. See, for example, "Personals," *Pacific Coast News* 1, no. 13 (Aug. 1921): 4; and "Society News," *Pacific Coast News* 4, no. 9 (May–June 1923): 12, MLICA.

112. "When 'Kidding' Does Real Harm," *Wells Fargo Nevadan* 2, no. 1 (Aug. 1920): 12–13, WFCA.

113. "The New Drink," *The New England Pilot* 14, no. 7 (Jan. 1929): 127, TNE.

114. The party lasted from the early evening of January 31, 1905, until the early morning of the next day, when a breakfast was served for the hardy souls who lasted the night. See Buley, *The Equitable*, 598–99.

115. There is some disagreement over the exact relation between James Hazen's behavior, the timing of press attacks on him, and the Armstrong investigation. Collier suggests that Hyde was almost singlehandedly responsible for raising the problems in the public mind; Buley reports that James Hazen believed the press attacks that led to the investigation were the result of his failure to invite Mrs. Joseph Pulitzer, the wife of *The World*'s publisher, to the party at Sherry's. Collier, *A Capital Ship*, 74–75; Buley, *The Equitable*, 92–131; Buley, *The Equitable*, 527–29, 598–605.

116. Stories about Hyde and the Equitable's internal struggles and financial dealings appeared in the *New York Times* from March 1905 until the investigation was over. See, for example, "Hyde Entertainments Paid for by Himself," *New York Times*, 30 Mar. 1905, 18; "Aggressive Action Ordered by Hyde," *New York Times*, 4 Apr. 1905, 1; and "Made No Restitution, Did No Wrong—Hyde," *New York Times*, 16 Apr. 1905, 1.

117. Transcript of proceedings, Meeting of House of Delegates, 5 Mar. 1913, PML; Minutes, Meeting of House of Delegates, 12, Mar. 1914, PML; Morris P. Capen, "Working with the Agent," *The New England Pilot* 7, no. 3 (Sept. 1921): 24, TNE.

118. Samuel L. Roth to Leroy A. Lincoln, 18 Apr. 1938; Leroy A. Lincoln to Samuel L. Roth, 20 Apr. 1938; Memorandum, Ernest H. Wilkes, Vice President, to Managers, 22 Apr. 1938, all MLICA.

119. "Provident Field Day," *Between Ourselves* 25, no. 6 (June 1937): 88–90; Photograph, soccer game, ca. 1932–35, PML.

120. See, for example, Willis Hatfield Hazard's unfavorable comments on the lack of intellect among most agents in "The Art of Personal Selling," *Manager's Magazine* 1, no. 3 (Jul. 1926): 22.

121. Smith, *That's the Way it Was*, 27. One can easily imagine Mae West playing Mrs. Allen in the movie version.

122. *The New England Pilot* 13, no. 2 (Aug. 1927): 26, TNE.

Chapter Six: An "Eve-less Paradise"

1. Elizabeth MacGibbon, *Manners in Business* (New York: Macmillan, 1937). See also Ruth Ashmore, *The Business Girl in Every Phase of Her Life* (Philadelphia:

Curtis, 1895); and Caroline Huling, *Letters of a Business Woman to Her Niece* (New York: F. R. Fenno. 1906).

2. Carole Srole discusses male clerks' perception that female workers lowered men's wages in the 1870s. She points out that, in reality, reductions were caused by general economic depression. " 'A Position That God has not Particularly Assigned to Men': The Feminization of Clerical Work, Boston, 1860–1915," part 1, (Ph.D. diss., University of California, Los Angeles, 1984), 100–110.

3. Vanse began working at the Equitable in the early 1890s. Charles H. Vanse, "How Well Do I Remember," *The Equitable Spirit* 1, no. 4 (23 Apr. 1934): n.p., ELASA.

4. John J. Conlon, "Wells Fargo Reminiscences, 1817–1960," typed ms., 5–6, WFCA. "The Romance of 32 Park Place" related the story of a fistfight between two male clerks at Metropolitan Life in 1889. V.F. H.O. 1876–1893, MLICA.

5. Vanse, "How Well Do I Remember."

6. George Frederick, "The Secretary-less Business Man," *The Office Economist* 14, no. 7 (Jul.–Aug. 1932): 4

7. The sense that women degraded the status of men's work or changed men's workplace behavior appeared in other work contexts. See, for example, Edwin Gabler, *The American Telegrapher: A Social History, 1860–1900* (New Brunswick: Rutgers University Press, 1988), 131–143.

8. See, for example, No. 1607, Box 33, Folder 384b; No. 1092, Box 31, Folder 371b; No. 1778, Box 33, Folder 384; and No. 1629, Box 33, Folder 383a, BVI.

9. Grace Robinson, "The Rocky Road to Secretarial Success," *Liberty* (21 Apr. 1928): 22.

10. Vanse, "How Well Do I Remember." Cindy Aron notes changes in the behavior of male clerks in federal offices as they adjusted to the introduction of female clerks in *Ladies and Gentlemen of the Civil Service: Middle-Class Workers in Victorian America* (New York: Oxford University Press, 1987), 164–65.

11. A Young Agent, "The Psychology of the Bull Pen," *Manager's Magazine* 3, no 3. (Jul. 1928): 18.

12. Quoted in Elizabeth Frazer, "Miss Graduate Hunts a Job," *Saturday Evening Post* (19 Oct. 1929): 15.

13. No. 911, Box 31, Folder 371b; No. 1093, Box 31, Folder 373, BVI.

14. Harriet A. Byrne, *The Age Factor as it Relates to Women in Business and the Professions*, Women's Bureau Bulletin no. 117 (Washington: Government Printing Office, 1934); Harriet A. Byrne, *Women Office Workers in Philadelphia*, Women's Bureau Bulletin No. 96 (Washington: Government Printing Office, 1932), 5.

15. A survey made by the Women's Bureau of the Department of Labor in 1931 showed that 63.5 percent of the female clerical labor force were under the age of twenty. Elyce Rotella notes that not only were female clerical workers young, they were younger overall than the general female work force; about half were between the ages of sixteen and twenty-four. Elyce J. Rotella *From Home to Office: U.S. Women at Work, 1870–1930* (Ann Arbor: UMI Research Press, 1981), 113. The Minnesota Department of Labor in 1919 showed six female "children" (between ages ten and sixteen) employed as stenographers or typists. In 1920, the depart-

ment reported fourteen female "children." In neither year were male "children" reported in those categories. *Seventeenth Biennial Report of the Department of Labor and Industries of the State of Minnesota, 1919–1920* (Minneapolis: Syndicate Printing, 1921), 118.

16. Letter from Miss Annie R. Walford to Miss Emma Hirth, Director of BVI, 29 May 1925, Box 31, Folder 373, BVI.

17. Photographic files, MLICA. *A Wonderful Village,* company brochure, Nov. 6, 1911, 2, V.F. Employees, 1867–1960 (I), MLICA.

18. *Welfare Work for Employees,* company brochure, 1915, 7, MLICA. Federal census reports of 1920 indicate that female "clerks" between the ages of seventeen and twenty-four were 51 percent of all female clerks. Men between seventeen and twenty-four constituted 35 percent of all male clerks. For stenographers and typists, the federal census showed a smaller range but a tendency toward younger women. Of all male stenographers and typists, 55 percent were between seventeen and twenty-four. For women, that figure was 62 percent. Byrne, *Age Factor,* 17. The census figures were computed from table 6, Bureau of the Census, *The Fourteenth Census of the U.S. Taken in the Year 1920,* vol. 4, *Population 1920, Occupations* (Washington: Government Printing Office, 1922). The category included all clerks except clerks in stores, and shipping and weighing clerks.

19. Donald R. Makosky, "The Portrayal of Women in Wide Circulation Magazine Short Stories" (Ph.D. diss., University of Pennsylvania, 1966), 37.

20. Rosabeth Moss Kanter has observed that "stereotyped informal roles" such as mother, "pet," "seductress," and "iron maiden" entrap women's sexuality, defusing and containing its potential for disrupting the workplace. *Men and Women of the Corporation* (New York: Basic Books, 1977), 233–34.

21. Letter from President Haley Fiske to Third Vice-President Francis M. Smith, 8 May 1928, V.F. Haley Fiske, Personal, MLICA.

22. See, for example, *The Metropolitan Life Insurance Company: Its History, Its Present Position in the Insurance World, Its Home Office Building, and Its Work Carried on Therein* (New York: Metropolitan Life Insurance Company, 1908), MLICA; "Handling the Metropolitan Mail," *The Home Office* (1918), V.F. Managers to 1939 (I), MLICA; and organizational chart, "Mailing Department," June 1921, E. I. duPont de Nemours Papers, HM&L.

23. One of the earliest women's stock brokerage firms was Woodhull, Claflin & Co., established in 1870. Deborah S. Gardner, "The Architecture of Commercial Capitalism: John Kellum and the Development of New York, 1840–1875" (Ph.D. diss., Columbia University, 1979), 142. On female stock-brokers, see William Worthington Fowler, *Ten Years in Wall Street; or, Revelations of inside Life and Experiences on 'Change* (New York: J. D. Denison, 1870).

24. Photograph, Mrs. Hattie Burke, NCM; Elsa Barkley Brown, "Womanist Consciousness: Maggie Lena Walker and the Independent Order of Saint Luke," *Signs,* 14, no. 3 (Spring 1989); 610–33.

25. Olive F. Vore, "Women in the Banking World," *Coast Banker* 15 (Dec. 1915): 490, WFCA; Mrs. William Laimbeer, "The Women's Department in a Trust Company," address delivered before the trust company division at the annual

convention of the American Bankers' Association, 20 Oct. 1920, BVI. Laimbeer was an assistant secretary for the United States Mortgage & Trust Company, New York City.

26. This has been the traditional explanation given within Metropolitan Life for the appearance of its first female agents in the 1890s. Personal communication from James Mann, former archivist for Metropolitan Life, 10 Dec. 1985.

27. See, for example, "For Women," *The Equitable News* 96 (18 Feb. 1909), 8, ELASA.

28. For an exposition of this argument, see Edith Johnson, *To Women of the Business World* (J.B. Lippincott, 1923), 241.

29. Anne Seward, "Forging Ahead—The Women in Banking," *The Burroughs Clearing House* (Sept. 1923): 15, BVI. Seward was the manager of the Hamilton National Bank's women's department and a prominent national banking figure.

30. Seward, "Forging Ahead," 15.

31. "Women in American Business: Women in the Banking Field," *American Business & National Acceptance Journal* (20 Aug. 1920): 33, BVI.

32. "Business Building Department: Teaching Women to Bank" *Coast Banker* 14 (Jan. 1915): 28, WFCA; Seward, "Forging Ahead," 15–16.

33. In organizing this bank, Walker became the first female bank president in the United States. Brown, "Womanist Consciousness," 616.

34. *The [Insurance] Investigator* (Jul. 1893): 617–20, in Walter C. Wright Scrapbook, 1883–1896, TNE.

35. Obituary, New York *Times*, 4 Aug. 1934, section 4, 11.

36. Eleanor Ames, "How Equitable's Ablest Woman Agent Won Success in Insurance," *Hearst's Boston American* (8 May 1905), 4; Clippings on female agents, File 4/c/1; *The Little Upstart* (June 1916–May 1918); "Women Who Have Won Out," Dayton *Daily News* (2 Nov. 1913), ELASA. Agency department report, *Records of Paid-for Business, 1920,* Jan. 1921, TNE; *Souvenir Commemorating the Dedication of New York Life Insurance Company's Home Office Building, Madison Square New York,* June 1929, HM&L.

37. "Women in Insurance," *The Equitable News* 42 (June 1903), 11, ELASA; Laimbeer, "Women's Department" and "What the Woman in the Bank Thinks of the Bank as a Place for Women," *The Literary Digest* (Jul. 17, 1920): n.p., BVI.

38. Unfortunately, no copies of this newsletter survive. However, it was quoted in *The Equitable News* 50 (Feb. 1904): 10, ELASA.

39. Editorial in *The Little Upstart* 1 (Jul. 1916): 1, ELASA. This and *The Little Sister* are the only newsletters I have found published by women's agencies. Since company newsletters were common throughout the industry, however, there is no reason to believe these were unusual.

40. *The Little Upstart* 5 (Nov. 1916): 1, ELASA.

41. Ibid.

42. Pamela N. Warford, "The Social Origins of Female Iconography: Selected Images of Women in American Popular Culture, 1890–1945" (Ph.D. diss. St. Louis University, 1979), 3–5.

43. Judith Smith, "The 'New Woman' Knows How to Type: Some Connections

between Sexual Ideology and Clerical Work, 1900–1930," paper presented at the Berkshire Conference on Women's History, Radcliffe College, Boston, 1974. Smith emphasizes a change from repressive to freer sexuality denoted by women's office dress. Valerie Steele has argued that the shift in women's clothing styles between 1860 and 1930 was from one sort of erotic expression to another, rather than from prurience to sexuality. See her *Fashion and Eroticism: Ideals of Feminine Beauty from the Victorian Era to the Jazz Age* (New York: Oxford University Press, 1985), 240–42.

44. Lauretta Fancher, "His Secretary Speaking," *Collier's* 83 (13 Apr. 1929): 28, 40; Merle Thorpe, "The Lady's Engaged," *Collier's* 83 (25 May 1929): 43, 70. The issues of women's dress and their emphasis on marriage were constant themes in the company journals of life insurance. See, for example, *The Pacific Coast News* 1, no. 9 (22 Apr. 1921): 3–5, MLICA.

45. Edward Kilduff, *The Private Secretary: The Duties and Opportunities of the Position*, rev. ed. (New York: Century, 1924), 59.

46. Ashmore, *Business Girl*, 8–9. The first edition of this work appeared in 1895.

47. Valerie Steele, in her analysis of Victorian clothing, observes, "The clerk's shiny black suit functioned both as a badge of respectability and as an involuntary sign of his relatively humble position in the social order." *Fashion and Eroticism*, 83.

48. *The Little Upstart* 1 (Jul. 1916): 5, ELASA.

49. *The Little Upstart* 11 (May 1917): 2, ELASA.

50. *The Little Upstart* 3 (Sept. 1916): 1, ELASA.

51. E. Marie Little, *Life Insurance*, Nov. 9, 1915, 9, 11, BVI. For the prevalence of this argument, see Johnson, *To Women*, 235ff. For a recent analysis of this same phenomenon, see Robin Leidner, "Serving Hamburgers and Selling Insurance: Gender, Work, and Identity in Interactive Service Jobs," *Gender & Society* 5, no. 2 (June 1991): 154–177.

52. *Items for Agents* 2 (14 Jan. 1909): 7, ELASA. See also John R. Hegeman, *To the Superintendents and Assistant Superintendents of the Metropolitan Life Insurance Company*, 25 December 1891, V.F. Managers to 1939 (I), MLICA.

53. Annie A. Russell, "Her Garden," *The Little Upstart* 3 (Sept. 1916): 3, ELASA. See also "Policies and Posies," *The Little Upstart* 9 (Mar. 1917): 5, ELASA.

54. Imogen Burnham, "An Appreciation," *The Little Upstart* 5 (Nov. 1916): 2, ELASA.

55. For the persistence of this belief, see Ann Hughey and Eric Gelman, "Managing the Woman's Way," *Newsweek* (17 Mar. 1986): 46–47, in which they argue for a distinct female management style based on "natural" or "instinctive" female qualities such as "sympathy," "sensitivity," and "a lack of the killer instinct."

56. Maude Radford Warren, "Green Timber," *Saturday Evening Post*, part I, 188 (20 Nov. 1915): 3–5, 38–39, 41–42; part II, 188 (27 Nov. 1915), 19–20, 52, 54. See also F. Charles Schwedtman, *The Ideal Business Woman* (1918), PML. Schwedtman was vice-president of the National City Bank of New York.

57. No. 862, Box 31, Folder 372a; No. 1641, Box 33, Folder 384b, BVI.

58. Burnham, "An Appreciation," 2.

59. Little, "Life Insurance," 3.

60. For the development of female professions, see Sheila Rothman, *Woman's Proper Place: A History of Changing Ideals and Practices, 1870 to the Present* (New York: Basic Books, 1978), 42–60; and Daniel Walkowitz, "The Making of a Feminine Professional Identity: Social Worker in the 1920s," *American Historical Review* 95, no. 4 (Oct. 1990): 1051–75. See also Faye Dudden, *Serving Women: Household Service in Nineteenth-Century America* (Middletown, Conn.: Wesleyan University Press, 1983), 156.

Conclusion: The Gender of Business

1. Elsa Barkley Brown, "Womanist Consciousness: Maggie Lena Walker and the Independent Order of Saint Luke," *Signs* 14, No. 3 (Spring 1989): 610–33.

2. On current conditions, see Cynthia Crossen, "Sex and Power in the Office" and "Women in the Work Force," *Wall Street Journal,* 18 Oct. 1991, B1, B3; and Joann S. Lublin, "Rights Law to Spur Shifts in Promotions," *Wall Street Journal,* 30 Dec. 1991, B1, B4.

3. On the contemporary sense of office work's possibilities for women, see "Women in American Business," *American Business and National Acceptance Journal* (20 Aug. 1928), Banking, Reel 3–78, BVI; and Ames, "How Equitable's Ablest Woman," 4, ELASA.

BIBLIOGRAPHICAL ESSAY

The issues covered in this book bridge a diverse body of primary and secondary sources and several scholarly disciplines. The following essay represents only those sources I found most useful in understanding the relationship between gender and the development of corporate work.

Primary Sources

Primary sources include manuscript materials from several corporate archives. The Metropolitan Life Insurance Company's enormous historical holdings are strongest in employment policy, agency newsletters, the history of health, corporate sports programs, architectural history, and the papers of company executives. The Equitable Life Assurance Society of the United States Archives' collection of newsletters, agency journals, architectural information, and materials on the early history of New York financial industries is excellent, although records before World War I are thinner than those after the war. The New England's collection of papers and ephemera is rich and is still being catalogued. The Wells Fargo Corporate Archives are an excellent source on early banking, with a nearly complete collection of trade magazines, advertising, and information on banking in the West.

The Hagley Museum and Library in Wilmington, Delaware, houses what is arguably the finest collection of business records in the United States. In particular, the E. I. duPont de Nemours Papers, the Provident Mutual Life Insurance Company Papers, the papers of the Farmers and Mechanics' Bank of Philadelphia, the extensive Trade Catalogue Collection, and the Pamphlet Collection were extremely useful. The Baker Library at the Harvard Graduate School of Business Administration has some holdings on life insurance. The Bureau of Vocational Information Papers, housed at the Schlesinger Library, Cambridge, Massachusetts, is an extensive collection of manuscript questionnaires filled out in 1925 as part of a survey of office workers. The collection also contains letters from employers, transcripts of speeches on vocations for women, and newspaper and magazine clippings on women and employment. It is now available in microform.

Collections of papers of businessmen and businesswomen are scattered around the country in a variety of archives. The William R. Perkins Library at Duke University contains some of the most extensive collections on insurance, and some papers (such as those of Rencher Harris and Fannie Rosser) on African American businesses. The North Carolina Mutual Life Insurance Company is reported to have an extensive collection of papers on the company's history. Unfortunately, these were not available during the time I did my research. However, I did have access to their collection of photographs and to the expertise of Howard Clement III, a third-generation Mutual officer, who has a wide knowledge of the company's history and its relation to the community.

The number of books and articles published between 1870 and 1930 on the issue of men and women and office work is enormous. Some of those I found most useful include Elizabeth Kemper Adams, *Women Professional Workers: A Study Made for the Women's Educational and Industrial Union* (New York: Macmillan, 1921); Ruth Ashmore, *The Business Girl in Every Phase of Her Life* (1895); Loire Brophy, *If Women Must Work* (1936); W. W. Charters and Isadore B. Whitley, *Summary of Report on Analysis of Secretarial Duties and Traits* (1924); Irene Widdlemer Hartt, *How to Make Money, Although a Woman* (New York: J. S. Ogilvie, 1895); Edward Kilduff, *The Private Secretary: His Duties and Opportunities* (1919) and *The Private Secretary: The Duties and Opportunities of the Position* (rev. ed. 1924); Elizabeth Gregg MacGibbon, *Manners in Business* (1937); Agnes Perkins, ed., *Vocations for the Trained Woman: Opportunities Other than Teaching* (1910); and Dorothy Richardson, *The Long Day: The Story of a New York Working Girl as Told by Herself* (New York: Century, 1911). For a vivid, albeit fictional depiction of the precorporate office, see Herman Melville's *Bartleby the Scrivener: A Story of Wall Street,* first published in 1853 and reprinted in *The Shorter Novels of Herman Melville* (1956), 107–55.

On systematic management in offices, see Eugene J. Benge, "Simple Tests for Selecting Office Workers," *Industrial Management* 61 (1921):91–92; Paul Bourscheiudt, "A Central Stenographic and Typing Department," *Office Economist* 12 (1920):3–4, 12; Jacques Boyer, "Are Men Better Typists than Women?: Interesting Scientific Tests Made by J. M. Lahy," *Scientific American* 109 (1913):327–29; Hinton Gilmore, "Gingering Up Office Work," (1915); R. H. Goodell, "Saving 42% on Routine Work," (1920); James Hartness, *The Human Factor in Works Management* (New York: McGraw-Hill, 1912); Donald L. Laird, "Problems in Handling Women Workers," *Office Economist* 18 (1935): 4–5; Edward D. Page, "The New Science of Business: Making an Office Efficient," *World's Work* 12 (1906):76–83; and Frederick W. Taylor, *The Principles of Scientific Management* (1911; reprinted, New York: Norton, 1967).

Secondary Sources

Most scholars now make a distinction between sexuality and gender. The term *gender* denotes a category of analysis that includes sexuality, as sexuality is merely one expression of a person's socially and biologically defined gender. For an analysis of the socially defined basis of gender attribution, see the Introduction to Suzanne Kesseler and Wendy McKenna, *Gender: An Ethnomethodological Approach* (New York: John Wiley & Sons, 1978), 1–20. Ethel S. Person discusses the connection between self and sexuality in "Sexuality as the Mainstay of Identity: Psychoanalytic Perspectives," *Signs* 5, no. 4 (1980):605–30.

Although the historical literature on homosexuality has only begun to sort out the chronology, the evidence presented so far suggests that the association of particular expressions of sexuality with "deviance" was a turn-of-the-century phenomenon. Most important in the context of my argument, the major cultural shift in defining homosexuality as a condition rather than an activity expressing a part of the self paralleled the focus on gender as an individual attribute rather than a series of social roles. See, for example, Christina Simmons, "Companionate Marriage and the Lesbian Threat"; John D'Emilio, "Capitalism and Gay Identity," in *Powers of Desire: The Politics of Sexuality*, eds. Ann Snitow et al., (New York: Monthly Review Press, 1983), 100–113; and Jeffrey Weeks, *Coming Out: Homosexual Politics in Britain from the Nineteenth Century to the Present* (New York: Quartet Books, 1990).

An excellent review of the political implications of replacing *woman* or *sex* with *gender* is Joan W. Scott's "Gender: A Useful Category of Historical Analysis," in her *Gender and the Politics of History* (1988). For examples of gendered expression in political and social realms, see Scott, *Gender;* Paula C. Baker, "The Domestication of Politics: Women and the American Political Society, 1780–1920," *American Historical Review* 89, no. 3 (June 1984):620–47, and *The Moral Frameworks of Public Life: Gender, Politics, and the State in Rural New York, 1870–1930* (New York: Oxford University Press, 1991); Mary P. Ryan, *Women in Public: Between Banners and Ballots, 1825–1880* (1990); and Elizabeth Faue, *Community of Suffering and Struggle: Women and Men in the Labor Movement in Minneapolis, 1915–1945* (1991).

Sex role theory has come under intense criticism from feminist scholars, who cite its main weakness as the inability to account for differences between biological sex and social gender. See, for example, Joan Acker, "Hierarchies, Jobs, Bodies: A Theory of Gendered Organizations," *Gender & Society* 4, no. 2 (June 1990):139–58; Tim Carrigan, Bob Connell, and John Lee, "Toward a New Sociology of Masculinity," *Theory and Society* 14, no. 5 (1985):551–604; and Helena Z. Lopata and Barrie Thorne, "On the Term 'Sex Roles,'" *Signs* 3, no. 3 (1978):718–21). For reviews of sociological theory and the current debate on sex role formation see Carrigan, Connell and Lee, "New Sociology of Masculinity"; and Lopata and Thorne, "On 'Sex Roles.'" On social definitions of gender and their relation to power, see Scott, "Gender." On the connection between social systems and change, see Michelle Z. Rosaldo, "The Use and Abuse of Anthropology: Reflections on Feminism and Cross-Cultural Understanding" (1980) and Clifford Geertz, *The Interpretation of Cultures: Selected Essays* (New York: Basic Books, 1973).

On using language to explore cultural meaning, see Naomi Quinn and Dorothy Holland, eds., *Cultural Models in Language and Thought* (New York: Cambridge University Press, 1987): George E. Marcus and Michael M. Fischer, *Anthropology as Cultural Critique: An Experimental Moment in the Human Sciences* (Chicago: University of Chicago Press, 1986); and Jennifer Coates and Deborah Cameron, eds., *Women in Their Speech Communities* (New York: Longman, 1985). Quinn and Holland argue that metaphor and metonymy are modes of cognition. Metaphor "maps structures from one domain to another," and metonymy "structures a domain in terms of its elements." For example, metaphor links physical and abstract understanding. Metonymy provides "salient examples," ideals, or stereotypes, which are then enacted and socialized through ritual. Thus, ritual is a code that links the typical to the particular. On the theory and application of deconstructive methods, see Geertz, *Interpretation of Cultures;* Joan W. Scott, "Deconstructing Equality-versus-Difference: Or, the Uses of Poststructuralist Theory for Feminism," *Feminist Studies* 14: no. 1 (Spring 1989):33–50; and Lloyd S. Kramer, "Literature, Criticism, and Historical Imagination: The Literary Challenge of Hayden White and Dominick LaCapra," in *The New Cultural History,* ed. Lynn Hunt (Berkeley: University of California Press, 1989). For examples of textual analysis applied to historical understanding, see Faue, *Community;* and Mary Poovey, *Uneven Developments: The Ideological Work of Gender in Mid-Victorian England* (Chicago: University of Chicago Press, 1988). On "natural attitudes" as a window on cultural formations, see Kesseler and McKenna, *Gender.*

The relationship between work and workers first articulated in E. P. Thompson, *The Making of the English Working Class* (New York: Pantheon, 1963), has become a common theme of virtually all labor history. While Thompson confined his analysis of this relationship to the formation of class, I have argued that it was central to the development of connections between gender and office work. A recent example of the popular or "common sense" acceptance of this viewpoint can be found in Michael Maccoby, *The Gamesman: The New Corporate Leaders* (New York: Simon & Schuster, 1977), 174–75: "At the top of the organization, you might conclude that the chief executive officer's behavior is determined 'psychologically' by the way his personality responds to pressures, opportunities, etc., but that conclusion would leave out the fact that his personality has been selected exactly because it fits the requirements of the role."

The secondary literature on social constructions of gender and office work is large. Useful sociological studies of gender and corporate work include Rosabeth Moss Kanter, *Men and Women of the Corporation* (1977); and Hilary Callan and Shirley Ardener, eds., *The Incorporated Wife* (1984). On the relationship between gender and organizations, see Acker, "Gendered Organizations"; Gibson Burrell, "Sex and Organizational Analysis," *Organization Studies* 5, no. 2 (1984):97–118 and "No Accounting for Sexuality," *Accounting Organization and Society* 12, no. 1 (1987):89–101; Robert K. Merton, "Functions of the Professional Association" (1958); David Collinson and David Knights, " 'Men Only': Theories and Practices of Job Segregation in Insurance," in David Collinson and David Knights, eds., *Gender and the Labour Process* (Hampshire, England: Gower, 1986), 140–78; Robin Leidner, "Serving Hamburgers and Selling Insurance: Gender, Work and Identity in Interactive Service Jobs," *Gender & Society,* 5 no. 2 (1991):154–77; and Barbara J. Thomas, "Women's Gains in Insurance Sales: Increased Supply, Uncertain Demand," in Barbara Reskin and Patricia Roos, eds., *Job Queues, Gender Queues* (Philadelphia: Temple University Press, 1990), 183–204.

The relationship between ideas about manhood and womanhood and the work experience is explored in various workplace contexts in Ava Baron, ed., *Work Engendered: Toward a New History of American Labor* (1990). Important studies of female clerical workers include M. Christine Anderson, "Gender, Class and Culture: Women Secretarial and Clerical Workers in the United States, 1925–1955," (1986); Cindy S. Aron, *Ladies and Gentlemen of the Civil Service: Middle-Class Workers in Victorian America* (1987); Margery Davies, *Woman's Place is at the Typewriter, 1870–1930* (1982); Ileen DeVault, *Sons and Daughters of Labor: Class and Clerical Work in Turn-of-the-Century Pittsburgh* (1990); Lisa Fine, *The Souls of the Skyscraper: Female Clerical Workers in Chicago, 1870–1930* (1990); and Carole Srole, " 'A Position That God Has Not Particularly Assigned to Men': The Feminization of Clerical Work, Boston 1860–1915" (1984).

Anderson, Davies, DeVault, Fine, and Srole center on patriarchal structures, female workers, or issues of class formation rather than gender as either a cultural system or a category of historical analysis. DeVault, Fine and Srole focus on geographical areas rather than a particular industry or economic sector. Aron's study of federal Treasury workers analyzes the public rather than the private sector and does not deal with the ways in which gender acted as an integral part of an institutional system. Both DeVault and Aron incorporate male clerical workers into their studies. Fine's study of Chicago charts the demographic and ideological feminization of clerical work. On the changing nature of women's office education, see Fine, *Souls of the Skyscraper*, chap. 6; and DeVault, *Sons and Daughters*, chap. 2. For a synthesis of some of this material, see Sharon Hartman Strom, *Beyond the Typewriter: Gender, Class, and the Origins of Modern American Office Work, 1900–1930* (1992). The best work on the demographics of office labor at the turn of the century is Elyce Rotella, *From Home to Office: U.S. Women at Work, 1870–1930* (1981). For useful studies of gender typing in other industries, see Edwin Gabler, *The American Telegrapher, A Social History, 1860–1900* (New Brunswick: Rutgers University Press, 1988); John N. Schacht, *The Making of Telephone Unionism, 1920–1947* (New Brunswick: Rutgers University Press, 1985); and Kenneth Lipartito, "When Women Were Switches: Technology, Work and Gender in the Telephone Industry, 1890–1920," *American Historical Review* (forthcoming).

The general literature on women and work assumes the dichotomy of experience for males and females known as *separate spheres*. For a summary and critique of this ideal, see Sheila Rothman, *Woman's Proper Place: A History of Changing Ideals and Practices* (1978); Linda K. Kerber, "Separate Spheres, Female Worlds, Woman's Place: The Rhetoric of Women's History," *Journal of American History* 75, No. 1 (June 1988):9–39; and Susan M. Reverby and Dorothy O. Helly's introduction to their collection of essays, *Gendered Domains: Rethinking Public and Private in Women's History* (Ithaca: Cornell University Press, 1992) 1–24. Explorations of women at work outside the home in the twentieth century—where, it was once argued, they were liberated or emancipated from domesticity—find that the nature of wage labor for both single and married women reinforced rather than challenged the predominant domestic experience. See, for example, Davies, *Woman's Place;* Maurine Weiner Greenwald, *Women, War, and Work: The Impact of World War I on Women Workers in the United States* (Westport, Conn.: Greenwood Press, 1980); Alice Kessler-Harris, *Out to Work: A History of Wage-Earning*

Women in the United States (New York: Oxford University Press, 1982); Jacqueline Jones, *Labor of Love, Labor of Sorrow: Black Women, Work and the Family from Reconstruction to the Present* (1985); Lois Scharf, *To Work and to Wed: Female Employment, Feminism, and the Great Depression* (Westport, Conn.: Greenwood Press, 1980); and Leslie Woodcock Tentler, *Wage-Earning Women: Industrial Work and Family Life in the United States, 1900–1930* (New York: Oxford University Press, 1979).

Historians have begun to explore the history of manhood. For an analysis of the so-called masculine identity crisis of the late nineteenth century, see Joe L. Dubbert, "Progressivism and the Masculinity Crisis," in *The American Man*, eds. Elizabeth Pleck and Joseph H. Pleck (Englewood Cliffs, N.J.: Prentice Hall, 1980), 305–20; and James McGovern, "David Graham Phillips and the Virility Impulse of Progressives," *New England Quarterly* 33 (1966):334–55. Overviews of the history of middle-class manhood include Peter Stearns, *Be A Man! Males in Modern Society* (1979): and Peter Filene, *Him/Her/Self: Sex Roles in Modern America* (1986). For a review of the historical literature on nineteenth-century masculinity, see Clyde Griffen, "Reconstructing Masculinity," in *Meanings for Manhood: Constructions of Masculinity in Victorian America*, eds. Mark C. Carnes and Clyde Griffen (1990), 183–204. E. Anthony Rotundo attempts an overview of ideas about middle-class white manhood in the nineteenth- and twentieth-century United States in *American Manhood: Transformations in Masculinity from the Revolution to the Modern Era* (1993). On masculinity and fraternal organizations, see Mary Ann Clawson, *Constructing Brotherhood: Class, Gender, and Fraternalism* (1989); and Mark C. Carnes, *Secret Ritual and Manhood in Victorian America* (1989). On men in retail organizations see Alan R. Raucher, "Dime Store Chains: The Making of Organization Men, 1880–1940" (1991).

A good general source on both the ancient and modern history of life insurance is J. Owen Stalson, *Marketing Life Insurance: Its History in America* (1942). On banking, see Benjamin J. Klebaner, *Commercial Banking in the United States: A History* (1974) and *American Commercial Banking: A History* (1990); Thomas C. Cochran, *Business in American Life: A History* (1972); Amos Fiske, *The Modern Bank: A Description of Its Functions and Methods and a Brief Account of the Development and Present System of Banking* (1923); and Naomi Lamoreaux, *Insider Lending: Banks, Personal Connections, and Economic Development in Industrial New England, 1784–1900* (forthcoming). Two classic statements of progressive business history are Alfred D. Chandler, *The Visible Hand: The Managerial Revolution in American Business* (1977); and Robert Wiebe, *Businessmen and Reform: A Study of the Progressive Movement* (1962). On professionalism, see Burton J. Bledstein, *The Culture of Professionalism: The Middle Class and the Development of Higher Education in America* (New York: Norton, 1976). For the relationships among office organization, new technologies, and forms of communication, see JoAnne Yates, *Control through Communication: The Rise of System in American Management* (1989).

Historians of business have yet to incorporate analyses of gender into their discussions of the late-nineteenth- and early-twentieth-century workplace, with the exception of two monographs. Olivier Zunz, in *Making America Corporate, 1870–1920* (1990), focuses on the cultural dissemination of corporate forms and experience and includes information on both men and women, as well as an analysis of corporate space. Gender is not, however, a primary focus of this work. Stuart Blumin's *The Emergence of the Middle Class: Social Experience in the American City, 1760–1900* (1989) looks at the urban experience and includes a perceptive discussion of the ideology of separate spheres. However, class and urbanization rather than gender and work remain at the center of his analysis. On women and management, see Sara Alpern, "In the Beginning: A History of Women in Management," in *Women in Management: Trends, Issues, and Challenges,* ed. Ellen A. Fagenson (Newbury Park, Calif.: SAGE, 1993), 19–51.

For material culture theory, see Dell Upton and John Michael Vlach, eds., *Common Places: Readings in American Vernacular Architecture* (Athens: University of Georgia Press, 1986); Jules Prown, "Mind in Matter: An Introduction to Material Culture Theory and Method," *Winterthur Portfolio* 17, no. 1 (Spring 1982):1–19; Henry Glassie, "Structure and Function, Folklore and the Artifact," *Semiotic* 7 (1973):313–51; and Bernard Herman, *The Stolen House* (Charlottesville: University Press of Virginia, 1992), especially the Introduction. On material culture and gender, see Angel Kwolek-Folland, "Gender as a Category of Analysis in Vernacular Architecture Studies," in Carter L. Hudgins and Betsey Cromley, eds., *Perspectives in Vernacular Architecture V* (Knoxville: University of Tennessee Press, 1994); Kenneth L. Ames and Katharine Martinez, eds., *The Material Culture of Gender/The Gender of Material Culture* (New York: W. W. Norton, 1994); Dolores Hayden, *The Grand Domestic Revolution: A History of Feminist Designs for American Homes, Neighborhoods, and Cities* (Cambridge, Mass: MIT Press, 1981) and *Redesigning the American Dream: The Future of Housing, Work, and Family Life* (New York: W. W. Norton, 1984); the entire issue of *Built Environment* 10, no. 1 (1984); and Leslie K. Weisman, *Discrimination by Design: A Feminist Critique of the Man-Made Environment* (1992). Two useful essays on office workers and work space are Thomas J. Schlereth, "The World and Workers of the Paper Empire," in his *Cultural History and Material Culture: Everyday Life, Landscapes, Museums* (Ann Arbor, Mich.: UMI Research Press, 1990), 145–78; and Frank Duffy, "Office Buildings and Organisational Change," in Anthony D. King, ed., *Buildings and Society: Essays on the Social Development of the Built Environment* (1980).

Some historians concerned with relations between workers and employers have stressed efforts to control experience in both public and private space. They have addressed the process of negotiation and compromise that underlies workplace struggle. As yet, their efforts have not resulted in a theoretical model that would make transparent the historical relationship between gender and the work environment. Efforts in this direction can be found in Susan Porter Benson, *Counter Cultures: Saleswomen, Managers, and Customers in American Department Stores, 1890–1940* (1986). On the functions of space, see Shirley Ardener, ed., *Women and Space: Ground Rules and Social Maps* (1981); Edward T. Hall, *The Hidden Dimension* (1966); Yi-Fu Tuan, *Topophilia: A Study of Environmental Perception,*

Bibliographical Essay

Attitudes and Values (1974); David Stea, "Space, Territory and Human Movements," *Landscape* 15, no. 1 (Autumn 1965):13–16; William H. Jordy, "PSFS: Its Development and Its Significance in Modern Architecture," *Journal of the Society of Architectural Historians* 21 (1962):47–83; and Frank Duffy, "Office Buildings" (1980). On the early development of financial architecture in New York City, see Deborah S. Gardner, "The Architecture of Commercial Capitalism: John Kellum and the Development of New York, 1840–1875" (1979).

There are relatively few scholarly works on African American business history. An important early survey is M. S. Stuart, *An Economic Detour: A History of Insurance in the Lives of American Negroes* (1970). Several company histories are available: Alexa B. Henderson, *Atlanta Life Insurance Company: Guardian of Black Economic Dignity* (1990); William J. Kennedy, *The North Carolina Mutual Story: A Symbol of Progress* (1970); Walter B. Weare, *Black Business in the New South: A Social History of the North Carolina Mutual Life Insurance Company* (1973); and Robert E. Weems, Jr., "The History of the Chicago Metropolitan Mutual Assurance Company: An Examination of Business as a Black Community Institution" (1987). An excellent resource on African American businesswomen is Elsa Barkley Brown, "Womanist Consciousness: Maggie Lena Walker and the Independent Order of Saint Luke" (1989). On African American women as workers, see Jacqueline Jones, *Labor of Love, Labor of Sorrow: Black Women, Work, and the Family from Reconstruction to the Present* (1985). Two useful sources on the development of class among African Americans are Willard B. Gatewood, *Aristocrats of Color: The Black Elite, 1880–1920* (1990) and Stephanie Jo Shaw, "Black Women in White Collars: A Social History of Lower-Level Professional Black Women Workers, 1870–1954" (1986).

Index

Library of Congress Cataloging-in-Publication Data
Kwolek-Folland, Angel.
  Engendering business : men and women in the corporate office,
  1870–1930 / Angel Kwolek-Folland.
    p.   cm. — (Gender relations in the American experience)
  Includes bibliographical references and index.
  ISBN 0-8018-4860-1
    1. Women in business—United States—History—19th century.
  2. Women in business—United States—History—20th century.
  3. Sexual division of labor—United States—History—19th
  century. 4. Sexual division of labor—United States—History—
  20th century. 5. Man-woman relationships—United States—
  History—19th century. 6. Man-woman relationships—United
  States—History—20th century.
  I. Title. II. Series.
  HD6053.K85 1994
  331.4'8165'00973—dc20   94-7518